The Ambition to Rule

THE AMBITION TO RULE

Alcibiades and the Politics
of Imperialism in Thucydides

STEVEN FORDE

CORNELL UNIVERSITY PRESS

Ithaca and London

First published 1989 by Cornell University Press.

International Standard Book Number 0-8014-2138-1
Library of Congress Catalog Card Number 88-47919

Printed in the United States of America

*Librarians: Library of Congress cataloging information
appears on the last page of the book.*

*The paper in this book is acid-free and meets the guidelines for
permanence and durability of the Committee on Production Guidelines
for Book Longevity of the Council on Library Resources.*

Contents

CONTENTS

Acknowledgments

MY work on this book has been facilitated by support from a number of sources. I thank Dartmouth College and the faculty of the Dartmouth Department of Government for the year I was able to spend in idyllic New Hampshire as a Culpepper Fellow. I must also thank Dalhousie University and the Dalhousie Department of Classics for a fruitful year of research on this and other projects as a Killam Fellow in Nova Scotia. I am grateful to the staff of James Madison College of Michigan State University for help in preparing the manuscript, and especially to Professor Richard Zinman for his advice on parts of this project. My greatest debt, however, and the one that I take most pleasure in acknowledging, is to my teachers. They are in a sense responsible for this work as a whole, or at least for what is good in it. Clifford Orwin provided me with the most salutary help with the interpretation of Thucydides in detail; one could not find a wiser and more astute adviser, nor a truer scholar in every sense. Thomas Pangle has given me much support and advice, always of the most welcome and incisive kind, as one would expect from a thinker and an individual of such stature. My gratitude to Allan Bloom I acknowledge last because, going beyond the merely academic, it is beyond the scope of this note to express. The help I have received from him encompasses all the finest elements of friendship, manifested in all kinds of circumstances; this is the greatest and most noble form of debt, one that can only be alluded to here.

STEVEN FORDE

THE AMBITION TO RULE

Introduction:
The Problem of Thucydides
and the Problem of Alcibiades

THIS book is a study not of the historical Alcibiades but of Thucydides' understanding of Alcibiades, of Alcibiades' place in Thucydides' writing and of his relation to the deepest of Thucydides' themes. I have focused on Alcibiades because I believe that Thucydides' presentation of Alcibiades brings us closer to the heart of Thucydides' understanding of the human and political world than does almost any other part of his work. Ultimately, this study aspires to be an exercise of the kind that I believe Thucydides sought to inspire in his readers: we begin with an interpretation of Thucydides' text but engage as well in broader reflections on the themes that his History introduces us to. I believe that the real reason we study Thucydides is to let him guide us in reflections of this kind. Before confronting the enigmas of Alcibiades, therefore, we need to consider the problem of Thucydides and his writing.

Thucydides appears at first glance to be an ordinary historian. Indeed, that is the title scholars have traditionally conferred on him. Yet Thucydides never calls himself a historian and never calls his work a "history."[1] And even those who identify him as the intellectual ancestor of

---

[1]See Leo Strauss, *The City and Man* (1964; rpt. Chicago: University of Chicago Press, 1977), p. 143; Christopher Bruell, "Thucydides' View of Athenian Imperialism," *American Political Science Review* 68 (1974):11–18. See also John H. Finley, Jr., *Thucydides*

modern historians acknowledge Thucydides to operate according to rules quite different from those followed by his putative descendants. Thus, present-day students of Greek history can use Thucydides as a "historical source" only with the greatest caution: his narrative is incomplete or selective, he fails to comment on whole classes of phenomena that modern historians deem crucial to the understanding of events, and he gives extraordinary emphasis to some seemingly minor incidents.

Indeed, Thucydides' work is not a history in the modern sense, but rather a quasi-historical work governed by an investigative and didactic purpose of its own. This purpose dictates the striking omissions and emphases and is meant to be revealed indirectly through them.[2] Of course, all historical writings necessarily emphasize some things at the expense of others; no history can include literally everything. In ordinary historical works the selection of events and the relative emphasis given them inevitably reflect the historian's overall interpretation of the period being examined. Thucydides raises this discrimination to the level of art, taking it far enough to remove his writing from the genre of history as we conceive of it today.[3] Thucydides has something to teach us and this teaching, rather than the historical task more narrowly defined,

---

(1942; rpt. Ann Arbor: University of Michigan Press, 1963), p. 3n, followed by Lowell Edmunds, *Chance and Intelligence in Thucydides* (Cambridge: Harvard University Press, 1975), p. 6, who refers to the use of the title *History* for Thucydides' work as "a useful convention." I have referred to it throughout as the History, capitalized but not underlined, to accentuate its conventionality. It should be noted that the Greek word *historia* does not convey what we usually mean today when we speak of history and historians: it signifies to begin with no more than an "inquiry" or "investigation." Thucydides' book can be called a political history in that sense.

[2]Some of the more important references in the literature to the "purposiveness" of Thucydides' writing are: F. M. Cornford, *Thucydides Mythistoricus* (London: Edward Arnold, 1907), p. 198; J. B. Bury, *The Ancient Greek Historians* (London: Macmillan, 1909), p. 87; Werner Jaeger, *Paideia: The Ideals of Greek Culture*, vol. 1, trans. G. Highet (Oxford: Oxford University Press, 1939), pp. 386, 394, 400; Finley, *Thucydides*, pp. 299, 318; F. E. Adcock, *Thucydides and His History* (Cambridge: Cambridge University Press, 1963), p. 47; Jacqueline de Romilly, *Histoire et raison chez Thucydide* (Paris: Société d'Editions "Les Belles Lettres," 1956), p. 299, and *Thucydides and Athenian Imperialism*, trans. P. Thody (1947; rpt. New York: Barnes & Noble, 1963), p. 3; Peter R. Pouncey, *The Necessities of War: A Study of Thucydides' Pessimism* (New York: Columbia University Press, 1980), p. ix.

[3]On this point, see also W. Robert Connor, *Thucydides* (Princeton: Princeton University Press, 1984), pp. 7–8; Friedrich Meinecke, "Values and Causalities in History," in F. Stern, ed., *Varieties of History*, trans. Franklin (New York: Meridian Books, 1956).

governs his writing. This is not to say that Thucydides has no allegiance to the ideal of factual accuracy. He claims that he does, explicitly distancing himself from the poets, who create their own situations the better to convey their teachings. Thucydides strives to retain all the richness of the particular while pointing us toward universal truths.[4]

This is what Thomas Hobbes, who translated and admired Thucydides, meant when he said that Thucydides is "accounted the most politic historiographer that ever writ"; for "he filleth his narrations with that choice of matter, and ordereth them with that judgment" that the reader is allowed, indeed compelled, to "draw out lessons to himself."[5] Thus, for example, Thucydides treats at length the Melian Dialogue, an incident clearly of minor historical importance, because it shows us something about Athenian imperialism and the arguments used to justify it. Thucydides' account of the plague follows directly upon the delivery of Pericles' splendid Funeral Oration, compelling the reader to raise questions about the relationship between them. Moreover, the History is notoriously silent on all sorts of matters pertaining to the economic, cultural, and intellectual developments of the period, except insofar as they are strictly related to Thucydides' political theme. This silence should be understood not as oversight but as the author's tacit means of conveying the precept that such things are not relevant to understanding the war and what is most important about the war.[6] For all these reasons, the art of interpreting Thucydides is a matter of developing a sensitive eye for emphases and juxtapositions, as well as for those

[4]See e.g., 1.20–22. References to Thucydides will henceforth be given in parentheses in the text by book, chapter, and, where relevant, section number, in the standard fashion. Book citations are omitted where the reference is clear.

On Thucydides' quarrel with the poets, see e.g. 1.9.3, 10.3, 11.2. I do not agree with Cornford (*Mythistoricus*) that Thucydides is weaving a semi-mythic tale out of the Peloponnesian War, on the model of Aeschylean tragedy. On Thucydides' combination of concern for particulars and for universals, see Finley, *Thucydides*, p. 73; Strauss, *The City and Man*, pp. 142–44.

[5]Translator's introduction "To the Reader," in Richard Schlatter, ed., *Hobbes's Thucydides* (New Brunswick: Rutgers University Press, 1975), p. 7.

[6]On economic factors in relation to the events of the period, see Cornford, *Mythistoricus*, p. 30; Romilly, *Athenian Imperialism*, pp. 72–73; Finley, *Thucydides*, pp. 117, 317; Strauss, *The City and Man*, pp. 153–54. Thucydides' virtual silence about the Megarian Decree as a cause of the war, in contrast to the opinions of some his contemporaries and much of modern scholarship, falls into this category.

explicit judgments that Thucydides occasionally makes, and an ear even for silences, insofar as these things are useful in guiding us to an awareness of Thucydides' purpose. This is the method I have followed,

In the opening of his work Thucydides suggests that he is uniquely able to combine factual accuracy with the revelation of universal truth because his subject, the Peloponnesian War, is a historical event that has proved especially revealing of permanent truth. Thucydides says that he began his project at the very beginning of the war, for he expected that the war would be a great war, the "most noteworthy" up to its time (*axiologōtaton* 1.1.1). And indeed, he continues, the war did prove to be the greatest "motion" or tumult that had ever beset the Greeks. Thucydides defends these claims about the war in the Archaeology, the first section of his History (1.1–19). The Archaeology details the Greeks' long, painstaking acquisition of wealth and power, from their original condition of poverty and dispersion to the peak attained just before the commencement of this war. It also describes the parallel rise of Greek civilization or culture out of barbarism. Both these developments appear central to Thucydides' claim about this war's greatness. The war squandered much of the combatants' carefully accumulated human capital, impoverishing, weakening, and finally threatening even to throw them back into barbarism. The struggle against the Persians, chronicled by Herodotus, was also a great fight, but it did not precipitate such a catastrophe, such a great "motion" among the Greeks.[7]

The Peloponnesian War of course differed from the Persian War in that it was a fratricidal war, fought not against a foreign enemy but among the Greeks themselves. The internecine quality of this war only increases its noteworthiness in Thucydides' eyes. Since the distinction between friend and enemy was not so clear as in other wars, the issue of justice was blurred in a way that finally became evident to many. During the Peloponnesian War, speakers could not easily rely on the kind of patriotic bluster that was adequate justification during the Persian Wars. Many of Thucydides' speakers appeal to the heroic deeds of the Persian Wars, for that period was perhaps the last time that a genuine common good, and hence a universally acknowledged justice, existed

[7]See 1.1.2. On self-destructiveness as an element of the greatness of this war see A. W. Gomme, *Essays in Greek History and Literature* (1937; rpt. Freeport, N.Y.: Books for Libraries Press, 1967), pp. 116–21; Finley, *Thucydides*, p. 220.

among the Greeks. But appeals to those times and those deeds did not suffice during the Peloponnesian War; Thucydidean speakers thus find themselves forced to grapple with ambiguous and intractible issues in speeches that shed especially revealing light on the fundamental problem of justice in wartime. The desperate speech of the Plataeans in Book Three of the History is paradigmatic (3.53–59). The new and openly immoral doctrine of power and justice proclaimed and acted upon by the Athenians exerts a similar compulsion on those who are forced to confront the Athenians in the war. Thus the Melians are prevented by the Athenians, and by the circumstances in which the Athenians place them, from appealing to the justice of their cause as a way out of their predicament (5.85–113). For Thucydides, the Peloponnesian War is uniquely worthy of attention in part because, more sharply than any other war, it exposed the grave ambiguities that attend the character, and the force, of justice in relations between states. From the point of view of the Greeks this was a war uglier perhaps, certainly less glorious, than the Persian Wars; but precisely for that reason it is for Thucydides and for us "more noteworthy" than other wars.

Thus one of Thucydides' great themes, one that the Peloponnesian War uniquely lends itself to, is the adequacy of the moral categories and qualities, such as justice, upon which conventional political understanding is built. The investigation of this theme is one of the purposes that inform Thucydides' History and govern its composition. This purpose may help account for Thucydides' decision to include speeches in his narrative. The speeches, as much as anything in Thucydides, show us people trapped by the fateful ambiguities of justice. The speakers reveal these ambiguities especially when they are compelled to make defective arguments while attempting to proclaim themselves simply and clearly in the right. The Plataeans and the Melians are again emblematic.

The speeches in the History exemplify the noteworthiness of this war in another respect as well. As presented by Thucydides, they indicate that during the Peloponnesian War the Greeks became conscious to an unprecedented degree of the problems that Thucydides has made his theme. The Peloponnesian War was in this sense the most self-conscious war, one in which at least some of the combatants were forced, or enabled, to move beyond the conventional, patriotic or moralistic, understanding of justice. The careful reader of Thucydides is led to do likewise.

This "enlightenment," for Thucydides' protagonists and readers alike, is not confined to the sphere of international politics and war: it extends also to the world of domestic politics. Indeed, the Peloponnesian War unsettled the conventional understanding of domestic politics and morality more thoroughly than it did the corresponding understanding of international politics. Thucydides' harrowing accounts of the plague in Athens and of the civil wars that overtook many cities in Greece during this time show how justice, along with piety and all the moral virtues that make political life and the city possible, came to be utterly overthrown (2.47–54; 3.82–83). Thucydides' accounts of these events, and the emphasis he accords them, raise troubling questions about the status of the civic qualities so easily trodden underfoot by "human nature" (3.82.2). They force us to wonder how firm the foundations of political life or the city can be. Such questions generally go unasked in times of peace and prosperity, but the rough schoolmaster war reveals them as permanent underlying issues in political life.

The figure of Alcibiades in Thucydides' History is of the greatest interest with regard to these themes. Alcibiades, in defiance of justice, unabashedly advances his city's ambition to rule over other cities. He is Athens' most vociferous advocate of the Sicilian expedition, the most daring attempt at imperial expansion by the city in perhaps two generations. All the questions of justice and power in international politics are thrown into high relief by this episode, and by the career of Alcibiades in general.

My study focuses on Alcibiades in part because he is key to Thucydides' treatment of these issues. Thucydides' presentation of Alcibiades thus cannot be separated entirely from his treatment of such broader themes as the character and justification of Athenian imperialism. We shall find that Thucydides' treatment of these themes shares all the ambiguity of his presentation of other aspects of the war. What makes Athenian imperialism, and Alcibiades' participation in it, ambiguous rather than simply deplorable is the fact that the Athenians' defense of their imperialism has some merit. The Athenians proclaim that their imperialism is a product of universal compulsions of human nature and international politics; they assert that powerful cities or nations will always respond as they do to these compulsions (e.g., 1.75–76). Thucydides' own account of Greek history provides some significant support for this view.

Moreover, the motivations that drove Athenian imperialism from its start are not entirely ungenerous.

Alcibiades is also important to Thucydides' investigation of the moral ambiguities of domestic politics, especially the question of how the political ambition of the individual statesman, and leadership itself, impinge on the political community. Alcibiades stands at the center of this question for Thucydides. A brilliant leader, he invariably aroused the strongest misgivings in those he led. He made extravagant claims to supremacy in the city, he lived in blatant disregard of conventional standards of modesty and self-restraint, and he proved willing to serve his city's enemies in time of war. But what makes Alcibiades ambiguous rather than simply sinister (there are sinister characters enough in Thucydides) is his unique ability to perform the greatest services for the city, and his complete willingness to do so, until the city exiled him. Thucydides clearly indicates that only Alcibiades could have saved the city from its enemies (6.15) and that Athens doomed itself to defeat when it condemned him. Yet one also sees from Thucydides' account the inevitability of Athenians' reaction against him. And the fact remains that perhaps the single most striking thing about Alcibiades' relation to Athens is his willingness not only to leave the city but to serve its enemies in time of war.

Alcibiades maintains that his willingness to serve Athens' enemies is justified because the city has turned against him. This argument, part of a well-developed outlook on politics as a whole, is remarkable for its redefinition of the traditional relationship between the political community and its greatest leaders. Alcibiades' understanding gives leaders important claims against the community, placing leader and community almost on a par, rather than making the leader subordinate to the community, as all other citizens are. This view is the key to understanding Alcibiades' claims for himself, and his behavior vis-à-vis Athens, as developed in the History. Because Thucydides insists that Athens was dependent on Alcibiades for its success and survival, Alcibiades' argument cannot be simply dismissed. Alcibiades' arguments, his abilities, and his actions compel Thucydides seriously to reconsider traditional views of the place of statesmen in political society and of their legitimate obligations to the community.

Pericles is the conventional candidate for the ideal of statesmanship

7

in Thucydides. The achievements of Pericles are indeed impressive, and must be kept in view when we study Alcibiades. Pericles, in contrast to Alcibiades, was modest and self-effacing, seemed to put the good of the city before his private interest, and inspired implicit trust in the Athenians. Pericles subscribed wholeheartedly to the conventional view of the relationship between statesman and city. However, Thucydides' presentation raises the question whether Pericles' adherence to this view may have stemmed in part from a degree of ignorance on his part of the vital role he played in the city. Pericles' modesty may derive in part from a misunderstanding of the role that leadership plays in a city like Athens. For this reason, among others, Pericles is a somewhat dubious counterpoise to Alcibiades. Alcibiades, meanwhile, seems to be the man of greater natural brilliance, just as he is clearly the man of fewer conventional encumbrances. Alcibiades' ambition is the highest, if only in the sense of the most extreme, and the purest, if only in the sense of the least inhibited, form of political ambition. He is not typical, but much can be learned about the nature of ambition from the spectacle of an individual and an ambition like this. In his arguments and in his actions as presented by Thucydides we see something of the predispositions of great political ambition and talent as such.

Within the context of the History as a whole, Alcibiades is the last in a line of memorable statesmen produced by the city of Athens, from Themistocles on. The Athens of Thucydides is a city that prides itself on its freedom and its individualism, and it is distinguished from all other cities by its enshrinement of these concepts at the very center of its political order. Thucydides' Athens can even be seen as a study in the long-term consequences of building a city on these foundations. The Athenians allowed human nature freer rein than did any other city, and they encouraged fuller development of individual human faculties. The city's uniquely brilliant leaders were products of this milieu. Alcibiades is the latest and most "liberated" of the Athenian leaders, and this is one reason that his case is so significant. In Alcibiades we see Athenian individualism, if not human nature itself, in its purest state.

Thus if Alcibiades' ambition is destined by its very extremism to detach itself from its native city, and almost to transcend the city as such, that circumstance will teach us important lessons about the ways of political ambition at its limit and about the true relationship between such ambition and the political community. If Alcibiades' ambition on the level of domestic politics proves so voracious as to provoke resentment and to stifle political life or dissolve it in grand rivalries, another set of important questions arises. If Alcibiades' conspicuous disregard for conventional morals proves a natural accompaniment of his ambition and his individualism, the political ramifications of that combination need to be explored. If Alcibiades' ambitions and his aspirations threaten the integrity of the city, we must consider how that circumstance affects our final evaluation of Alcibiades and of the city both. The tension between Alcibidean ambition and the city may prove to be another instance of the ambiguous relation between human nature and political life. Unlike the politically corrosive facets of human nature seen in the plague and the civil wars, however, this tension involves some of the finest, rather than the most corrupt, elements of human nature.

Much of Thucydides' reflection on the fundamental dilemmas and ambiguities of morality in politics is concentrated in his portrayal of Alcibiades. Thucydides is able to use the figure of Alcibiades in this way because Alcibiades' career reveals some of those ambiguities so clearly, and because he is a late figure in Thucydides' History. Alcibiades' career took place in the period during which the war and the internal dialectic of Athenian politics were bringing these dilemmas and ambiguities into the open. Alcibiades is also situated in the part of Thucydides' narrative that is itself more frank about these problems and the doubts they cast on the conventional moral–political perspective. This last point needs to be explained, and it brings us back to the problem of Thucydides' writing.

Thucydides, by dint of reflection on the grave doubts that the war cast on the ordinary understanding of politics, came to believe that this ordinary understanding was inadequate to a true appreciation of political reality. The History embodies this discovery and seeks to transform the understanding of those readers who have not yet realized it, especially those who remain captivated by the conventional outlook. Thucydides, it has sometimes been said, is an educator. Moreover, since he was at least for a time a political man, and since practical politics is his exclusive theme, Thucydides' educational project is best conceived of as directed primarily to practical political men.[8] Now, when undertaking to educate

---

[8]That Thucydides is an educator was of course the opinion of Hobbes; see also Jaeger, *Paideia*, p. 388; Finley, *Thucydides*, pp. 18, 309; Strauss, *The City and Man*, p. 202n;

such men, or any class of human beings for that matter, one must take account of their moral and intellectual presuppositions and proceed cautiously with regard to those views if one hopes to overcome or transform them. The existence of such presuppositions among ordinary political men, the character of these views, and their resistance to change comprise one of Thucydides' themes. For him, a city like Sparta and a man like Nicias display these characteristics most powerfully. In order successfully to educate or transform men of Nicias' type, to alert them to the inadequacies of some of their most cherished beliefs, a serious writer such as Thucydides would see that he must proceed very delicately, moving gradually from the inadequate understanding to the adequate one. This task is facilitated in Thucydides' case by the fact that the very logic of the war reveals the truth with gradually increasing clarity. Thucydides' presentation deliberately mimics this attribute of the war in such a way that his judgment seems to shift as the war progresses and as new problems come to light. These shifts are dictated by the delicacy of Thucydides' educational task. He seems to begin with relatively greater sympathy for Sparta, the bastion of the conventional moral outlook, and gradually moves toward a greater appreciation of Athens.[9] He seems to begin with greater sympathy for Nicias and disdain for Alcibiades, only gradually to show us the inadequacies of that point of view.

Many modern commentators have noted shifts of language and perspective within Thucydides' work. These discoveries have led to a school of interpretation that attempts to trace the inconsistencies to changes in Thucydides' own understanding that are incompletely integrated into the fabric of the History as we have it.[10] On the other hand, there have always been scholars willing to defend the essential consistency of the work and its teaching.[11] The hypothesis I have outlined accounts for

---

Bruell, "Athenian Imperialism," p. 11; John A. Wettergreen, "On the End of Thucydides' Narrative," *Interpretation* 9.1 (1979):93.

[9]Cf. Strauss, *The City and Man*, pp. 145–54, especially 151–52; 177; 179; p. 202n89 and context; Bruell, "Athenian Imperialism," p. 12.

[10]Romilly surveys the early literature on this subject, dubbed by some the "Thucydides question" (*Athenian Imperialism*, pp. 3–10), and some of the later literature (ibid., pp. 369–79). See also Virginia Hunter, "The Composition of Thucydides' History: A New Answer to the Problem," *Historia* 26 (1977):267–94. For a detailed overview of the arguments involved, see K. J. Dover, "Strata of Composition," in A. W. Gomme, A. Andrewes, and Dover, *A Historical Commentary on Thucydides*, 5 vols. (Oxford: Clarendon Press, 1945–81), vol. 5, app. 2, pp. 384–444.

[11]See again Romilly's survey in *Athenian Imperialism*. One of the most influential of

systematic changes in Thucydides' presentation but explains them in terms of an underlying unity of purpose.[12] This approach enables one to characterize certain positions taken by Thucydides as "early" or "late," referring not to changes of attitude on Thucydides' part but to shifts mandated by the plan of the work itself. Although this book does not devote itself systematically to developing this argument about the composition of the History, it supports and makes use of it in direct and indirect ways.

This book is divided into four chapters, in a scheme of organization that I hope does some justice both to Thucydides' treatment of Alcibiades and to the Thucydidean themes closely connected to him. The first chapter treats rather generally of Athenian imperialism, which attains a kind of "Alcibidean" peak in the voting on the Sicilian expedition. The second begins an investigation of Alcibiades' own ambitions and his political understanding, for the most part as these are revealed in his speeches. The third chapter moves to the scene in Book Eight, after the demise of the Sicilian expedition, in which Alcibiades moves from the Spartan to the Persian to the Athenian camp. These developments provide the basis for a reinvestigation of Athenian imperialism and Athenian politics, and of the practical repercussions of Alcibiades' ambitions and his political understanding. Chapter 4 offers a final account of Alcibiades' politics and makes a final judgment, guided by Thucydides, on those politics and on Alcibiades himself. We should not be surprised if the final estimation of this man, whose career and whose very existence breathe ambiguity, contains some irreducible measure of that ambiguity itself.

---

these defenses is that of Finley (especially *Three Essays*, chap. 3). See also James Boyd White, *When Words Lose Their Meaning* (Chicago: University of Chicago Press, 1984), p. 88 and n39; Connor, *Thucydides*, p. 10.

[12]Romilly combines the "unity" and "changefulness" hypotheses in a different way (*Athenian Imperialism*), tracing a uniform concern with Athenian imperialism throughout the work but identifying different periods of composition at which Thucydides' attitude toward it changed. I argue that such changes as do take place over the course of the History are there by design. Romilly speaks of "layers" of composition visible within passages; I argue that Thucydides in earlier passages has already begun sowing the seeds of later reevaluations. I do not propose, however, to account in this way for every putative change of judgment that has been alleged in Thucydidean scholarship. The great majority of them seem simply false discoveries. This is the burden of Finley's defense of the unity of the History, which I believe is substantially correct (see above, note 11).

1

The Alcibidean Moment

THE moment of the Sicilian expedition, the moment when Alcibiades and Athens come together to decree what is the most daring scheme of the Peloponnesian War, is a climactic one in Thucydides' History. This event, which takes place almost exactly halfway through the war, is pivotal not only in the course of the war but also in the life of the city of Athens. It is climactic in part because it represents a culmination of the long and astonishing history of Athenian imperialism in Thucydides' work. The most daring of cities and the boldest of its bold commanders set in motion an imperial scheme of the greatest audacity. What results is the most spectacular single instance of Athenian imperialism that Thucydides describes at any length in his book. It is also the last: the grand and extravagant Sicilian project issues in a disaster that signals the decline, and eventual destruction, of Athenian power. In the end, the Sicilian expedition represents perhaps the most important single vindication of Thucydides' expectation, which he says he had at the beginning of the war, that the Peloponnesian War would be a great war (1.1). The stormy relationship between Athens and its statesman Alcibiades has much to do with both the inception of the scheme and its disastrous outcome for the city.

The Sicilian expedition has a significance in Thucydides that goes beyond the purely strategic to touch on broader themes, indeed the broadest. The most comprehensive spectacle that Thucydides' History presents is the slow and painstaking rise of human civilization out of a poor, weak, and barbarous past; toward increasing power and wealth, order, and civilization; and into a war that squanders that precious human accomplishment. The war between Athens and Sparta precipitates a permanent decline of Greek power and to some extent even returns the Greeks to barbarism.[1] Before the Sicilian expedition, Athens is close to the peak of her power, wealth, and self-assurance, but the destruction of the Athenian force in Sicily leaves no Greek city able to support any comparable undertaking. The scale of the war itself seems diminished thereafter. Of greater concern is the potential return to barbarism. Its most notorious apparent manifestation, the Melian Dialogue, precedes rather than follows the Sicilian expedition in Thucydides' presentation. In fact, Thucydides never lets us lose sight of the paradox that Athenian imperialism, while representing a kind of peak in human achievement, is also gravely unjust. Thucydides' presentation of the Sicilian expedition reflects faithfully both the splendid and the unjust. In fact the Athenians themselves do not seem to be spared this insight: the combined spectacle of the extravagant Alcibiades and a grave impiety committed in the city leads them, in a reflex of self-doubt, to repudiate Alcibiades and entrust the conduct of the expedition in effect to the pious and conservative Nicias.

Alcibiades, the most uncompromising advocate of the Sicilian expedition at Athens and also the very incarnation of what we might call the Sicilian spirit in the city, embodies the fundamental ambiguities of that spirit. Interpretators have never agreed whether Thucydides' Alcibiades represents the flower of Athenian and Greek development or its final corruption. This is a question that must be approached with the greatest care and subtlety, and only with the proper preparation. Alcibiades, in his speech championing the expedition to Sicily, asserts that he is merely a successor to an eminently honorable tradition of great statesmen (6.16.5–6). Alcibiades clearly sees his former guardian, Per-

[1]On the decline of Greek culture as one of Thucydides' themes see Paul Shorey, "On the Implicit Ethics and Psychology of Thucydides," *Transactions of the American Philological Society* 24 (1893):66; Leo Strauss, *The City and Man* (Chicago: University of Chicago Press, 1977), pp. 156–57; W. Robert Conner, *Thucydides* (Princeton: Princeton University Press, 1984), p. 105; James Boyd White, *When Words Lose Their Meanings* (Chicago: University of Chicago Press, 1984), chap. 3.

icles, as one of his predecessors, but Alcibiades' advocacy of the Sicilian expedition represents the final overthrow of Pericles' policy for the war—only the first of the ways he turns the example of Pericles on its head.

Pericles' war policy was essentially a defensive one. He anticipated, or hoped, that the war would not be a great war but a small series of skirmishes, perhaps damaging the Peloponnesians peripherally but leaving the Athenian empire essentially unchanged. Accordingly, he urgently advised the Athenians not to undertake any new conquests while the war was under way (1.143–44; 2.65.7, 11–13). The vote on the Sicilian expedition, which we may justly call the Alcibidean and non-Periclean moment at Athens, is the final triumph of a new war strategy, but it is also an emblem of the post-Periclean epoch in Athenian politics. That at any rate is the way Thucydides treats it in his eulogy of Pericles, where he first makes mention of the expedition (2.65). Apart from the obviously disastrous military consequences that the Sicilian defeat had for Athens, Thucydides there connects the entire debacle, in a way that is not made entirely clear, to popular license and factious demagogues, which later became the real cause of the city's downfall (2.65.10–13). Yet Thucydides conspicuously refrains from saying in his eulogy that the Sicilian expedition was a mistake: he claims only that it was poorly carried out (2.65.11). Indeed, Thucydides insists throughout his presentation of the expedition that Athens could easily have prevailed if it had not removed from command and exiled Alcibiades (2.65.7, 11; 6.31.6; 6.15.4).

It is by no means correct to say that Thucydides, even in his eulogy of Pericles, unambiguously endorses Pericles' war policy. Pericles after all, unlike Thucydides, failed to foresee the extent and duration of the war, two things that doomed his cautious policy to failure. Alcibiades meanwhile, in his speech in favor of the expedition, plausibly poses as a conservative, if a peculiarly Athenian one, by arguing that such an undertaking is the most typically Athenian thing to pursue. His position echoes Thucydides' insinuation in his eulogy of Pericles that the expedition was predictable under the circumstances (2.65.11). Alcibiades argues that, aside from the fact that prudence compels imperial powers to overthrow all potential rivals, Athenians in particular are required by their way of life to be continually enterprising. Inactivity for a city like Athens is not only uncharacteristic but positively dangerous, for both internal and external reasons (6.18.3, 7).

14

The Sicilian expedition, in which the ambitions of Alcibiades and Athens come together most powerfully and for the first time in Thucydides' History, is the appropriate beginning point for a study of Alcibiades' significance. The evaluation of Alcibiades cannot be separated from an evaluation of Athenian imperialism, which recieves its fullest expression in Thucydides in the Sicilian expedition. To what extent Thucydides agrees that the Athenian character or way of life compels the city to undertake this project; to what extent the Periclean policy of keeping still actually courted danger for Athens, from within and without; and to what extent Alcibiades is a proper leader for this city and this enterprise are questions we can evaluate only by looking more closely at Thucydides' understanding of Athenian imperialism and the Athenian way of life. Such an examination will put us in a better position to resolve the ambiguities that surround the Sicilian expedition and to begin properly to evaluate Alcibiades and even Pericles.

The theme of Sicily as an object of Athenian longing or desire seems to develop as a crescendo in Thucydides' History, reaching its peak at the moment the expedition is decided on. According to Thucydides, Sicily was at the back of Athenians' minds before the war broke out, and it even made a certain contribution to the coming of the war: the Athenians contracted their provocative alliance with Corcyra in part because Corcyra was conveniently situated for an assault on Sicily (1.44.3; 1.36.2). Early in the war, at the request of some Sicilians, Athens sent a small expedition to the island, professedly on the grounds of their kinship to some cities there that were being oppressed, but also in part to test whether the affairs of Sicily could be brought under their control (3.86.4). Not much later they sent out a larger force to augment the first (3.115.4; 4.2.2).

Thucydides' presentation suggests that the longing for faraway Sicily began as something almost hypothetical and became sharper as the war progressed. The Athenians responded to it almost sheepishly at first, by sending ships in the respectable name of kinship. The Athenians doubtless would not have refused Sicily if it had fallen in their laps—indeed there are signs that they furtively wish it would[2]—but they are willing

[2]The strongest such sign is the ire they display when their generals return from the early mission to Sicily without having established Athenian influence there—in spite of the fact that their original charge (at least as Thucydides relays it) had not clearly proposed any such goal for the mission (3.86, 3.115, 4.65).

15

neither to undertake the effort nor, it seems, fully to confront the thought of subduing it (note even 6.8.2). After the conclusion of the Peace of Nicias, however, the Athenians begin to think more seriously about Sicily. At the beginning of Book Six of the History, the Athenians wish unambiguously to conquer Sicily, by sending out a larger armament than they sent before (6.1.1). It is in this spirit that they first decree the expedition—although it is still on the pretext of helping their friends in Sicily against the Syracusans. Five days later, in an assembly devoted to settling the details of the expedition, Nicias begs a reconsideration of the whole issue, and his speech and that of Alcibiades, opposed to and in favor of the expedition, follow. It is in this debate that the project of subduing and ruling all of Sicily is presented and defended publicly for the first time in Thucydides' History; the man who proposes the plan is Alcibiades.[3]

In approving Alcibiades' speech, which they immediately do, the Athenians seem for the first time to confront their Sicilian ambition without pretext. The significance of their choice goes beyond this, however, for the debate about the expedition between Nicias and Alcibiades is in reality a far-ranging one between opposed political understandings at the very poles of Athenian politics, the only contest of this kind in Thucydides. The Athenians' approval of Alcibiades involves the rejection of Nicias' counsel in equal measure; and Nicias is the only major advocate of restraint remaining in Athens. After the choice is made, the inept Nicias, still attempting to dissuade the Athenians, proposes an armament so huge that its only possible goal can be the domination of all of Sicily (although Nicias persists in hoping for less: 6.47), an armament the size of which appears to guarantee the safety and success of the project. The Athenians embrace the Nician amendment, and in doing so they fall in love with the enterprise. In one of the most striking passages of the History, Thucydides says that at that moment an erotic passion to sail

---

[3]We know from other sources that there were all along in Athens politicians who openly cherished dreams of expansion westward (Aristophanes *Knights* 174, 1303; *Peace* 250; cf. Plutarch *Alcibiades* 17). See John H. Finley, *Thucydides* (Ann Arbor: University of Michigan Press, 1963), p. 213; Connor, *Thucydides*, p. 35n35. Thucydides' treatment of Athenians' longing for Sicily nevertheless has the character indicated. See also Jacqueline de Romilly, *Thucydides and Athenian Imperialism*, trans. P. Thody (New York: Barnes & Noble, 1963), p. 195; H. D. Westlake, "Athenian Aims in Sicily, 427–424, B.C.," *Historia* 9 (1960):385–402.

away fell on all alike (6.24). Thus the peak or consummation of Athenian imperial daring coincides with an outburst of erotic passion directed at alluring and distant Sicily.

The power of Thucydides' description of Athenian eagerness at this moment can only create in us a sense of the utter futility of Nicias' hope, which was also Pericles' hope, that the Athenians could be turned away from such projects. It reminds us of Thucydides' suggestion, in his eulogy of Pericles, that this was just the sort of thing to be expected from a city like Athens. At any rate, when the moment finally comes, readers of Thucydides are not surprised by it, and not only because we were alerted to it at that early juncture. The passion for Sicilian conquest is the culmination of the theme of Sicily in the History, as well as the triumph of some distinctive Athenian traits themselves themes of Thucydides. His treatment of these traits forms the core of Thucydides' understanding of the impetus behind the Sicilian project and of the sources of Athenian imperialism.

The Athenian Character and Athenian Imperialism

To inquire about the causes of Athenian imperialism in Thucydides' work is necessarily to consider the Athenian character. That "national character" is central to Thucydides' account of Athenian imperialism has always been recognized, but there have been few serious attempts to explore Thucydides' account of the Athenian character. His account provides us with an explanation not only of how the distinctive Athenian character came into being, but also of its grounding in permanent and universal human traits. One of these is the erotic passion seen at the moment of the Sicilian expedition.

The Athenian character receives a great deal of attention in Thucydides' History. Friends and enemies of the city alike speak of the Athenian character when called upon to explain Athenian imperialism, indeed Athenian behavior in general; Thucydides in his own portrayal does likewise. If we look at the whole of what is said about the character of the Athenians in the History, a remarkably consistent portrait emerges. By all accounts the Athenians are restless, adventurous, bold beyond measure and beyond precedent. This seems to account for both their astounding imperial success, and the threat they pose to other cities. The Corinthians in Sparta before the war are the first to speak of the

17

Athenian character; they make all these points (1.68–71); using the word *daring* to denote the driven, almost frantic character of the Athenians (1.70.3), as do almost all who broach the subject subsequently, Athenians and non-Athenians alike. *Daring* in fact is reserved almost exclusively in Thucydides for descriptions of Athenian acts and the Athenian character—it is practically a technical term.[4] The Athenians are daring, the Spartans are the opposite (8.96.4–5); Brasidas is the single Spartan exception (5.7.2; 2.87; 2.89.5). The Syracusans alone succeed in driving back the Athenians; they do so by becoming daring (6.69.1; 7.21.3–4; 8.96.5). Daring is one of the traits that lies at the core of the kinetic, expansive Athenian character. But what exactly does it signify in the quasi-technical usage of the History? Daring may be a good word to describe the Athenian character as it unfolds in Thucydides, but as a political trait it seems both insubstantial and enigmatic. Yet because it seems to supplant other, more traditional qualities in the Athenians, in particular courage.[5] The shift to daring in imperial Athens is clearly significant, but it is also something that requires further interpretation. Its clarification requires consideration of passages that are scattered through the first parts of the History.

The best place to begin an investigation of this peculiar Athenian trait is with the most famous description of the Athenian character in Thu-

---

[4]The word I translate as "daring" is *tolma*; the patterns of its use can be traced with the help of any word index to Thucydides, for example that of E. A. Bétant (*Lexicon Thucydideum* [Hildesheim: Georg Olms, 1961]). The patterns are quite striking, though to my knowledge they have gone virtually unnoticed. See Pierre Huart, *Le vocabulaire de l'analyse psychologique dans l'oeuvre de Thucydide* (Paris: Librairie Klincksieck, 1968), pp. 431–36. Interpreters have often noted that Thucydides' presentation of Athens revolves around certain significant words—e.g., *polypragmosyne* for Ehrenberg (Victor Ehrenberg, "Polypragmosyne: A Study in Greek Politics," *Journal of Hellenic Studies* 68 [1947]:46–67), *gnome* and *techne* for Edmunds (Lowell Edmunds, *Chance and Intelligence in Thucydides* [Cambridge: Harvard University Press, 1975]), and a whole vocabulary of words for White (*Words*, chap. 3). Almost all of these arguments are justified. *Tolma* is one of these significant words, and in some respects, I shall argue, the most important. See also J. Peter Euben, "The Battle of Salamis and the Origins of Political Theory," *Political Theory* 14 (1986):359–90.

[5]It should be noted that the Greek word *tolma* covers the same range as the English word "daring," from courage to rashness ("courage" is in Greek *andreia*). In fact, the rarity with which the word "courage" is applied to the Athenians in Thucydides is quite as striking as their corner on daring (see n. 6 below). This fact is lost or blunted in all the translations I am aware of, which are as likely to translate "courage" as "daring" for *tolma*.

cydides, the Funeral Oration of Pericles. The Funeral Oration is an extravagant praise of the Athenian character, which Pericles identifies as one of the prime causes of Athenian greatness and accomplishment. Because his is a speech in praise of men who died in war, Pericles' virtual failure to mention courage as one of the virtues of the Athenian character is quite striking. Where we might expect him to speak of Athenian courage, he speaks instead generically of the "virtue" of his countrymen or, more pointedly, of their daring.[6] The daring of the men who died, he says, should be the model for those who survive (2.43.1). The Athenians as a race are characterized by a native daring that allows them, without effort, to be the equal of others who take great pains to cultivate virtue (39.4). The greatness of the empire, which makes the city of Athens uniquely worth dying for, was built according to Pericles by the daring and dutifulness of the present Athenians' ancestors (43.1). Pericles goes so far as to boast that the Athenians have "compelled" every sea and every land to yield to their daring, enabling them to leave "immortal" monuments of themselves "everywhere" (2.41.4).

Pericles presents the daring of the Athenians not only as one of their most praiseworthy traits but as a trait very closely connected with their empire. The primary effect of Athenian daring seems to be the empire. Indeed, if we reflect on the difference between courage and daring as suggested by the remarks of Pericles or the Corinthians, we see that daring is adventurous and expansive, willing to go where courage will not; it is a specifically imperial or imperialistic quality. Athenian daring and Athenian imperialism seem so closely related in fact that we are led to wonder whether they are not coeval. The Athenian empire, after all, had a definite genesis in the not-too-distant past. The empire was built by one of the generations Pericles speaks of. We thus might find clues in Thucydides' account of the origin of the Athenian empire as to the nature of Athens' characteristic imperialism.

The theme of the birth and growth of the Athenian empire is developed with great care by Thucydides. Book One of the History is systematically devoted to the inevitability of the Peloponnesian War; the rise of the Athenian empire, and the fear it struck into the Spartans, is

---

[6]Pericles mentions courage only once, when he is developing a specific contrast to the Spartans (2.39.4; cf. 39.1). This, if I am not mistaken, is the only time the word is applied directly to Athenians in the History (cf. 2.64.2).

the real cause of the war in Thucydides' exposition. Thucydides shows the Athenian empire growing out of circumstances connected with the second great Persian invasion of Greece. During this invasion the Athenians, in order to help defend the Greeks, were driven to abandon their homeland and fight the enemy at sea. That moment was in fact a watershed in Athenian history. Before it, Athens was not a particularly great power in Greece; afterward its naval power and empire grew dramatically and with astonishing rapidity (cf. 1.14.3). Pericles, in a speech prior to the Funeral Oration, explains the general sequence of events in the following way: the present Athenians' ancestors, beginning literally with nothing, not even their homes and possessions, succeeded both in defeating the Persians and building the empire by dint of resolve and daring more than luck or power (1.144.4). In Pericles' view, the Athenian deeds in the Persian Wars are of the same stuff as the imperialism that followed on their heels. As to daring itself, Pericles contends that it somehow creates power, or at any rate allows those who possess it to accomplish more than their power otherwise would allow. This is a feature on which the Corinthians also agree (1.70.3).

Thucydides' own presentation of Athens' rise as an imperial power in Book One bears out and expands on the link suggested by Pericles between Athens' accomplishment in the Persian Wars and its subsequent imperialism. Athenian daring is visible everywhere in Book One, and everything points back to the moment of the Persian Wars. Before the wars, what little we hear of Athens makes no reference to daring; afterward, daring is Athens' most characteristic trait. Of the pivotal moment itself Thucydides says, the first time he mentions it, that as the massive Persian force advanced, the Athenians resolved to abandon their city; packing up their goods, they embarked on their ships and "became seamen" (*nautikoi egenonto*, 1.18.2). It seems that this particular moment or action somehow transformed the character of the city of Athens. This transformation had much to do with Athens' subsequent career.

Thucydides' brief yet pregnant remark is not an idle one. Nor are he and Pericles the only Athenians to attribute to the feat of abandoning the city to fight the Persians a special significance. That attitude was in fact common in the city, as Thucydides indicates by giving perhaps the fullest description, and the greatest praise, of those deeds to certain anonymous Athenian envoys who speak at Sparta before the war. The anonymity of these envoys appears designed in part to indicate that they

20

speak for the city as a whole.[7] These Athenians, like Pericles, d
the extraordinary character of their city and its citizens as a means oɪ
demonstrating its greatness.[8] Like Pericles, they make Athenian daring
a primary theme of their argument. But their presentation places the
greatest emphasis on the daring displayed by the city during the Persian
Wars. The way they introduce their account of these actions shows that
they believe the Athenian actions at that juncture to be paradigmatic,
illuminating for anyone who desires to know what kind of a city Athens
is. They will refrain, they say, from speaking of ancient things that are
not to the point,[9] but they are "compelled" to mention the deeds of the
Persian Wars: they are repeating the story only because it is indispensable
to the point of their speech, the demonstration of Athenian greatness
and power. The fact that Athens participated in the fight against the
Persians at all was, as the envoys correctly point out, a sign of the most
extraordinary zeal. Indeed it was a zeal, they say, of the most extreme
daring[10] that led the Athenians, when all the cities up to its borders had
already been enslaved by the Persians, to abandon their homeland yet
not disperse, to embark as it were from a city that was no more and
rely on themselves as their last, slender hope of facing the Persian throng
(1.74). Their hope proved not so desperate as they had thought: they
and their allies defeated the Persians at Salamis, thus paving the way for
the liberation of all of Greece.

We learn from Thucydides and the anonymous Athenians both that
the alliance of cities forged after this event for the final expulsion of the
Persians from Greece became the basis of the Athenian empire, as the
Athenians took increasingly exclusive control of it. Thucydides, how-

---

[7]On this point, see Romilly, *Athenian Imperialism*, pp. 108, 242; Peter R. Pouncey,
The Necessities of War: A Study of Thucydides' Pessimism (New York: Columbia University
Press, 1980), p. 62. For a different view, see Werner Jaeger, *Paideia: The Ideals of Greek
Culture*, vol. 1, trans. G. Highet (Oxford: Oxford University Press, 1939), p. 393.

[8]The anonymous Athenians' speech is devoted (according to the speakers and to
Thucydides) to a demonstration of Athenian power: they point to the Athenian character,
rather than to the city's wealth or to the number of its ships, to demonstrate that power
(1.72.1, 73.1, 73.2–4, 74). See also A. E. Raubitschek, "The Speech of the Athenians
at Sparta," Philip A. Stadter, ed., *The Speeches in Thucydides* (Chapel Hill: University of
North Carolina Press, 1973); Strauss, *The City and Man*, p. 171.

[9]Narrations of quasi-mythic ancient deeds were in fact common in speeches of a
certain kind. The Scholiast here mentions possible tales about the Amazons or the Her-
aclids. See, e.g., Isocrates *Panegyricus* 20–32, 68–72.

[10]This appears to be the only occurrence of the superlative *most daring* in the History.

ever, tells us, as the anonymous Athenians do not, that the Greek cities regarded Athens with some apprehension not only after they became an imperial power but immediately after the Persian defeat at Salamis. Although the allies were glad to make use of Athenian zeal against the Persians, Thucydides indicates that something about that zeal disturbed them. Thus when the Athenians returned to an Athens devastated by the Persians and undertook among other things to rebuild its walls, the other cities opposed it fearing, Thucydides says, not only the size of the newly enlarged Athenian navy but the daring that had "come into being" in the Athenians during the Persian invasion (1.90.1). The Athenians thus were not alone in viewing their own actions during that crisis as a great watershed and a catalyst in the transformation of their character. The other cities saw this and were not heartened by the sight. The great period of Athenian imperialism followed.

The question that arises on the basis of this account of the birth of the Athenian imperial character is how we are to understand the traumatic moment of the second Persian invasion to have given the Athenian character the volatile and expansive daring that became its hallmark. To review Thucydides' terse, early formulation, the Athenians at that moment packed up their things, got onto their ships, and became seamen (1.18.2). The fact that Athens was a naval power is sometimes taken to be a sufficient explanation of the Athenian character and imperialism,[11] but Corinth and the islanders were maritime cities as well, and none of them resembled Athens in its daring or its imperialism. Not seafaring as such, but seafaring as it came into being at Athens, explains the Athenian character and Athenian imperialism. Only the Athenians became seamen in the course of a struggle in which they lost, if only temporarily, their connection with their homeland. For no other city did "becoming nautical" involve such a baptism; no other citizens became seamen in so complete, or so literal, a sense.

In order to grasp the political significance of the Athenians' actions, we must first think of all the things that a fixed location, a piece of ground, mean to a city and what it would mean to give all that up.

[11]Suggestions of this kind have been made by Albert Thibaudet, *La campagne avec Thucydide* (Paris: Editions de la Nouvelle Revue Française, 1922), p. 79 (cf. pp. 84–85); Romilly *Athenian Imperialism*, pp. 67–70; and John H. Finley, Jr., *Three Essays on Thucydides* (Cambridge, Mass: Harvard University Press, 1967), p. 143; Finley, *Thucydides*, p. 90.

From that point of view it seems that in becoming, however briefly, men without place, the Athenians severed in some way their connections with all the fixed things that the life of a city normally revolves around, that normally serve as its stable, conservative base.[12] But the ramifications of this action go further: there is another aspect of the matter to which we must give equal if not greater weight, an aspect that is to some extent peculiar to the Greek cities and that has to do with Greek piety.

Generalizations about Greek piety are difficult to make because that piety consisted of numerous elements, some of which were in conflict with one another, and others of which are not fully known to us.[13] Nonetheless, some of the elements significant especially for the life of the city were inextricably bound to place: to sacred ground, to temples or shrines, to ancestral graves. From the point of view of this piety, the

[12]The traumatic character of the abandonment of the land can be judged in part from 2.15; for interpretations of that passage relevant to our purposes, see Thibaudet, *La campagne*, p. 199; Michael Palmer, "Love of Glory and the Common Good," *American Political Science Review* 76 (1982):827. On the general point, see also Euben, "Battle of Salamis"; and, for an ironic but important view, pseudo-Xenophon *Constitution of the Athenians* 2.14.

[13]See, e.g., E. R. Dodds, *The Greeks and the Irrational* (Berkeley: University of California Press, 1951), esp. chaps. 2, 6; G. B. Grundy, *Thucydides and the History of His Age*, 2 vols. (Oxford: Blackwell, 1948), 2:87–88; Gustave Glotz, *La solidarité de la famille dans le droit criminel en Grèce* (Paris: Albert Fontemoing, 1904). The following discussion owes much to Fustel de Coulanges, *The Ancient City*. Some of his premises or conclusions concerning ancient piety have been called into question by recent scholarship on the ancient city that questions our understanding of the role of piety in forming the community of the cities. The point on which Fustel is held to be weakest is his argument concerning the importance to ancient piety of the *gens*, the family or extended family. But this point is not directly connected to the role of piety in forming the community of the city. For brief reviews of this problem, see the introductions by Arnaldo Momigliano and S. C. Humphreys to *The Ancient City* (Baltimore: Johns Hopkins University Press, 1980). Fustel treats the piety of the city to some extent as an extension of the piety of the *gens*, but he also sees it as a modification of the latter. The piety and the institution of the *gens* sometimes notoriously conflicted with the community of the city.

The traditional piety at the core of the Greek city's community was surely somewhat attenuated by the middle fifth century, especially in such a large and cosmopolitan city as Athens. To that extent, considerations of the kind I am advancing to help account for the transformation of the Athenian character would be less significant. It would be a grave mistake nevertheless to underestimate the importance of piety, especially given the role it plays in Thucydides' History as a whole. Although piety certainly eroded in Athens over the course of the fifth century, I shall argue that according to Thucydides the erosion was due in large part to the corrosive incubus of imperialism, which owed its own birth in turn to a crucial weakening of the impulses of piety.

city was constituted in effect by common rites and sacred festivals, and citizenship was identical with competence to participate in the common cults. These festivals and rites took in the guardian divinities belonging to the city as well as the generations of its ancestors, divine and spiritual beings who more or less immovably inhabited the places associated with their cults. Those familiar with Greek piety only through the rather rarefied sorts of myths that grew up as the heritage of all the Greek cities in common are not likely to appreciate this fact, although it is a fact of special relevance to the point now under discussion. When the Athenians abandoned their city to the Persians, therefore, they also abandoned their holy places, the abodes of their gods, and their ancestral graves. It would be a real question within Greek piety whether a city could have any being at all under such circumstances; and this in fact seems to be behind the anonymous Athenians' emphasis on the fact that the Athenians did not simply disperse, did not consider the city to have been ruined or dissolved, and joined the common fight although they were issuing in effect from a city that was no more (1.74.2–4). The Athenians did not disband, and went on to glorious victory instead; but the principle or foundation of their community could not help being altered by the experience.

From the point of view of the other Greek cities, the unexampled zeal exhibited by Athens in the Persian Wars would thus have had not only an admirable but a terrible or shocking quality as well. The Athenians' astonishing deed, which seems to display the greatest courage, also bears a certain tincture of impiety. It might go beyond what is permitted to human courage. It is audacity; it is daring. In any event, it is certainly mistaken to assume—as the Athenians sometimes do (e.g., 1.74.4; 6.82.4)—that the cities that refused to abandon their land to the Persians surrendered purely out of cowardice.

It is sometimes said that the defeat of the Persian hordes ushered in a new era of Greek self-assurance by indisputably proving the superiority of the polis and of freedom to barbarism and Persian despotism.[14] Thucydides suggests that the Athenians in particular gained self-assurance

[14]See Victor Ehrenberg, *From Solon to Socrates* (London: Methuen, 1968), p. 177; J. B. Bury, *The Ancient Greek Historians* (London: Macmillan, 1909), p. 44; Arnaldo Momigliano, *Essays in Ancient and Modern Historiography* (Middletown, Conn.: Wesleyan University Press, 1977), pp. 164–65; Hegel, *The Philosophy of History*, trans. J. Sibree (New York: Colonial Press, 1900), p. 257. See also Euben, "Battle of Salamis."

of a revolutionary kind from this experience. Perhaps one of the things they discovered as a body on their ships was the enormous potential of what we may call purely human power, standing on its own and bereft of its traditional supports, terrestrial or otherwise. In the traditional scheme of things, those suppports function also as restraints: the gods do not countenance every undertaking. Insofar as daring among the Athenians represents a transformation of and a replacement for traditional courage, therefore, it is an innovation predicated in part, if not wholly, on overcoming the inhibitions imposed by piety. Those inhibitions include restrictions, in the name of justice, on the accumulation and exercise of power. Immorality is thus at the core of the significance of daring in Thucydides' Athenians. The revolution represented by the replacement of courage with daring is in the first instance what we might call an intellectual revolution, based on a revolutionary discovery or awareness. This is seen later in the highly sophisticated rationale for empire that the Athenians develop. The earlier consequences of this revolution, however, are quite concrete, as the Athenians turn from the daring displayed against the Persians to the expansion of their own power.

If the essential features of Athenian imperialism were forged in the crucible of the Persian Wars, it was the statesman Themistocles who more than any other individual was responsible for guiding Athenian daring immediately after the war and creating the proper conditions for a rapid increase in Athenian power.[15] He succeeded in rebuilding the walls of Athens in spite of Greek, especially Spartan, opposition, and he persuaded the Athenians to devote serious attention to the Peiraeus (1.89–93). It was Themistocles, in Thucydides' phrase, who first "dared" tell the Athenians after the war that they should take to the sea (1.93.4). He first perceived the enormous potential for power connected with becoming a nation of seamen, and he started the Athenians down that path.

[15]A peculiar feature of Thucydides' presentation is that he does not connect Themistocles with the fateful decision to abandon the city in the Persian Wars, though Plutarch does so in recounting Themistocles' famous interpretation of the oracle of the "wooden walls" (Plutarch *Themistocles* 9, 10). Thucydides has Themistocles only as the mastermind of early imperial policy after the Persian Wars. Whatever we may say about Thucydides' motive in tailoring his account this way, it does give the decision to abandon the city more the appearance of spontaneous choice, while also depriving it of any divine or oracular sanction.

Once under way, the Athenians rose astonishingly quickly to the position Themistocles foresaw for them. After dwelling rather pointedly on the events of the Persian Wars and their immediate aftermath, Thucydides quite briefly narrates the roughly fifty years' history that passed between the end of the Persian Wars and the beginning of the Peloponnesian War. His brevity is surprising because this is the period of Athens' imperial expansion proper. The great compression of Thucydides' account, the *Pentekontaetia* (1.89–117), serves only to exaggerate our impression of the rapidity of Athens' rise.[16] It also suggests that Thucydides believes the essence of Athenian imperialism to be sufficiently elucidated in earlier events, the subsequent drama being, therefore, merely an unfolding of the forces created or unleashed there. The drama is quite an astonishing one. The Athenians push the Persians out of Ionia and Asia Minor, establish firm control over their allies, and undertake major expeditions to Cyprus and Egypt, all apparently with no further provocation than their own character and ambition. Thucydides suppresses the names of virtually all the statesmen who would have counseled these enterprises, strengthening the impression of complete spontaneity in the city's actions. Indeed, on the basis of his account, is scarcely seems possible to give reasons or motives for any particular enterprise during the period, so daring and promiscuous are the Athenians. Athenian enterprise seems inexhaustible; the Athenian empire is built before our eyes in a veritable explosion of activity that begins with the Persian invasion of Greece.

The Athenians emerge from the activity of these fifty years in firm possession of an empire and sufficient power to threaten the Spartans and their allies. Much of that power and that threat lies simply in the Athenians' daring character. This is the period during which the anonymous Athenians praise their city at Sparta. What they say there shows that their daring has indeed liberated itself from the restraints that the Greeks and others thought applied to cities' relations among themselves,

---

[16]It has been recognized that the *Pentekontaetia* is a highly selective exposition, even by Thucydidean standards, tailored to create a certain impression or demonstrate a point. See for example Romilly, *Athenian Imperialism*, pp. 61–64; F. E. Adcock, *Thucydides and His History* (Cambridge: Cambridge University Press, 1963), p. 2; Christopher Bruell, "Thucydides' View of Athenian Imperialism," *American Political Science Review*, 68 (1974):14. Cf. also Connor, *Thucydides*, p. 42; Ehrenberg, *Solon to Socrates*, p. 187; White, *Words*, p. 87.

in particular divine restraints and restraints of justice. The Athenians at Sparta say nothing about the gods, or any higher sanction for their actions; they are the first to voice their city's notorious thesis that, in establishing an empire and enslaving their fellow Greeks, they are simply acting in accordance with certain necessary and universal compulsions of fear, honor, and profit (1.75–76). Hence, they say, they cannot be blamed for their actions. The Athenians do temper their argument with the assertion that they hold their empire "not inappropriately" (1.73.1)—that they are in some sense worthy of rule (1.76.2) and that their rule is "more just" than is necessary under the conditions. These considerations are undoubtedly important to the Athenians, at least at this moment in their history, and to their understanding of their empire. But they are not meant to disguise the fact that the empire, and Athenian speech about the empire, represent an unapologetic overturning of the principles of justice that are ordinarily supposed to apply to relations among states (1.76). The Athenians refuse altogether to submit to justice, and in this respect at least their position does not differ significantly from that voiced later by the Athenian envoys on Melos.[17]

Pericles, one of the few commanders mentioned by Thucydides in his account of the fifty years, is entirely in accord with the new Athenian manner. Pericles is the successor to Themistocles and a staunch imperialist. Although his policy for the Peloponnesian War is cautious, its ultimate purpose is to preserve the empire he helped to build. Pericles himself has nothing but praise for Athenian daring. His Funeral Oration is devoid of any serious reference to the gods, which is particularly striking in light of the fact that that speech is a eulogy over those who have died in war. We should not forget that Pericles shows by deed that he is willing to abandon Attica, for the first time since the Persian Wars. In connection with that policy, Pericles tells the Athenians in effect that they should consider the land as something of no significance for the city: human beings are what make the city what it is (1.143.5). In the

---

[17]5.85–113. The Athenian remarks on Melos are of course much nastier than those in Sparta, and they do reflect a changed vision of Athenian rule. There is a wide range of opinion in the literature on the precise character and significance of this change, which I discuss more fully below. To me the conclusion seems inescapable that the extenuations the Athenians offer at Sparta represent an undigested tension or contradiction in their attitude toward empire, a tension that is resolved—in the predictable direction—by the time they reach Melos.

Funeral Oration he depicts Athens, Athenian power, and Athenian great-ness, purely as monuments of human virtue and endeavor. His reduction of the city completely to its human beings, indeed, to the present gen-eration of its human beings (cf. 2.36.1–3), is to be sure typical of this imperial Athens; but that only underscores its revolutionary character. Pericles' "humanism" (of which these remarks are primary examples) is often noted by commentators; the radically anti-traditional and even impious background of this humanism have received much less attention. Yet they are as important as any other facts in Thucydides' evaluation of Periclean Athens. They also prove crucial in explaining the problems with Pericles' policy and the fate of Athens after his death.[18]

Another aspect of Athenian humanism or liberation relevant to our inquiry, is the unprecedented internal freedom that characterizes Athe-nian democracy as a regime. In Pericles' Funeral Oration, the fact that the city as a whole has freed itself from the restraints traditionally applied to cities is less conspicuous than the fact that the Athenians individually have been liberated from the constraints that men are ordinarily sub-jected to within cities. The Athenians are a race of independent, indeed self-sufficient, men. Each of them is most capable of accomplishing an admirable variety of things on his own (2.41.1). The proof of this, according to Pericles, is the great power of the city (41.2): it is precisely the liberation of individual talent and individual initiative that has al-lowed the city of Athens to grow so great. Athens' greatness is thus built not only on purely human foundations but on the abilities and talents of human beings as individuals.

The fact that democratic Athens allows each of its citizens a remarkable degree of individual freedom is conspicuous to all in the History. The

[18]On Pericles' "humanism" see David Grene, *Man in His Pride* (Chicago: University of Chicago Press, 1950), p. 90; Grundy, *Thucydides*, 2:7–8; Bury, *Historians*, p. 146. On its impiety, see Charles Norris Cochrane, *Thucydides and the Science of History* (New York: Russell & Russell, 1965), pp. 32, 55; Edmunds, *Chance and Intelligence*, pp. 26, 39, 45–46, 76, 82; Connor, *Thucydides*, p. 74n54; Euben, "Battle of Salamis."
As Edmunds in particular makes clear, the Athenians' humanistic focus on *gnōmē* and *technē* ("intelligence" and "art," roughly) as means of mastering fate both is predicated upon and advances the undermining of piety. This, it seems to me, is why that strain of the Athenian character denoted in Thucydides by *daring* and traced to the very beginning of the "new" Athens of the fifth century, must be considered the more fundamental stratum of Thucydides' analysis. The notion that this somehow intellectual liberation grew out of a specifically political experience is in keeping with Thucydides' unremittingly political view of things: cf. Bury, *Historians*, p. 78; Jaeger, *Paideia*, pp. 380–81.

Corinthians, once again, are the first to introduce this theme, in a way that anticipates rather closely the remarks of Pericles (1.70.6). Thucydides himself makes a theme of individual Athenians' unique ability to think and to act on their own. Anonymous Athenians at Sparta are able to speak extemporaneously on behalf of their city. The native genius of Themistocles proves far more versatile than that of his Spartan counterpart, Pausanias, when each is tested outside his native city (1.128–38). The liberation of individual talent and initiative is in fact a trait as unique as any other in the city of Athens, and as important to her success. We might even say that the democratic Athens depicted by Thucydides is the nearest approximation to "individualism" in ancient politics, which was not in general characterized by or dedicated to anything of the kind.[19]

The Athenian experiment with "individualism" produced a city of great energy and many devices. But Athens must also confront the one great problem that is always connected with individualism, the problem of political cohesion. For if individuals are independent or self-sufficient, they are independent in some measure of the city itself. The restrictions placed on individuals in most cities in part serve the function of solidifying political order. The Corinthians' brief description of the Athenian regime does not allude to any problem of this kind: the mind of each Athenian is completely his own, they say, but his body is utterly at the service of the city (1.70.6). They are speaking of the tremendous success that Athens has enjoyed up to the time of the Peloponnesian War. Thucydides, on the other hand, draws our attention as early as his Eulogy of Pericles to the fact that Athens was later devastated by internal quarrels and factionalism, the real reason it lost the war (2.65.7, 10–12). These problems came into the open only after Pericles' death; nevertheless, Pericles is clearly alive to the problem of political order and cohesion, seeing it as peculiarly Athenian, and in the Funeral Oration he attacks it in a number of ways. Pericles claims that despite their unexampled individual freedom, Athenians obey the laws and the salutary conven-

---

[19]Individualism is sometimes supposed to be the exclusive preserve of modern politics. On individualism as characteristic of Periclean Athens see Cochrane, *Science of History*, p. 23; Grundy, *Thucydides*, 1:171, 2:xv; A. W. Gomme, *More Essays in Greek History and Literature* (Oxford: Blackwell, 1962), pp. 139–55; Finley, *Thucydides*, pp. 49, 301; see also Hegel, *Philosophy of History*, p. 238. For somewhat different views, see Adcock, *Thucydides and His History*, p. 50; Grene, *Man in His Pride*, p. 31.

tions of the city out of a kind of fear or reverence for them (*deos*, 2.37.3) that is not merely a dread of punishment. Along with their native and irrepressible daring, the Athenians have a certain native decency and law-abidingness; they seem to obey the laws of the city spontaneously and voluntarily.[20]

Pericles emphasizes this spontaneous respect for law in his account of what allows for the internal order of Athens as a city. He does not, however, threat it as sufficient in itself to dedicate the individualists he has described and praised to the good of the city as a whole. We must bear in mind that in the Funeral Oration, Pericles is confronted with the problem of dedication in its most extreme form: he must find something that will make the Athenians willing to die for their city, as have those who are eulogized in the speech. Pericles' final response to this problem is quite striking and serves to introduce an important theme in Thucydides' treatment of Athens. Throughout his speech, Pericles appeals to the Athenians' love of glory: Athens is the most glorious of cities, a monument to the virtue and daring of her citizens. Contemporary Athenians, in serving and even dying for the city, share in that glory.[21] Since Athens is uniquely glorious, it is uniquely capable of reflecting glory on those who sacrifice themselves for the city. But this argument proves inadequate, if only because glory of the kind described—glory in common, so to speak—is scarcely glory at all, particularly from the point of view of true individualists. Therefore Pericles, at the climax of his speech, has recourse to quite another appeal, one that appears as novel as the problem that it is meant to address: Pericles appeals to erotic passion. In the passage in question, he exhorts his audience to show no less daring than the men who have already fallen in the war. He allows that calculations of advantage should not be excluded in serving the city; but in the final analysis, he says, Athenians

---

[20]The passage in the Funeral Oration I am drawing from here is a difficult one, but it is obviously important for Pericles' view of the city as a whole. It is not clear exactly how Pericles understands the salutary Athenian *deos* (fear or reverence) that he speaks of, although I believe what I have said about it can be confidently asserted. It seems likely in addition that Pericles' confidence in the innate self-restraint of the Athenians is connected more broadly to his humanism and expresses a confidence in human nature itself which he sees as vindicated by Athens. See Finley, *Thucydides*, pp. 146–49; Edmunds, *Chance and Intelligence*, p. 59.

[21]2.42.1, 43.3. See Michael Palmer, "Love of Glory," for a fuller discussion of this part of Pericles' argument.

should become devoted and willing servants of the city, by beholding its power, manifested every day in deeds, and becoming lovers of it.[22] It is by means of a kind of erotic attachment, therefore, that each Athenian should ultimately become a patriot.

Pericles' sudden recourse to erotic passion as the centerpiece of Athenian cohesion is striking because we are not accustomed to thinking of patriotism in these terms—although it is a seldom-noticed fact that eros is a significant if somewhat concealed theme in Thucydides' work.[23] The word *erōs* and its derivatives appear only seven times in the History, but each appearance is at a crucial juncture, and each plays a significant role in Thucydides' treatment of Athenian imperialism and the political psychology of Athens.[24] With regard to the present passage, we might upon reflection agree that an appeal to this kind of passion is appropriate to the Athenian case of all cases, particularly given the warmth of Pericles' praise of the city. Erotic passion, after all, may be the one thing capable of attaching the most individualistic of human beings to something outside themselves. In any event, it is clear that Pericles, whose Athens has largely forsaken traditional supports to community and patriotism, must have recourse to extraordinary devices. Patriotism or "love of city" (*philopoli*) of the ordinary kind, grounded in such things as traditional civic piety and subordination of individuality, is no longer sufficient as a grounds for community at Athens.[25] The Athenians have all but aban-

[22]2.43.1. I have attempted in my paraphrase to retain an ambiguity of the original: it is not clear whether Pericles exhorts his listeners to become lovers of the city or of its power.

[23]One of the few studies to take this theme seriously is F. M. Cornford, *Thucydides Mythistoricus* (London: Edward Arnold, 1907), but he takes it in a "mythic" sense which I believe is unjustified. See Bury, *Historians*, p. 124; also W. P. Wallace, "Thucydides," *Phoenix* 18 (1964):256; Dodds, *Greeks and the Irrational*, p. 186; Huart, *Vocabulaire de l'analyse psychologique*, p. 391.

[24]The seven appearances are at 2.43, 3.45, 6.24, 6.54 (twice), 6.57, and 6.59, not counting one reference by Nicias to *duserōs*, bad or unhealthy erotic passion, at 6.13. All of these references will be discussed in this chapter.

The Greek notion of *erōs*, of course, is broader than ours, embracing potentially all objects of desire, but it still differs from other kinds of desire both in its intensity and in its unexpungeable sexual reference. Pericles' appeal to *erōs* would therefore be striking and paradoxical to Greek audiences, although somewhat less so than to modern ones. See Euripides *Phoenissae* 359, and Finley, *Three Essays*, who refers to Euripides *Erechtheus* fg. 360.54.

[25]Some perceptive observations in this vein regarding Pericles' appeal to erotic passion may be found in Cochrane, *Science of History*, p. 55, who speaks of eros here as a substitute

doned public piety; their individualism owes its very existence to the abandonment of the kinds of conventional strictures that cement the political community in a city like Sparta, for example. Pericles' appeal to eros thus circumvents or supplants those conventional mechanisms of community and seeks to bind the Athenians, as individuals, directly and passionately to the city.

But is this new alternative, proposed or supported by Pericles, sufficient to the task of keeping Athens under his direction and guided by his policy? According to Thucydides, Pericles' leadership of the city was restrained (2.65.5). The vision of the city that he bids the Athenians fall in love with, the vision presented in the Funeral Oration, is brilliantly splendid to be sure, but not extravagant; there is a certain measure to it that Pericles insists upon (esp. 2.40.1). Within the context of the Funeral Oration, Pericles appeals to the Athenians the way he does in order to bind them to his policy for the war, which is itself restrained: keep quiet within the city's walls, do not confront the Spartans directly, and above all refrain from any great attempts at expansion for the duration of the war (1.144.1; 2.65.7). Pericles thus exhorts the Athenians to become erotically attached to a policy and a vision of the city that is relatively measured or restrained.

The Athenians of course did not follow this advice; in fact, as Thucydides' eulogy of Pericles makes clear, after the statesman's death the Athenians did "everything" contrary to his views (2.65.7). The most conspicuous of their abandonments of his policy was the launching of the Sicilian expedition. The expedition, when it is launched in Book Six of Thucydides' History, represents the reassertion of all the imperialistic impulses in the Athenian character in their most extravagant form. Thucydides connects the whole Sicilian enterprise to Athenian erotic passion. His remark that an erotic passion fell upon the Athenians to sail for Sicily (6.24) is in fact Thucydides' only explicit reference to the eroticism of the city as a whole in his own name. The passion for Sicily was so overwhelming, he says, that if anyone still opposed the vote, he was cowed into silence by the "excessive" desire in the citizenry as a whole (6.24).

---

for ordinary patriotism based upon piety; Thibaudet, *La campagne*, p. 25, speaks of an unusual "crystallization" of erotic passion at Athens; and Henry R. Immerwahr, "Pathology of Power and the Speeches in Thucydides," in Stadter, ed., *The Speeches in Thucydides*, pp. 27–28, connects it to the "pathological" course that Athenian policy later took.

Pericles bid the Athenians fall in love with the city or the power of the city in the name of a general policy of restraint; but when that policy is finally and definitively overthrown by Athenian eros, the development in retrospect looks all but inevitable. When Athenian passion reaches its height, forcing its way to the surface of Thucydides' narrative, so to speak, it expresses itself as a longing for the most spectacular increase of power, the most audacious project of imperial expansion, since well before the Peloponnesian war. Nicias, in his futile speech against the expedition, pleads with the Athenians, at least the old Athenians, not to succumb to a perverse erotic passion (*duserōs* 6.13.1) for things far away. But his hope is as vain as the hope of Pericles—indeed, erotic passion is naturally enflamed more by the splendid, the distant, and the grand than by any vision of restraint. It powerfully resists domestication, even by a man of Pericles' stature. And this passion lies at the core of the city's imperialism. The Sicilian expedition is the most erotic, as it is the most daring, of all Athenian undertakings during the war (cf. 6.31.6), the peak of what Athens represents in the History.

For this reason, it is not inappropriate that Thucydides should use the sequence of events surrounding the Sicilian expedition to reveal more clearly than he does elsewhere his own understanding of the regime of democratic individualism at Athens. The expedition shows the failure of the Periclean policy of imperial restraint; Thucydides' understanding of Athens, as opposed to Pericles,' accounts not only for the inevitability of an undertaking like the Sicilian expedition but also for the decline and eventual failure of Athens. For Thucydides, Athenian imperialism grows out of a volatile combination of erotic passion and daring, two unusual qualities woven into the fabric of the regime. Thucydides understands the dynamics of this combination better than does Pericles or, indeed, the Athenians themselves. The last point is of interest because it is the reason Thucydides gives for inserting a peculiar but very significant digression to the legendary tyrannicides Harmodius and Aristogeiton into his narration of the Sicilian expedition (6.53, 54–59, 60). The digression, he tells us, is intended to correct some important defects in the Athenian self-understanding.[26] It draws our attention not only

[26]Thucydides makes brief mention of the Harmodius and Aristogeiton story near the beginning of the History (1.20.2), in order to indicate that men may be mistaken not only about remote and foreign things, but also about things most close to home. On this point, see also Strauss, *The City and Man*, pp. 163–64.

because it deals with crucial aspects of the Athenian character, but because its subject turns out to be Athenian daring and Athenian eros both; it contains more references to eros in particular than are found in the entire remainder of the History.[27]

The Athenian characteristic immediately in question at this point in the History is the notorious suspicion shown by the Athenian democracy toward its most outstanding leaders—one of the gravest defects of the Athenian regime. Here, the Athenians have recalled Alcibiades from Sicily after sending him out as commander, a move which breaks the alliance between Alcibiades and the city and dooms the expedition to failure. Alcibiades is charged with certain impieties, and the Athenians also fear that he desires to establish a tyranny in the city. Their dread and suspicion are excessive, according to Thucydides, because of their earlier suffering under the tyranny of the Peisistratids, which provoked the famous attack of Harmodius and Aristogeiton. But according to Thucydides, the tyranny was actually rather mild until attacked (6.54.5–6, 59.2); the Athenians are also mistaken about the story of Harmodius and Aristogeiton itself. Thucydides begins his account by saying that the "daring deed" of Harmodius and Aristogeiton was actually undertaken incident to a love affair (6.54.1; cf. .56.3, .59.1). Aristogeiton was the lover of Harmodius whom Hipparchus, brother of the tyrant Hippias, tried to seduce. Aristogeiton became excessively agitated, as Thucydides would expect of a lover, (54.3)—all the more so because he feared that the tyrant's brother might, owing to his position, be able to force himself upon Harmodius. Therefore, pursuant to what was in its origin a private quarrel, Aristogeiton resolved to overthrow the tyr-

---

[27]There are four references to *erōs* in the digression, at 6.54 (twice), 6.57, and 6.59. There has been a great deal of scholarly commentary on this digression, much of which assumes that the passage does not have great significance for the History as a whole. See the summary in A. W. Gomme, A. Andrewes, K. J. Dover, *A Historical Commentary on Thucydides*, 5 vols. (Oxford: Clarendon, 1945–81), 4:317–29, which concludes with the suggestion that the digression derives from the historian's obsession with setting the record straight. Bury, *Historians*, pp. 89–90, believes its aim is simply to correct popular misconceptions, apparently of no great significance. Finley, *Three Essays*, p. 168, and Romilly, *Athenian Imperialism*, p. 217, suggest that the digression has a deeper significance, which, however, they do not attempt to identify. For other treatments that take the passage seriously, see Hunter R. Rawlings, III, *The Structure of Thucydides' History* (Princeton: Princeton University Press, 1981), pp. 100–113; Michael Palmer, "Alcibiades and the Question of Tyranny in Thucydides," *Canadian Journal of Political Science* 15 (1982):105–9; Connor, *Thucydides*, pp. 178–80.

anny. Provoked by Hipparchus' later insult to Harmodius' sister (for which Hipparchus did use the public power of the tyranny) the two lovers made their attack, failing to kill Hippias but managing to kill Hipparchus. The lovers and their deed, which Thucydides now characterizes as a piece of "irrational daring" (59.1), subsequently became so legendary in Athens that Hipparchus was falsely elevated in the popular mind to the position of tyrant, to magnify their accomplishment (55.4). Likewise, Harmodius and Aristogeiton, the supposed tyrannicides, came to be regarded as champions—practically founders—of the democracy at Athens after its reestablishment. Indeed, the "tyrannicide" came to occupy a place in Athenian lore as significant perhaps as that occupied by the memory of the city's heroism during the Persian Wars.[28] The legend became in effect a keystone of the democracy's self-understanding; Harmodius and Aristogeiton were revered by the Athenians, whose own love and defense of liberty drew inspiration from that of the lovers.

Thucydides' presentation of this episode controverts in one important respect the impression given in Book One that Athenian daring made its first appearance at the time of the Persian Wars. Thucydides here speaks of a daring in Athens from before that time, a daring connected with the foundation of the democracy. Thucydides seems in his account to agree with Athenians that the Harmodius and Aristogeiton story somehow captures the essence of the Athenian democracy and character. The story as formulated by Thucydides thus corroborates the view that Athens is characterized by a kind of erotically charged daring. But his rendition of the story, in precisely that respect, represents a fundamental correction of the popular understanding of things. The first and perhaps most important correction has to do with the motives the Athenians attribute to their heroes. The Athenians suppose them to have been public-spirited champions of democratic liberty; Thucydides shows that their motivation was private, even selfish, and aimed at public benefit only incidentally if at all. Thucydides grants that Harmodius and Aristogeiton hoped that once their attack was begun, in a public procession, bystanders would assist in gaining their own freedom (6.56.3); moreover, insofar as the lovers were seeking to ovethrow the oppressive

[28]Among other things, the Athenians erected a statue of the lovers in the Agora, not once but twice.

regime that threatened their own freedom, their action amounted to a certain advocacy of freedom for the city as a whole. But their primary concern and motivation was still private, not public. Thucydides' pointed praise of the regime of the Peisistratids even forces us to wonder whether the lovers' action was unambiguously in the public interest at all.

The tyranny was unbearable to Harmodius and Aristogeiton because of the particular kind of freedom they craved; their jealousy toward the tyrants was at bottom purely private and erotic; and the freedom they aimed at was primarily what we might call private erotic freedom. Within the context of Thucydides' retelling of the story, this conclusion implies first of all that although the Athenians' excessive suspicion of prominent men in the city (here Alcibiades) presents itself, and understands itself, as a laudable and public-spirited defense of liberty in the city, it is in fact rooted in a rather questionable private jealousy.[29] The basis of the jealousy moreover, and of the devotion to the democracy itself, Thucydides seems to suggest, is dedication not to the common good as such but rather to a kind of private freedom from restrictions, a freedom to follow where one's passions might lead. The force of this passion incites those under its sway to acts of the greatest daring on its behalf; the story suggests that daring itself is primarily a handmaiden, perhaps even a simple reflection, of liberated erotic passion in Athens.

Thucydides' rendition of the Harmodius and Aristogeiton story provides among other things a vivid and revealing image of Athenian individualism and the intense love of freedom that characterizes it. It is easy to recognize here the Athens of Pericles' Funeral Oration, a city whose citizens enjoy freedom in every direction and who feel a genuine erotic attachment to the city or the regime that provides it. But Thucydides' account casts this democratic Athens in a decidedly different light from that of Pericles, coming to very different conclusions about the stability of the regime, the security of its dedication to the public good, and even its ultimate praiseworthiness. For one thing, unjustified and harmful jealousy toward its greatest leaders is now seen as Athens' characteristic attitude, rather than the generous deference it showed to Pericles. In any event, it is certainly easier to understand from Thucyd-

---

[29]Consider for example *idia*, "privately," at 6.15.4, in a description of Athenian suspicions of Alcibiades. This word may refer either to the Athenians or to Alcibiades.

ides' presentation of the story of Harmodius and Aristogeiton than from the Funeral Oration why Athens was so prone to the kind of internecine strife that eventually destroyed it.

If Thucydides' account of Athenian eros, which reaches a climax of sorts in the digression on the tyrannicides, shows it to be more problematic than the Athenians or Pericles are aware, his treatment of the other distinctive Athenian trait of daring invites at least as many doubts. Here we must collect references scattered across the History. Pericles praises daring without qualification in the Funeral Oration, but in the plague at Athens, which Thucydides describes immediately afterward, daring shows itself in the city in a rather more questionable light. With an eye to the dissensions that later devastated Athens, Thucydides says that lawlessness was first introduced into the city by the plague, as men dared more openly to pursue their private pleasure in contravention of all restraint (2.53.1). Even more to the point is Thucydides' description of the civil wars that destroyed a great many cities during the war. In a famous passage detailing how moral categories, and the words that denote them, were eventually turned on their heads during these upheavals, the first, and perhaps the controlling, reversal is said to be the supplanting of loyal courage by "irrational daring."[30] The passage culminates in Thucydides' pronouncement that respect for the divine law finally ceased to be a basis of trust or community among men as oaths lost all their force under the pressure of almost universal lawlessness (3.82.6–7).

These remarks, some of Thucydides' most direct pronouncements on the character of daring, certainly give us pause when it comes to considering the case of Athens. Athens has replaced courage with daring in precisely this sense of disembarrassing itself of the traditional restraints of justice and divine law. The resulting freedom has allowed Athens to accumulate vast power and empire, running circles around their more traditional and inhibited opponents, in particular the Spartans. Daring undeniably represents the discovery of an "effectual truth" about the character of international politics. It also represents a very corrosive incubus in the city, although one that takes its time to develop.[31]

---

[30]3.82.4; cf. 82.6. The phrase *irrational daring* is used on only one other occasion—to describe the act of Harmodius and Aristogeiton (6.59.1).

[31]The point that the immorality of Athenian imperialism caused Athens to degenerate

The most characteristic features of the Athenian regime are thus more problematic for Thucydides than they are for Pericles. But there is one point of great importance on which Pericles and Thucydides agree: the Athenian regime, based on this unprecedented individualism, this liberation of human faculties repressed or restricted under the conditions of ordinary political life, has discovered a source of power broader and more explosive than that available to any other city known to their political experience. Athens even enjoys, to the time of Pericles and beyond, an unrivaled devotion from her ordinary citizens. It would be quite wrong to conclude from the defects Thucydides detects in Athenian democracy that he is blind to the charms and strengths of the regime. These strengths and countervailing weaknesses of Athens seem connected, if not inseparable: Athens' individualism and daring are the keys to its success but also the keys to understanding its eventual failure. The paradoxes here, important themes in the History, are central also to the case of Alcibiades.

The individual liberation brought about by the democracy at Athens, and the corresponding liberation of the city from many pious or moral restraints on its behavior, form the core of Thucydides' Athens. First the founding of the unique democracy, then the Persian Wars and the opportunities opened by the Persian defeat brought into being the erotic Athenian daring and everything that is connected with it: the impulse to empire, the immorality or impiety to release it, and the power to pursue it.[32] Thucydides' presentation of the sequence of events that set all this in motion carries a strong impression of inevitability; that is, an impression that a democracy characterized by such liberation of human faculties must inevitably become imperialistic. The Athenian exoneration of their empire likewise hinges on an assertion of inevitability. This issue

---

has been made before. See Grene, *Man in His Pride*, p. 32; Strauss, *The City and Man*, pp. 192–209; Ehrenberg, "Polypragmosyne," p. 53; Euben, "Battle of Salamis," pp. 361, 373, 375.

[32]Among interpretations that find the source of Athens' uniqueness simply in the democracy there is one that does some justice to these considerations. Grene, *Man in His Pride*, p. 35, suggests that the Cleisthenic revolution at Athens, which gave the democracy by and large its final form, and which took place in the generation following Harmodius and Aristogeiton, represents the decisive Athenian break with ancestral religion, blood ties to place, and so on. This view historically has much to recommend it (see Ehrenberg, *Solon to Socrates*, pp. 88–90; Glotz, *Solidarité de la famille*, pp. 399–400), but Thucydides emphasizes instead the "tyrannicide," before Cleisthenes, and the Persian Wars afterward. I have tried to follow Thucydides' indications in my own portrayal.

should be briefly reexamined in light of what we have learned from Thucydides' account of the roots of Athenian imperialism.

In retrospect, the specific character of the eros that possesses Thucydides' Athenians appears crucial in their turn to imperialism. We should carefully consider this passion and its place in the Athenian regime. If one lesson of Thucydides' digression on Harmodius and Aristogeiton is that democratic freedom in Athens is connected to the liberation of human eros in the city, it seems that the converse is also true: the first and perhaps the primary attachment of eros in Athens is the attachment to freedom itself. That is to say, in the Athenian case at least, eros comes close to revealing itself as a pure and promiscuous desire for freedom as such. The first historical step from the private, individual eros to imperialism would be the politicization of erotic passion within the city. Harmodius and Aristogeiton discovered that their private erotic freedom had to enter the public realm simply to defend and preserve itself. The restored Athenian democracy enshrined as a political form precisely that kind of freedom and passionate attachment to freedom. Indeed, once the democractic regime was made over in the image of Harmodius and Aristogeiton, it was inevitable that the Athenians fall hopelessly in love with this unprecedented order of things. Under these circumstances, it is perhaps no longer so surprising that the Athenians could be induced to abandon Attica and even the city itself rather than lose their beloved liberty. They loved their freedom more than did other Greek cities and more than the things that tied them to their land; they thus abandoned the land and with it perhaps the last remaining restraints on their daring.

After the Persians were defeated, the idea of empire, presented to the Athenians by their new position as coequal leaders of Greece, recommended itself to them first as a means of protecting the freedom that had so recently proved vulnerable to external attack. In fact the Athenians never lose sight of the defensive argument for empire (e.g., 1.75, 6.82). Beyond that, there is the sense in which rule or dominion over others is itself the greatest form of freedom—a fact we are not accustomed to acknowledging but which the Athenians seemed to relish.[33] The empire

---

[33]Romilly, *Athenian Imperialism*, pp. 80–82, makes this point but confines it to the Greek city-states. See also Timothy J. Galpin, "The Democratic Roots of Athenian Imperialism in the Fifth Century B.C.," *Classical Journal* 79 (1983–84):107–9; and Thu-

thus represents an extension of Athenian freedom, its crowning emblem and achievement. The democratic love and defense of freedom at Athens could have passed insensibly into the impulse to rule over others by a transformation more natural than we generally suppose. In any event, Thucydides concludes his digression on the attempted overthrow of the tyranny with the following terse summary of events: Hippias, after three more years as tyrant, was deposed, fled to the court of the Persian king Darius, and finally, as an old man, returned with the Persians on their expedition to Marathon (6.59.4). Thus the fight against Hippias and the tyranny was transformed literally at least into the fight against the Persians and its aftermath.

Thucydides' View of Athenian Imperialism

A final reference to erotic passion in Thucydides' History sheds important light on the connection between eros and Athenian imperialism, placing the whole in a wider and more theoretical context. It occurs in the speech of the Athenian Diodotus during the debate over the fate of the rebellious Mytilenaeans. Diodotus is one of three figures in Thucydides who give crucial speeches but play no other role and are otherwise historically unknown. In addition, they all have what might be taken to be unusually significant names in the light of the speeches they deliver.[34] Diodotus' speech is exceptional in the depth and systematic character of its theoretical reasoning—in remarkable harmony with what we have seen of Thucydides' own.[35]

---

cydides 8.68.4. We should also be cognizant of the fact that in some important respects the empire subsidized the Athenian democracy, making much greater freedom available to the populace at large.

More generally, we may cite here Plato's presentation of the tyrant in *Republic* Book 9. According to Plato, the tyrant is erotically driven; it is precisely the strength of his erotic longing for freedom or his longing for erotic freedom (these seem again to be two sides of a coin), an essentially private motive, that impels him into the political arena in order to secure his desire. The extreme love of freedom leads the Athenian *demos*, by the same logic, to behave tyrannically toward both its own leaders and its allies.

[34] The other two figures are Athenagoras of Syracuse and the Athenian Euphemus. Diodotus' name means "gift of Zeus." He succeeds in delivering the Mytilenaeans from slaughter and the Athenians from the kind of barbarism they later succumb to at Melos. Cf. Strauss, *The City and Man*, pp. 231–36; Bruell, "Athenian Imperialism," pp. 16–17.

[35] 3.45. Most of the commentators who address the issue agree that, within the context of the debate over Mytilene, Diodotus' speech reflects Thucydides' position. See Shorey,

Diodotus argues against the slaughter of the Mytilenaeans in part by arguing against the efficacy of capital punishment altogether, and he ties his critique of capital punishment to a theoretical analysis of human nature. Capital punishment is ineffective, he argues, because the causes of transgression are too deeply rooted in human nature (3.45). Human nature according to his analysis is essentially lawless, in the sense that no law can restrain it once it has wholeheartedly set itself upon some undertaking. The reason for this is that human nature is characterized by a powerful erotic impulse (45.5). Eros, Diodotus says, is "everywhere," setting on any and all objects. Together with hope, which is always in its train, it draws men into the most disastrous enterprises. Although invisible and unseen, eros and hope can and do prevail over visible terrors and punishments. The result is unquenchable ardor, "hubris," and "daring."[36] Diodotus' point is that it is futile to kill the Mytilenaeans in the hope that it will deter future revolts. Erotic and daring human nature will lead others to revolt at some time or other regardless of the treatment of the Mytilenaeans, and the specter of the death penalty will only make them desperate in their resistance.

Although Diodotus draws the Athenians' attention only to the case of their subjects, it cannot escape our attention that the core of his argument, dealing as it does with human nature in the most general terms, applies to all individuals and all cities, and in particular to the Athenians themselves. Indeed, although Diodotus has his reasons for not drawing the Athenians' attention to their own case—he wants them to indulge the Mytilenaeans, not themselves—his argument is if anything more applicable to them. It is the Athenians who have predicated their political life, and especially their foreign policy, on the release of precisely

---

"Ethics and Psychology," pp. 67–70; Romilly, *Athenian Imperialism*, pp. 329–30; Cornford, *Mythistoricus*, pp. 121, 135; Grene, *Man in His Pride*, pp. 59, 66; Ehrenberg, "Polypragmosyne," p. 51; Finley, *Thucydides*, p. 83; G. E. M. de Ste. Croix, *The Origins of the Peloponnesian War* (London: Duckworth, 1972), p. 21. There is disagreement as to whether Diodotus is uniquely close to Thucydides in his views. This is my interpretation. See Strauss, *The City and Man*, p. 231; Bruell, "Athenian Imperialism," pp. 16–17; Bury, *Historians*, p. 13.

[36]The precise connection between eros and hope on the one hand and hubris and daring on the other is not made clear in Diodotus' speech (it depends partly on what force we assign to *te* at 3.45.5). It seems to me that the only fair reading is to give eros the fundamental or leading role, both because of the way Diodotus makes his argument and because of the character of the things he is describing.

41

the impulses Diodotus speaks of. Diodotus' concluding statement here makes this as clear as it could be made without openly broaching the subject. Cities, he says, are even more prey than individuals to the workings of the impulses in question, for the reason that cities deal with the greatest objects, have much more power than individual men, and are thus exposed to the temptation of much grander and presumably more seductive designs. The objects that tempt them, he says, are freedom for some, and rule over others—empire—for those who have the power (3.45.6). This argument, of course, offers great support to the Athenians' own argument that empire is only the natural and inevitable ambition of every powerful city. Diodotus establishes a direct link between human eros and empire; empire according to him is a natural goal of erotic passion simply because it is the greatest of accomplishments. Diodotus would be no more surprised than is Thucydides that Athenian policy during the war should eventually lead to a project like the Sicilian expedition.

Diodotus' speech because of its great sophistication, reflects importantly on the thought of Thucydides himself. It has been remarked that Thucydides' use of the notion of eros bears some resemblance to the mythic psychology of Greek tragedy. Eros in Greek tragedy, a divine presence, is frequently a goad and deceiver, leading men inexorably to hubris, nemesis, and fall. This resemblance has given rise to the argument that Thucydides' perspective is dominated by categories and motifs that he absorbed from tragedy but that he might not be fully in command of.[37] It is clear from the foregoing, however, that Thucydides' use of eros is devoid of all mythic content; it is purely "scientific."[38] It goes

[37]The most important study to develop this line of argument is of course Cornford's *Thucydides Mythistoricus*. See also Finley, *Three Essays*, chap. 1, in a parallel but somewhat different vein.

[38]Edmunds in *Chance and Intelligence* makes in effect the same case for Thucydides' use of the notion of "chance." For a critique of Cornford's thesis on the "mythologizing" of Thucydides, see Bury, *Historians*, p. 124. Cornford's "scientific" alternative to Thucydides' allegedly mythologized treatment of the causes of the war—namely the proposal that its causes were primarily economic—suggests that Cornford is an unwitting pawn of nineteenth- and twentieth-century prejudices more than it proves anything about Thucydides. See Romilly, *Athenian Imperialism*, pp. 71–72. In general, the most famous thematic defense of the "scientific" Thucydides is Cochrane's *Thucydides and the Science of History*, which is a useful study from this point of view, though ultimately I find Cochrane's understanding of the scientific, of Thucydides, and of the scientific in Thucydides inadequate.

without saying that Thucydides could have learned from Homeric or Aeschylean psychology, for example, in the same way that a modern student might find insights of significance there. There are undeniably tragic elements in Thucydides' treatment of the Sicilian expedition: Athenian eros overreaches itself, scales the peak of hubris, and is crushed in humbling, if not awe-inspiring, fashion. But, aside from the fact that Thucydides continually insists that the Athenians could have prevailed if they had kept (the most hubristic) Alcibiades as their commander (2.65.7, 11; 6.31.6; 6.15.4), the presence and character of Book Eight in the History seems to preclude any simply tragic interpretation of Athenian imperialism.

Diodotus' argument, which is purely scientific in character, points to a view of the world not so much tragic as simply bleak. Diodotus depicts a world of human beings and cities driven by desires at once irrepressible and irrational, irreconcilable among themselves, or fundamentally at war with one another. Diodotus' perspective explains, indeed predicts, both imperialism and revolt; they are permanent political phenomena. He puts the Athenians in their splendor and the Mytilenaeans in their misery in a common world, even a common predicament. The compulsions he speaks of drive both the weak and the strong into pointless dangers. It is easy enough to understand on the basis of such a view why Diodotus, one of the most intelligent and eloquent speakers in the History, would choose not to pursue a career in the imperial politics of Athens or indeed the politics of any city. Thucydides, who shares Diodotus' view on the essential points, was likewise content to remain politically inactive after his exile from Athens.[39]

We must be cautious, however, in generalizing from the bleak view of political life implied in Diodotus' argument, and in attributing that

[39]Scholars do not agree on the interpretation of Thucydides' attitude in exile, but it seems a mistake to see Thucydides chafing bitterly at his exile, writing only out of enforced idleness, and allowing his narrative to be colored by resentment bred of his exile (the last suggestion made, e.g., by H. D. Westlake, *Individuals in Thucydides* [Cambridge: Cambridge University Press, 1968], p. 60). On the contrary, Thucydides indicates at the outset that he undertook the project at the beginning of the war (1.1.1); he mentions his exile only in order to explain that it allowed him to write and to gather information from both sides in the war with greater ease (5.26.5). On Thucydides' contentment to remain an onlooker, see also Ehrenberg, "Polypragmosyne," p. 52; Strauss, *The City and Man*, p. 236; cf. Romilly, *Athenian Imperialism*, p. 359; Andrewes, in Gomme, Andrewes, Dover, *Historical Commentary*, 5:383.

generalized view to Thucydides. Such a view is inevitably an element in Thucydides' perspective—he does not take at face value all the city's claims to seriousness, allegiance, or nobility. On the other hand, we should never overlook, nor underrate, the fact that Thucydides, in spite of his withdrawal, devoted himself to writing a book exclusively about the world of politics, a book he deemed worthy to be a possession for all time. Both the high and the low are eminently visible in his work. The argument of Diodotus, meanwhile, is tailored to a specific rhetorical situation; designed to portray the plight of the Mytilenaeans in such a way as to elicit pity from the Athenians. If we look at what Diodotus accomplishes, rather than at what he says, we might well conclude that the outcome of the Mytilenaean affair represents the Athenians' finest hour. This is highlighted by the context Thucydides places it in. Diodotus' speech is preceded by the indignant fulminations of Cleon, who advocates indiscriminate death for the rebellious city (3.37–40). And the Mytilenaean episode as a whole is followed by Thucydides' account of the Spartan treatment of the Plataeans, who were not even rebellious allies but vanquished enemies. The Spartans slaughter them indiscriminately (3.52–68). Diodotus, by appearing even tougher than Cleon, by claiming to cast aside considerations of justice in favor of pure expediency, succeeds almost surreptitiously in providing the Athenians with an outlet for their compassion. The Athenians, as the assembly begins, feel remorse at having previously decreed the death of all the Mytilenaeans (3.36.4–5; cf. 3.49.4); Diodotus gives them amply hardheaded reasons for rejecting Cleon's advice and voting with their hearts. This is wholly apart from the many ways in which justice inserts itself, unannounced, into his argument.[40]

Diodotus relies upon some truly exceptional Athenian virtues to spare the Mytilenaeans, virtues that we must include in any comprehensive account of the Athenian character. The central, theoretical part of his speech, tracing the Mytilenaean rebellion to compulsive erotic passion, not only serves to defuse the moral indignation Cleon appealed to, but communicates to Athenian sophistication and even self-knowledge. The Athenians elsewhere make arguments rather similar to that of Diodotus

[40]On the speech and tactics of Diodotus, see the excellent discussion by Clifford Orwin, "The Just and the Advantageous in Thucydides: The Case of the Mytilenaean Debate," *American Political Science Review* 78 (1984):485–94.

on their own behalf, justifying their imperialism by tracing it to certain universal compulsions. Diodotus' analysis of the imperial impulse is more penetrating—and sobering—but the point is that he succeeds, almost surreptitiously, in getting the Athenians to apply their sophisticated understanding of political things even-handedly to their opponents as well as themselves. If they excuse themselves, they are capable at least of allowing their enemies the same excuse. In spite of the fact that Diodotus barely succeeds in persuading the Athenians (3.49.1) and treads a fine line between playing on the Athenians' understanding of their own motives and bringing their own case too much to the fore, the Athenian action shows a rare kind of magnanimity indeed. The Athenians, in all their amoral sophistication, are capable of a kind of objectivity and fairness unmatched by other cities in the History. The counterpoint of the Spartans at Plataea illustrates this vividly. This remarkable capacity is linked not only to Athenian sophistication but to their unprecedented frankness about themselves.

Frankness of this kind must indeed be counted among the Athenians' foremost virtues. They eschew hypocritical pretexts and explanations for their self-aggrandizement at the expense of other cities. Aside from whatever admiration we might have for this trait as a purely intellectual virtue, it causes the Athenians to act in crucial situations significantly more fairly and gently than other cities would. Athenian treatment of other cities is at least free of the "pious cruelty" of which the Spartans in their moralism are capable. We should think in this connection not only of the Spartan judges of Plataea, but of the Spartan commander Alcidas (3.32) and the ephor Sthenelaidas (1.86): righteous concern with justice is frequently capable of much greater harshness than exclusive concern with amoral expediency.[41] This is true in part because the

---

[41]This is one of the primary lessons of Machiavelli, from whom the phrase *pious cruelty* is taken (*The Prince*, chap. 21). We can draw the same lesson from the Athenian debate over Mytilene, in which Cleon's call for the justice of indignation is the vindictive alternative ultimately rejected by the Athenians. This is one of a number of respects in which Cleon is almost Spartan in character (see chapter 3). It has been argued that the Peloponnesian War was marked by ever-greater "ideological" stridency as it progressed: see Marc Cogan, *The Human Thing* (Chicago: University of Chicago Press, 1981); and his "Mytilene, Plataea, and Corcyra: Ideology and Policy in Thucydides, Book Three" *Phoenix* 35 (1981):1–21. It seems to me that this thesis would have to be modified at least to take account of the differences between Athens', and Sparta's general approaches throughout the war.

city, especially during war, necessarily identifies justice with its own cause—but in fact things are rarely that simple, least of all during war. The Athenians, the only ones capable of rising above this kind of moralism, are correct when they say that all cities or nations are dominated by their interests, even to the point of imperialism. They are correct when they tell the Spartans in effect that they are hypocrites (1.76). Thucydides remarks that the Spartan action against Plataea (which is inaugurated and concluded with the most ostentatious displays of piety: 2.74; 3.68.3) was in fact taken to satisfy the hatred of the Thebans (3.68.4), whom the Spartans did not want to estrange because their services would be needed in the war (3.68.4).

The juxtaposition of the Mytilenaean and Plataean episodes is not the first occasion on which Thucydides indicates this important difference of "national character" between the Athenians and the Spartans. The earliest such occasion, in the *Pentekontaetia* in Book One, also merits some attention. Thucydides again juxtaposes parallel episodes, the revolt of Thasos against the Athenians and the revolt of the helots against Sparta at Mount Ithome (1.100–102). During the Thasian revolt, when the Athenians and the Spartans were still nominally allies, the Spartans agreed secretly to help the rebels against the Athenian forces. They were prevented only by the revolt of their helots at home, who garrisoned themselves on Mount Ithome. The Spartans, alarmed, requested help from their allies; the Athenians obliged along with many others. But the Athenians were turned away on a pretext, the real reason, according to Thucydides, being the Spartans' distrust of them. Thucydides calls this the first incident that brought Athenian and Spartan enmity into the open (102.3), but we should also note the devastating light the Lacedaemonians appear in. They underhandedly attack the Athenians; the Athenians openly agree to assist them and are unjustly scorned. Of greater significance is the fact, first alluded to by Thucydides in this passage, that the Spartans have an empire no less than the Athenians do. Their helot slaves in Messenia were victims of an old Spartan war of conquest. Only the antiquity of this imperialism, and the fact that the Spartans were no longer expanding it, make it invisible. The Athenians do not begrudge the Spartans their empire; they are even willing to help maintain it as allies, but the Spartans seek under cover of secrecy to attack the Athenians. The fact that the Spartans may have told themselves that they were acting on behalf of Greek freedom only confirms their own hypocrisy. In fact, the quasi-invisible Spartan empire is perhaps the most telling example of the Athenians' contention that all cities expand so long as they have the power.

All of this forces us to the conclusion that the Athenians' views on power and imperialism, in addition to being uniquely frank, are also correct. This is an even greater intellectual virtue than frankness. In any general assessment of Athens' portrayal by Thucydides, intellectual sophistication must figure prominently. The sophisticated Athenian thesis on power and rule is only its most conspicuous sign. The imperial Athenians have not only seen through the hypocrisy of ordinary professions of justice or piety in international affairs; they have also seen through the conventional character of a host of traditional restraints on human activity, domestic and foreign.

In fact, we may go so far as to say that the Athenian regime in Thucydides is revolutionary because it is based to an unprecedented extent upon the discovery of nature and the liberation of natural impulses as far as possible from traditional restraints. This fact must never cease to inspire us with wonder. The city discovers the impact of universal natural forces on international politics; it also discovers and liberates human nature within the city, and attempts to build its community upon that basis rather than upon the rigid conventional discipline of a city like Sparta. It is appropriate, on the basis of everything we have seen of Athens so far, to speak of the Athenian regime and Athenian imperialism as a great and unprecedented political experiment. It is an experiment in "enlightenment," dispelling many of the public illusions that are part of all ordinary politics, and an experiment in bringing both internal and external politics more into line with nature thus discovered. It is this fact that will have been of the greatest interest to the writer and observer Thucydides. His History is devoted in large part to interpreting this experiment and charting its course.[42]

[42]In connection with these general observations about Athens, we must not overlook the similarities between the insights of the Athenian regime as portrayed by Thucydides and the arguments of some of the sophists of this period. This connection has sometimes been commented on. We must bear in mind, though, that Thucydides is so far from proposing any causal link between the sophists and the Athenian doctrine that he never even alludes to the sophists or their teaching. Instead, I have argued, he traces this development to the peculiar foundations of Athenian democracy and to the Athenian experience in the Persian Wars. This is entirely in keeping with Thucydides' unremittingly political approach to things. Cf. Bury, *Historians*, p. 88.

47

The Athenian experiment is unprecedented of course, but it is also for Thucydides a quintessentially Greek phenomenon. This means not that its significance is limited to a certain historical period but rather that it reveals some of the highest possibilities of human culture. Thucydides devotes the first section of his work, the Archaeology, to an account of the rise of Greek civilization out of ancient barbarism, which sets the stage for the greatest and most noteworthy of wars. The first steps in that rise were a gradually more settled form of life than that of the earliest peoples, and the accumulation of greater wealth. These merely material preconditions make possible more important developments. The Athenians, in Thucydides' account, were the first people to give up carrying arms in consequence of the greater security and to adopt a softer or more luxurious mode of life (1.6.3). The Spartans, however, were the first to adopt a less ostentatious form of dress, "in the current manner" as Thucydides says, and to comport themselves in more reserved fashion in the city regardless of wealth (1.6.4). They also were the first Greeks to exercise and compete in the nude, abandoning the practice, still current among the barbarians of Thucydides' time, of wearing loincloths for these activities (1.6.5).

The Greeks, like all civilizations, arose only after a long period of accumulating wealth and power and increasing stability out of original chaos. Characteristic of the Greeks in particular is a return to simplicity, modesty, and reserve, on the level of developed culture rather than of primitive poverty, as a matter of choice rather than of necessity. This seems to be associated with the discovery, for the first time, of what we may call the beauty or nobility of unadorned humanity. From their learning to scorn the ostentatious and barbaric display of the past to the development of the institution of wrestling in the nude, Greek civilization discovered a more austere, more sublime aesthetic, an appreciation of the beauty inherent in humanity itself.[43] This ideal, pioneered by the Spartans but later adopted by all the Greeks, combines the appreciation of humanity with genuine moderation. One consequence of this implicit humanism might be a new and fiercer kind of pride.

Against this background, the regime of democratic Athens appears

[43]This is very close to Hegel's view of what defines the distinctive beauty of Greek culture (*Philosophy of History*, pt. 2, esp. p. 241). See also Thibaudet, *La campagne*, pp. 51, 164–65.

not simply unprecedented or revolutionary but in some respects merely a development of one aspect of the Greek ideal. This is particularly true if we can regard human pride as latent or implicit in that ideal. The Athenians stand for the most resplendent view of humanity. They have sought to allow human beings to develop all of their powers, free of restraints. They have dedicated themselves to pushing human power as far as it will go, in the name of ambitions that are grounded in human nature. There is something grand about this project. Thucydides describes Athenian ambition, at the moment when it reaches the erotic peak of the Sicilian expedition: The young and those in their prime longed to see far-off sights and spectacles; the majority saw employment and the prospect of sufficient power to provide them "everlasting pay" (6.24.3). Despite the almost comically pedestrian character of the longing of the majority, it is clear that Sicily represents for Athens more than simply another conquest in an ordinary imperial scheme. The lure of Sicily is the lure of a politically, even a humanly impossible fulfillment, the hope almost of transcending the human condition. The majority of the Athenians seem even to forget their own mortality in their erotic transports.[44]

There is something generous not only about this ambition but also about the Athenian political experiment that brought it forth, this bold attempt at human self-sufficiency. It represents an unmistakable peak of Greek civilization, of civilization as such. It is true that the Athenian project is close to hubris—the crime of going beyond the limits proper to human action, transgressing divine law to rival the gods or play the part of gods.[45] In retrospect, in light of the Athenian project, Greek

---

[44]I mean by this to capture some sense of the power of the Athenian longing for Sicily. We must not jump to the conclusion that Athenian eroticism, and therefore Athenian imperialism, is unqualifiedly noble. The uninspiringly material motivation reflected in the desire for "eternal pay" is indicative enough of this (see chapter 3).

[45]I follow Strauss in speaking this way of the divine law in Thucydides (*The City and Man*, esp. p. 147). The use of the term does not imply that the gods exist, or even that Thucydides believed that they did. It does imply the possible existence of some absolute, i.e., nonconventional, law or moral rule that applies to all human beings, hence to cities in their relations with each other. This rule is traditionally supposed to emanate from the gods; so for ordinary cities and human beings in Thucydides, it is the "divine law."

Virtually every commentator on Thucydides has been aware of his theme of individuals or cities overstepping the bounds of the permissible, whether this boundary is called the divine law or something else. And virtually all agree that one of the History's tasks is to explore or explicate the nature of this boundary; thus virtually all make use of this concept,

civilization may itself appear poised on the brink of hubris. The difficulty of assessing this lies partly in needing to know exactly where the line is between legitimate human self-assertion and hubris or disregard for the limits proper to humanity. With regard to Athens, it is too simple to say that the city's imperialism is a mere exercise in excess and crime. Generosity can be found in its sources; it might also be seen reflected in Athenian taste, a notion not entirely foreign to Thucydides' way of thinking, as his brief treatment of the rise of Greek civilization indicates. The monuments erected on the Athenian acropolis during the peak of the city's imperial splendor—monuments that Thucydides does not mention but that we can still see—are not the tawdry ornaments of barbaric culture but the very embodiment of classic reserve. In this spirit Pericles, in his Funeral Oration, praises Athens not simply for her wealth but for her modest use of it (2.40.1). He praises the Athenians in general for decency and reserve, qualities that allow Athenian freedom to flourish both gracefully and peacefully. Pericles views the Athenian empire as a fitting possession for such a great, yet modest, city (41.3).

Thus have the Athenians of Pericles' time, or at any rate of Pericles' Funeral Oration, appeared to solve the problem of maintaining balance between respect for human freedom and hubris, or the abuse of that freedom, both externally and internally. The balance cannot be sustained, however, and its decay is at the heart of Thucydides' treatment of the theme of Athens and hubris. Central is the problem of imperialism, that key product of the Athenian experiment and its unleashing of natural impulses. Pericles himself, in his final speech in the History, made under the sobering influence of the plague and the ongoing war, is forced to admit that Athens holds her empire as a tyranny (2.63.2). He maintains that the empire is nevertheless a glorious, even a noble thing to maintain (2.64.5–6). But precisely in this context, the empire reminds us instead of Diodotus' claim that eros, especially when tempted by the greatest objects, is lawless by nature, leading men into daring and hubris (3.45.4–5). Since Athens is a strong city, not subject to the law of any other, the only law she could break, according to the sense of Diodotus' argument, is divine law or the law of justice in its universal sense.

---

under various names. I prefer Strauss's formulation because it is true to the way that the problem of absolute restraints is formulated and worked out in Thucydides' work itself. I make use of the classical term *hubris* for the same reason.

Regardless of how matters stood in Pericles' time, Diodotus' argument, together with Thucydides' darker hints on the consequences of daring, point strongly to the possibility that imperial Athens, having transgressed this law, would become ever more excessive and barbarous over time. This is indeed what happens to Athenian imperialism, and to some extent Athenian civilization, after Pericles' death. Athens' fate accords with Thucydides' view that punishment for transgressions of the divine law comes primarily through barbarization and political decay rather than through intervention by the gods. The close connection between the flowering of Greek civilization in Athens and the problem of hubris points to one of the ways in which that civilization bore the seeds of its own decline.

The Melian Dialogue stands as an epitome of the barbarization of imperial Athens. The Athenians' position on Melos, however, has roots that go back to the time of Pericles, if not further; its foundations are fully visible in the original Athenian thesis on power and rule, dating from before the war. What is missing in the Melian restatement of this thesis is any argument to the effect that, in addition to being the most powerful, the Athenians are in some more elevated way worthy of rule. The argument about "worthiness"—insisted upon by the anonymous Athenian envoys to Sparta and by Pericles—represents at least some allegiance to an ideal higher than that of mere power and self-interest. It was important to those Athenians that the city should deserve its position in some more elevated sense—but this desire was never completely reconcilable with the other and primary argument concering power and self-interest, and perhaps by the time of Melos it simply died a natural death.[46] To those Greeks who were always suspicious of the

---

[46]Interpreters have always struggled with the Athenians' diverse rationales for empire, especially early in the History, and with the question of whether or in what way the Athenian argument changes by the time of Melos. Romilly claims that the Athenian argument does not so much change as move between two strains present in it from the beginning (*Athenian Imperialism*, pp. 59, 65). The anonymous Athenians at Sparta refer to "worthiness" in order to exempt Athens from harsher arguments about the rule of the stronger and the nonapplicability of justice (pp. 255–57). For some of the scholarly opinion on this issue, see Arthur W. H. Adkins, *Merit and Responsibility* (Oxford: Clarendon, 1960), p. 222; Andrewes, in Gomme, Andrewes, Dover, *Historical Commentary* 4:184; Connor, *Thucydides*, p. 153; Ehrenberg, "Polypragmosyne," p. 52; Romilly, *Athenian Imperialism*, pp. 65, 250; de Ste. Croix, *Origins*, p. 14; White, *Words*, pp. 77, 81; A. Geoffrey Woodhead, *Thucydides on the Nature of Power* (Cambridge: Harvard University Press, 1970), p. 17; Cogan, *Human Thing*, p. 89; Jaeger, *Paideia*, pp. 401–

Athenians, the Athenian arguments probably sounded from the start like what we hear on Melos. The reality of empire, after all, is always rule by force. From this point of view, the Athenian innovation on Melos is only greater frankness to themselves as well as to their adversaries, and the reservations or qualifications characteristic of their earlier statements are simply an Athenian version of the moral hypocrisy with which they tax the Spartans and others. On Melos, their open claim to do what the gods do rather than what the gods are supposed to have said (5.105.2) brings the Athenians finally to the very pinnacle of hubris.

When we move from the Melian Dialogue to the launching of the Sicilian expedition which Thucydides juxtaposes to it, a more subtle tableau confronts us. The expedition itself overthrows the Periclean policy of strategic restraint during the war; in addition, it is described as a showcase for the gratuitous display of Athenian wealth. The splendor of the fleet to Sicily is so extravagant in Thucydides' account (6.30–31) as to raise the question whether the Athenians have not overstepped the bounds of Periclean restraint in every sense. The lavishness with which the fleet was outfitted in fact bore little enough relation to the purely military task at hand, Thucydides says, that the whole thing seemed as much a display for the benefit of the other Greeks as a purely military undertaking (6.31.4; cf. 31.6). He adds that part of the reason for the ostentatious display was private rivalry among the commanders and outfitters to produce the most splendid appearance for their vessels (31.3–4).

Such private rivalry on an occasion like this reflects a distracting and unseemly concern for personal preeminence in the very context of a great common undertaking. The extravagance itself, moreover, is questionable in light of the ideal of reserve that has informed the best of Greek culture from its inception. The Athenians' ostentation at this moment embodies and confirms the problematic character of their ambition for Sicily and signals their abandonment of the notion that restraint of any kind is appropriate to human beings. Their ambition and their splendor are signs of Athenian arrogance or hubris. They recall the Spartan commander Pausanias' ill-fated plot after the Persian Wars to become tyrant over Greece with the help of the barbarians, a plot that was pointedly

---

2; Finley, *Thucydides*, p. 89. The Athenian remarks on Melos are of course much meaner in tone than the earlier statement, which does reflect a changed vision of Athenian rule.

accompanied by his abandonment of all modesty or restraint in manners and dress (1.130). Pausanias betrayed the Greeks in more ways than one.

In the Athenian case it is more difficult to speak of betrayal for the reason that their activity can still be seen as a manifestation of the ideals of Greek culture adumbrated by Thucydides. The Athenian case reveals a tension within that culture that can be traced to its combined appreciation of humanity for its own sake and its dedication to modesty. We are near the core of Thucydides' analysis when we realize that these two things are at odds for him. It was the exquisite achievement of Athens in Pericles' day to combine them in a golden balance between humanism and dedication to restraint. The beauty of this balance, at the heart of what makes Periclean Athens such a pleasing spectacle, should not blind us to the fact that it was to some extent an illusory balance and one that could not endure.

If there are two divergent and perhaps contradictory ideals at the center of Greek culture, it becomes difficult to speak of a single peak to which that culture aspires. And indeed, Greek culture engendered not one but two great political alternatives—Athens and Sparta. The Spartans, by pursuing an austere and disciplined nobility, obtained a species of political perfection not attained elsewhere, especially not in Athens. The Spartans, after all, invented the aspect of the Greek ideal connected to moderation; the Athenians undertook to test whether humanity, when freed as much as possible from conventional restaints, will become an enemy to all restraint and thus return to barbarism. Athens illuminates more clearly the delicate balance the Greeks struck between the cultivation of humanity and noble austerity. It is a balance that Thucydides strives also to maintain in his own work.[47]

---

[47]This is true with regard to Thucydides' even-handed treatment of the virtues and vices of Athens and Sparta in his work, but it can also be seen in Thucydides' style of writing, which has drawn attention since the time of the ancient commentators. It is highly mannered in a sophisticated or even sophistic fashion, containing elaborate parallelisms, shifts of tense and of grammatical form, striking uses of words in unexpected contexts, and so on. Yet it is simultaneously so terse as to be practically opaque at points, even to the ancient grammarians. This combination has sometimes brought Thucydides harsh criticism on the grounds that his style is artificial or even "crabbed," but I believe this style can also be seen as indicative of Thucydides' own synthesis of the poles of culture represented in the History. His style is what one would expect from a fundamentally Laconic taste operating on the highest level of Athenian sophistication—which

The necessarily tenuous or unstable character of this balance explains much about Athens' career during the war and the city's tendency to develop ever greater extremism in speech and action. The Athenian character is full of hidden dangers, something that the best Athenian statesmen are aware of in the History. Diodotus deflects the Athenians' attention from true understanding of their own case, implicitly on the grounds that enlightening them could serve to fuel their excessive tendencies. There are also signs that Themistocles, as much the founder of Athenian imperialism as any individual, practised a similar kind of reticence.[48] More to the point is the case of Pericles. We learn from his own mouth, in his third and final speech, given near the end of his career, of something that he has always taken care to conceal from the Athenians, something he believed it was better for them not to know. To encourage the Athenians, disheartened by the combined force of the war and the plague, Pericles discloses for the first time the truly immense power that their control of the sea affords them. For of the two usable departments, he says, the sea and the land, they have absolute mastery over one; hence their power extends in reality not only over their present allies, as they think, but to wherever else on the sea they wish to take it (2.62.1–3). Pericles claims that although this fact is in a way obvious, the Athenians never really reflected on it before; and he never spoke of it because, he says, it represents a rather boastful claim. In other words, Pericles concealed the full significance of the Athenians' naval power in order to prevent the possibility of a too-boastful spirit arising among them.[49]

In the light of this late and telling confession we may say that Pericles'

is also as fair a description as any of Thucydides' essential attitude in the History. On the question of Thucydides' style, see Dionysius of Halicarnassus, *De Thucydide*, 21–51; Shorey, "Ethics and Psychology," pp. 80–85; Jaeger, *Paideia*, p. 389; Finley, *Three Essays*, chap. 2; Bury, *Historians*, pp. 109–13.

[48]Describing the policy of Themistocles, Thucydides says that he first promoted naval power because of the facility with which the Persians could invade by sea (1.93.7). It is not clear whether Themistocles was struck by the need of a fleet for defense or by its potential for conquest. In either case, all that he "often advised" the Athenians was that if they were hard pressed by land, they should go down to the Peiraeus and defend themselves against all attackers with their fleet. His exhortations seem modestly to have emphasized the defensive, though they do contemplate the abandonment not only of Attica but of the city itself in favor of the Peiraeus as an adjunct of sea power (this was before the long walls were built linking Athens and the Peiraeus).

[49]On Pericles' reticence and its purpose, see also Finley, *Three Essays*, pp. 159–60.

management of the city throughout his career kept an eye on the problems inherent in the Athenians' volatile character, as he saw them. I remarked earlier that when Pericles told the Athenians in the Funeral Oration to gaze upon the power of the city and become lovers of it, it was in the service of a general policy of restraint. We now see that he took care all the while actually to minimize the power of the city in their eyes, not only to help keep the city quiet during the war, but in order to prevent boasting. But exactly how Pericles understood the danger or problem of boastfulness is something of a puzzle.

We know that Pericles in his time was one of the foremost proponents of empire at Athens. Yet we find that he shrank from certain extremes in inflaming the Athenian mind or passion, on the basis of some notion of limits improper for the city to cross. Pericles seems aware of the problem of hubris in the imperial politics of Athens. The "boastfulness" that he tries to keep the Athenians away from seems to be, not the idea of any particular conquest, but the idea of essentially limitless conquest— the notion that awareness of universal control of the sea points to. Given Pericles' formulation, it seems that the boastfulness of a city that was fully conscious of this power would consist in the ambition to conquer indiscriminately on the basis of the mere conviction that it had the power to do so. This is precisely the tendency that Thucydides identifies in the Athenian character, and it is doubtless to Pericles' credit, from Thucydides' point of view, that he has recognized it. The depth of his awareness, however, and the consistency of his policy as a whole, is open to question. Once again, Pericles was a great imperialist; he is one of the few commanders visible in Thucydides' account of the fifty years of imperial expansion before the war, and his role there is unmistakable.[50] If Pericles did consider boastfulness a danger at Athens, therefore, it would be difficult to say on the basis of his words and actions as a whole exactly what he thinks is objectionable about it. He does not say it would be

[50]1.111, 114, 116, 117. The only other Athenian commander who is as visible in the *Pentekontaetia* is Cimon, from the generation before Pericles (1.98, 100, 102, 112). Pericles, as opposed to Cimon, presides over the period when Athenian rule is becoming increasingly despotic. One peculiar but significant feature of Thucydides' presentation of the two men in the *Pentekontaetia* is that Cimon is always shown attacking barbarians, or aiding fellow Greeks, or both, while Pericles is shown only fighting fellow Greeks, to consolidate Athenian power over them. This corresponds to some extent to the actual character of the two men's careers. See Plutarch *Cimon* 18, 19; Romilly, *Athenian Imperialism*, p. 62.

impossible or imprudent to push Athenian power beyond the limits he considers appropriate (2.62.2). He openly praises and nurtures Athenian daring. Pericles is the apostle of Athenian individualism, liberation, and eros, though he tries to rein in the last. He censures inactivity severely (2.40.2, 63.2, 64.4) and never so much as alludes to "moderation,"[51] or to the gods in any way that would serve to restrain the Athenians. In fact, in the Funeral Oration Pericles' claims for Athenian achievement seem to rival any boasts he might fear from them.[52]

Pericles wants it both ways. He makes unflinching use of the power and the dynamism produced by the characteristic Athenian qualities, but he seeks to combine them with restraint. To be sure, Pericles, or any other Athenian in his position, would have to base his policy on these characteristic qualities of the city, since they are hardly to be ignored or turned aside. But Pericles embraces them wholeheartedly. A peculiar combination of circumstances finally leads him to break his silence on the subject of the true extent of Athenian power, the silence that in his view constituted a significant prop to Athenian restraint. He does so in order to save the city from despair brought on by the plague and the war. One of the additional causes of the city's despondency, Pericles makes clear, is sorrow at abandoning homes and lands in Attica (2.62.2–3). Pericles is in the difficult position of having to reconcile the Athenians to deserting the lands they have not deserted since the Persian Wars. He does so by making bold to show them the immense prospect of their power on the seas, in spite of the fact that that prospect will lead easily to boasting. These are almost Pericles' last words in Thucydides. We might foresee in the doubly daring war strategy he feels compelled to lead the Athenians in—abandoning the land and being consoled with the universal control of the sea—the fate of his hope that the Athenians will keep still during the war. We might also find it a fitting epitaph to his uncertain stewardship of restraint in the city.

[51]It is characteristic of the History that Thucydides does not use the word *sōphrōn* (moderate) in connection with Pericles or Athens. He does sometimes use the word *metrios* (measured) to describe them, which is a lower-order form of self-restraint. Palmer, "Love of Glory," p. 834n, points to one revealing exception to this rule. See 8.1.3 and chap. 3 below for another exception, though of a qualified sort.

[52]See especially 2.41.4 (discussed earlier), where Pericles proclaims that the Athenians have compelled "every sea and every land" to yield access to their daring and have left "immortal" monuments of their activity "everywhere." It is hard to see how any future Athenian claim could top this.

The Parting of the Ways:
Alcibiades and Athenian Retrenchment

In moving from Pericles to Alcibiades we seem to leave altogether the realm of concern with restraint or modesty. Alcibiades, and Athens at the Alcibidean moment of the Sicilian expedition, are in love with the extravagant and unrestrained. Yet, as I remarked before, Alcibiades in proposing the expedition poses plausibly as a conservative, championing the kinetic, expansive traits of the Athenian character than can now be called, paradoxically, traditional for the city (6.18.6–7, 16.5–6, 18.1). Alcibiades is entitled to argue that continual motion and continual expansion are political imperatives derived from those traits as they exist in the city. Whether he is correct in his views regarding the advisability, the proper role, and the charms of modesty in politics is a question that awaits fuller discussion of Alcibiades. For now we will leave it that Thucydides does not in any simple or unambiguous sense regard Alcibiades, or Alcibidean Athens, as a degradation of Athenian culture or Greek civilization.

There is nothing unambiguous, meanwhile, about the judgments of Alcibiades and Athens on the propriety of the Sicilian expedition, at least not at the moment of its decree. That moment is a moment of complete good conscience at Athens, especially if we exclude the weak voice of Nicias. This insouciance, however, barely survives the public deliberations over Sicily, and Nicias becomes much more significant in later events. Readers of Thucydides are already schooled in the questionableness of Athenian imperialism, most pointedly by the Melian episode that immediately precedes the Sicilian one. In light of that jarring juxtaposition, Athenian good conscience, on which the city's charming exuberance so much depends, is seen to depend in turn on a certain blindness to Athens' own kind of moral hypocrisy. At the moment when the Athenians fall in love with the idea of sailing to Sicily, the most generous of the motives Thucydides ascribes to them is the longing of the young for faraway sights and spectacles (6.24.3). What the young seem to forget, however, is that the first sight they implicitly hope to see is a great battle in which many will be killed and entire cities will be enslaved. Similarly, the majority of Athenians, who yearn for eternal pay, do not seem to contemplate the eternal servitude of the human beings who will be forced to provide it. It is safe to say that the freedom and splendor of their city obscures the Athenians' appreciation of the subjection that it is built upon. Even their compassion toward the Mytilenaeans, as Diodotus knows well, cannot extend to ending their oppression as subjects of Athenian rule.

The Athenians long tempered their imperial rhetoric and self-understanding with the notion that they were worthy of rule in some measure beyond the title that power confers. Athenian frankness, even when it admitted (in the mouths of Pericles and Cleon) that its empire was a tyranny, never fully confronted the implications of Athens' rule over other human beings by force. This oversight is crucial also to the good conscience that presides over the Athenians' decision to make an attempt on Sicily. But the event that immediately follows this most ambitious of Athenian resolves in Thucydides' narrative is a shocking sacrilege perpetrated in the city—the defacing of some sacred statues of Hermes—which shatters Athenian complacency and throws the city into extreme consternation. The Athenians are inspired by something akin to panic, both because of the cloud that the sacrilege seems to cast over the expedition and because they fear that the act augurs a conspiracy against the democracy (6.27.2–3). The Athenians react to this event with the most conspicuous outpouring of pious concern that we have witnessed in the city to this point. They inaugurate an investigation not only of the mutilation of the statues but of any other impiety that might have been committed in the city (6.27.2). It is in connection with the latter that Alcibiades is implicated (6.28.1–2) and the sequence of events put in motion that leads eventually to Athens' repudiation of Alcibiades, the collapse of the partnership between them, and the subsequent Athenian disaster in Sicily.

The accord between Alcibiades and Athens was based partly on the fact that Alcibiades stands practically as the incarnation of all those qualities in the Athenian character that triumphed at the moment of the decision to sail for Sicily. The triumph of Alcibiades over Nicias in the debate is both the symbol and substance of this development. Renewed Athenian suspicion of Alcibiades, partly pious in character, and the city's subsequent recoil from him, necessarily reflects a retreat from what he represents as well. Under the circumstances, it is fair to say that the newfound Athenian aversion to Alcibiades results in part from the shock of self-recognition. The Athenians most dislike or mistrust in Alcibiades the very qualities that they most share with him.

But the Athenian reaction to Alcibiades, however inevitable under the circumstances, is not immediate. Influenced in part by scheming dema-gogues (6.29.3), Athens first sends Alcibiades out, along with Nicias and one other, to command the expedition to Sicily. Only later do the Athenians, still in great consternation over the impieties and allegations of impieties and falling further under the influence of the demagogues, recall Alcibiades with the set intention, according to Thucydides, of putting him to death (6.61.4). Alcibiades escapes to the Peloponnesus instead, leaving Nicias effectively in command of the expedition.

It was Nicias who most vehemently opposed the idea of the expedition at Athens when Alcibiades spoke in favor of it. In his speech against it, Nicias implied that the Athenian desire to sail could be attributed to an unhealthy erotic passion for things far away (6.13.1)—Nicias' only ref-erence to eros in Thucydides. The perverse longing in question is found primarily in the Athenian youth, who are thus mostly to blame for goading Athens into accepting the expedition. In his speech, Nicias expresses the fear that some of the older men too will vote for it, not only for shame lest they appear cowards before the young, but also because some of them share the blameworthy passion of the young. Nicias has grave doubts as to whether his position will be appreciated; he confesses from the outset that he will confine himself to speaking against sending the expedition at this particular moment because he believes it would be futile to make any more general objection to it (6.9.3). In fact, he says that before men with characters like the Athe-nians' it would be futile to make the argument, which is reminiscent of the Periclean argument about the war, that the city should strive to secure its present possessions rather than risking them for the sake of unseen and future things.[53] Nicias' experience of the years after Pericles' death, and particularly of his own inability to restrain the Athenians the way Pericles had done, has given him an insight into the character of

---

[53]There is of course this difference between the situations of Pericles and of Nicias: Pericles was giving advice for the war, while Athens at the time of the Sicilian expedition was officially at peace. Thucydides' verdict on the status of the peace, however, is well known: in effect it was no peace; the Peloponnesian War was a single, long war. Hence the Periclean advice would apply to this period as well. Nicias is fully aware of the shaky character of the peace, and he fears with reason that the expedition will help destroy it (6.11.6). But Nicias would likely go beyond Pericles in extending this cautious policy even into times of secure peace.

Athenian politics that Pericles did not have. He is more aware of the intractability of the Athenian character, of its hostility to restraint, and of the impossibility of curbing it in any fundamental way.

As a result of his insight, Nicias is pessimistic about the Athenians' accepting his good advice. More broadly, he doubts they will listen to him because he knows that in a profound sense they are optimists while he is a pessimist. According to Nicias, Athenian optimism here consists in the willingness to risk present possessions for future and unseen gains. He is thinking precisely of Athenian daring, which implies optimisim of just this kind (see also the remarks of the Corinthians: 1.70). On the basis of what we have already ascertained about this Athenian quality and of what is readily observable about Nicias by any reader of Thucydides, we may say that the optimism of the one and the pessimism of the other imply or even constitute opposing views of the world in general and of the gods in particular. Most simply stated, Nicias' pessimisim involves the belief that man's ultimate fate is not in his own hands but in the hands of gods, gods who may be capricious. Every undertaking is to him a gamble, regardless of the justice of the cause or the competence of the commanders (5.16.1; 7.77.2). These doubts are multiplied if there is any question as to the justice of the enterprise. This attitude is more or less that of traditional piety; it appears as pessimism only in the light of thoroughgoing Athenian optimism, which bespeaks human liberation from the control of the gods. Human destiny can be taken into human hands by those bold enough to wrest control of their fate from chance. Fortune herself, for she too is a goddess, is propitious to the truly daring.[54] The Athenians' optimism reflects their implicit belief in the possibility of human self-sufficiency and thus is one with the Athenian project or experiment altogether. Needless to say, this attitude appears to someone like Nicias as the greatest presumption or hubris.

---

[54]This attitude of the Athenians, and their optimism in general, foreshadow Machiavelli's view that at least most of what is called fortune or god can be conquered by the especially audacious. See, e.g., *The Prince*, chap. 25. In both cases an intellectual revolution provides the setting for a revolution in politics.

On the serious theme of optimism and pessimism in Thucydides, which I only touch upon here, see also Edmunds, *Chance and Intelligence*, which does not, however, follow quite the tack I do in exploring this issue.

The gulf between Nicias and the Athenians is not, however, so great as it might appear. The shock of the mutilation of the Hermae, and the Athenians' contemplation of everything that is most questionable in Alcibiades, succeed after all in bringing Nicias into the ascendency. His rise seems symptomatic of an even deeper shift in public sentiment in the city; which is reflected in a peculiar speech given under Nicias' command in Sicily, the speech of the Athenian Euphemus at Camarina (6.82–87). Euphemus' is the first political speech given by an Athenian after the resurgence of pious concern in the city (one speech by Nicias to his troops intervenes: 6.68). The Camarinaeans, formerly allies of Athens, are being courted by both the Athenians and the Syracusans for the impending struggle between them; the ensuing debate pits Euphemus against the formidable Syracusan Hermocrates. Euphemus himself is one of those few Thucydidean speakers, like Diodotus, who are not known to us except through their single appearances in Thucydides, but whose speeches are highly significant in the History. Euphemus' name signifies not exactly "euphemism" but reticence, or even silence, about the evil and particularly the impious; his speech is in fact an interesting study in Athenian rhetoric drawn in the direction suggested by this name.

Euphemus' speech replaces that which Alcibiades would probably have been called upon to deliver in this situation if he had not already been exiled from the Athenian camp. Perhaps its most striking departure from what Alcibiades might have said is its elaborate and explicit denial that the Athenians have come to conquer. To be sure, neither Alcibiades nor any other Athenian could be expected openly to proclaim that ambition here, but Euphemus' protestations on this subject go considerably beyond the requirements of the situation. Alcibiades, like Brasidas in a similar situation (at Acanthus: 4.85–87), might have deftly mingled threats with appeals to fear of a common foe. Hermocrates himself, Euphemus' opponent, was astonishingly frank earlier about the desire of all powerful cites to rule and persuaded his listeners (4.59–64). But Euphemus' arguments, beginning with those concerning Athenian aims for Sicily, echo remarkably the arguments made by Nicias at Athens. Euphemus claims that the Athenians cannot have come to conquer Sicily because the island, as Nicias had suggested, would be impossible to hold, even if it were possible to take (6.86.3; cf. Nicias at 6.11.1). Euphemus speaks as

61

though the Athenian empire has reached its natural limits, a suggestion Nicias also made, though he was not entirely consistent on this point (6.85, 86.3; Nicias at 6.13.1, somewhat at odds with 10.5). Nicias used these arguments to recommend against the expedition altogether, while Euphemus uses them to make plausible his claim that Athenian goals in Sicily are strictly limited. Both Athenians espouse strangely conservative views of imperial politics.[55]

Euphemus' speech implies such a thorough revision of Athenian strategy for Sicily that only Nicias could be responsible for it. But not even Nicias has power to make such an alteration legitimately.[56] In fact, Euphemus' assertion that Athenian intentions for Sicily are innocuous must be a lie, unless his speech reflects in fact a change of heart in Athens itself, in the direction of the views of Nicias. Given the thrust of Thucydides' presentation from the mutilation of the Hermae to the moment of Euphemus' speech and beyond, this is a plausible interpretation. Certainly, one of the revelations that comes out of this episode in Athenian history is that there is more of Nicias in Athens than anyone, including Nicias himself, was aware. It is not entirely coincidental that this strain should become visible and attempt to assert itself precisely against the background of the most extreme and extravagant imperial undertaking in Athens in at least a generation. And it is not at all coincidental that its reassertion is in large part responsible for the crushing failure of that undertaking.

Considered in this context, Euphemus' speech is a strange mixture. It revises some of the foremost themes of Athenian rhetoric but does

---

[55]Nicias takes this so far as to maintain that if Syracuse were allowed to become master of Sicily, it would then be least likely to venture an attack on Athens: "it is not likely that an imperial city would make war against an imperial city" (6.11.3). The view behind this apparently preposterous statement is precisely that empires, once established, become fundamentally conservative or defensive. This is clearly the way Nicias would respond to imperial politics. This view, interestingly enough, does correspond to Spartan behavior, though not, of course, to Athenian.

[56]It is true that the only charge recorded by Thucydides to the commanders of the expedition was to aid the Egestaeans and Leontini, and, rather ambiguously, to arrange affairs in Sicily "in whatever way they judge to be best for Athens" (6.8.2), which might be construed within the limits of Euphemus' speech. This however is before the debate between Nicias and Alcibiades, in which the Athenians' views of what they want for Sicily become quite unmistakable. Nicias seems in his actual campaign to act on the goals so clearly mandated by the city. This makes the speech of Euphemus an even more interesting case of revisionism, due to its forlorn and ultimately fruitless character.

not repudiate them. Euphemus defends the Athenian empire explicitly, arguing that the compulsion of self-interest exonerates the Athenians in their imperialism (82.3, 83.2, 85.1–2), and he scorns any attempt on the part of his audience to tutor the Athenians, at this late date, in "moderation" (87.3). Perhaps most telling, he praises Athenian daring precisely for its willingness to abandon the city during the Persian Wars (82.4). But Euphemus makes use of this episode in Athenian history in a wholly unprecedented way. Because the Athenians thus dared, he says, while other Greeks sided with the Persians and in some cases even aided the attack, it was "not unjust" for the Athenians subsequently to enslave the Greeks (82.3). This modest "not unjust" keeps Euphemus within previous Athenian claims about justice and empire in one sense, but the argument that the allies' wickedness is part of Athens' justification for subjugating them is quite new. The anonymous Athenians speaking at Sparta make much of Athenian actions during the Persian Wars, but for the purpose of illustrating Athenian power and character, not Athenian moral superiority (1.73.2–74; cf. 1.75.1).

Euphemus recasts the Athenian arguments along more traditionally moral (or moralistic) lines, to give a quasi-moral justification for the empire. Nowhere does he claim that the Athenians rule because of power alone, according to a universal law of the stronger.[57] He does suggest, however, that before the growth of Athenian strength, the Spartans dominated Greece on the basis of power alone (82.3). In connection with that claim, Euphemus perpetrates his single most outrageous case of historical revisionism. The first motive that he advances for Athenian imperialism, in the opening passage of his speech, is the opposition of the Doric and Ionic races. This traditional or ancestral argument is all the more striking here because no other Athenian, with the possible exception of Nicias, ever makes use of it.[58] Euphemus is referring of course to the opposition between Athens and Sparta. He argues, quite fantastically, that not only did the Athenian empire spring largely from an initial attempt to escape Spartan hegemony but it is maintained in

[57]Cf. especially 5.89, on Melos, with Euphemus' almost comically weak echo at 6.83.2. Again, we note that Hermocrates, in a similar situation, got away with proclaiming this universal law.

[58]6.82.1; contrast 85.1. Cf. Nicias at 6.9.1 and Alcibiades' rejoinder, 6.18.1. Hermocrates precedes Euphemus in this general line of argument (6.77, 79, 80.3), but the use Euphemus makes of it is entirely his own.

its present scope in order to avoid falling back under that hegemony (82.3, 83.1). Thus the sole motive of imperial policy at Athens, aside perhaps from revenge on the Medizing islanders and others, has been fear of the Spartans. The desire to check Spartan power has of course been a conspicuous part of Athenian apologetics all along—it was a motive of paramount importance to Themistocles in particular (1.91.4–7)—but Euphemus' exclusive reliance on it significantly alters the Athenian posture.

While Euphemus does echo the argument that Athenian pursuit of self-interest justifies its imperial policy, his development of that argument gives it its most noncontroversial form. Fear of the Spartans is a much more obviously exonerating compulsion than honor or profit, the other self-interested motives named in the original Athenian argument (1.75.3, 76.2). Indeed, fear of the kind that Euphemus speaks of seems incompatible with the old motivation of honor. Euphemus says that the city of Athens is motivated like a tyrant (83.2), and apparently a feeble tyrant at that. Athens is driven by fear, even craven fear. Hence the Camarinaeans need not fear the Athenians, in whose narrow self-interest it is to keep its allies in Sicily strong and independent and to thwart the ambitions of Syracuse (85). The Camarinaeans should indeed be thankful for the opportunity, offered by the Athenians' presence in Sicily, to defeat the Syracusan menace. They should not think too much about why Athens should have sent a force out of all proportion to the limited task Euphemus speaks of (86.2; cf. 6.31.6).

The last argument employed by Euphemus, which seems almost an afterthought (he states it only in his concluding recapitulation: 6.87), is perhaps the most interesting and ingenious of all. Owing to their fear and their sense of vulnerability, Euphemus claims, the Athenians act throughout Greece, as now in Sicily, as a prop to the good, the innocent, and the weak against the wicked and ambitious. The oppressed and threatened everywhere know they can enlist the Athenians for support against their oppressors. The Athenians are compelled by their position to be the policemen of Greece, as it were. Precisely their meddlesome character—it is here that Euphemus alludes to their inveterate immoderation—forces the ambitious to respect their neighbors and to become moderate against their will, and delivers the unmeddlesome from danger. The Athenians thus turn out to be unjust champions of justice and immoderate enforcers of moderation, men on off-white horses, we might say, who whatever their motivation bring the boon of peace and order to the Greeks.[59]

Leaving aside for a moment the obvious problem that for many this peace is the peace of imperial servitude, that with friends like the Athenians many cities might well be able to do without enemies, this argument is quite ingenious, if Euphemus' goal is to defend Athenian behavior as much as possible in moral terms. Euphemus cannot and does not argue Athenian virtue; he nevertheless manages to produce an argument that defends Athenian actions very much in terms of traditional virtue and modesty. His concluding flourish is the clearest example of what he is attempting to accomplish throughout his speech. In striving as much as possible to defend Athenian behavior in moral terms, Euphemus does what all previous Athenian spokesmen had openly disdained to do. To be sure, he does not appeal to the gods any more than they, but he shows some respect, if almost nostalgic respect, for the old moral categories, and he definitely abandons the boastful notion of Athenian self-sufficiency and the peculiar kind of optimism that goes with it. It is in this that Euphemus is most Nician; his is a speech that Nicias himself might have delivered. Euphemus is filled with apprehension and diffidence of a kind that Alcibiades for example would never have felt. Nor is this diffidence forced upon him or justified in any way by the situation that confronts him in Sicily or the present balance of forces in Greece.

It is this diffidence as much as anything else that makes Euphemus seem non-Athenian. In fact, however, it has a significant predecent at Athens, even apart from the speech of Nicias against the expedition. This precedent appears precisely at the culminating moment of imperial ambition in the city, the voting of the Sicilian expedition. The Athenians

[59]A number of commentators have argued that the Athenian empire did bring many benefits to Greece and that Thucydides ignores the genuine justification for Athenian imperialism that these constitute. The benefits of Athenian imperialism are said to include those identified by Euphemus—namely, order and security—as well as general political unification and prosperity flowing from all of these factors. See Romilly, *Athenian Imperialism*, p. 95; Thibaudet, *La campagne*, p. 224; Finley, *Thucydides*, p. 247 (cf. p. 300); see also Isocrates *Panegyricus, Peace*. Euphemus' speech demonstrates that Thucydides was aware of these considerations, but for him the issue is the defensibility of unifying Greece and bringing all these benefits in the way Athens does. It is novel, and quite un-Thucydidean, to suggest that the objections to imperialism from the point of view of justice can be overcome by considerations of material benefit.

not only vote for but fall in love with the expedition; but the erotic passion descends on the city only after Nicias' second speech, in which he seems to promise that with a sufficiently vast armament the expedition will be secure. Nicias had hoped by this argument to dissuade the Athenians from undertaking such a burdensome affair, but they fall hopelessly in love with it instead, owing largely to the conviction, gotten from this speech of Nicias, that no real risk is involved (6.24). This is hardly unalloyed daring. The Athenians vote the massive armament Nicias recommends, then put Alcibiades and Nicias both at the head of it. Alcibiades himself after all had recommended that the Athenians choose them both, insinuating, somewhat satirically it is true, that Nicias would provide the good luck (6.17.1). Thucydides does not say why Nicias and Alcibiades both were chosen by the Athenians, especially since Nicias did not want to serve (6.8.4), but it would not be surprising if Alcibiades' witticism contains part of the truth. Nicias' personal connection with the expedition seems somehow auspicious. It is this reassurance, as well as that of the vast supply of arms, that the Athenians derive from Nicias on their way to falling in love with the project. This is something of a departure on both counts from the former imperial spirit at Athens, and certainly from that spirit as it is embodied by Alcibiades.

Thus it is somehow appropriate that, when Alcibiades is repudiated by the Athenians in connection with the alarming and inauspicious impieties committed in the city, that Nicias and the Athenians are left to themselves with their massive expedition. Nicias' presence may be auspicious and comforting to a newly ascendent aspect of the public mind at Athens, but Nicias' leadership under the circumstances proves to be disastrous. Even the overwhelming size of the expedition proves as much a disadvantage as an advantage, due to the difficulty of supplying it and the alarm it inspires in the Sicilians. Alcibiades' strategy, before the size of the expedition was determined, deliberately minimized the need for force (6.17.4), relying more on subterfuge, persuasion, and finesse, so to speak; and Alcibiades continues to advocate such a policy even after the expedition has been sent out (6.48). This policy, like almost everything else about Alcibiades, is more reminiscent of the Athens that defeated the Persians and built the empire than is that of Nicias. It is more daring in the specific sense that it boldly attempts a conquest beyond what appears justified by the forces at hand; it is more brashly optimistic about the prospects of success.

The condemnation of Alcibiades and the ascendency of Nicias and Euphemus might easily give us the impression that Alcibiades alone is left embodying, in exile, the old Athenian ideal of superlative daring and its corollary optimisim and belief in real human self-sufficiency. Alcibiades is the only one who seems still to believe that honor or grandeur is a properly ruling attribute. The Athenians, who had defied all the limits in international politics for so long, appear here to succumb to the unpleasant questions about their behavior that were evident to others all along. For the first time they experience the force of the traditional political limits. Those limits are largely internal.

The attitude and ambitions of imperial Athens suffer defeat in Sicily not from lack of power to match them but from lack of Alcibidean resolve. Alcibiades, who is surely aware of what men like Nicias would call the impious or hubristic character of his own and the Athenians' undertakings, alone retains the strength of soul to contemplate and to carry out such designs. Whether Alcibiades' attitude is real strength of soul or merely moral obtuseness is one of the most serious questions that arises in Thucydides in connection with him. The Nician attitude springs from a suspicion that the empire is indeed a tyranny, inevitably involving, implicitly or explicitly, the boast against justice that the tyrant's rule is fitting or appropriate. Perhaps Alcibiades is simply brazen enough to make this boast; that is what the Athenians suspect. Alcibiades certainly has no qualms about extending the city's empire or about pursuing his own rather great ambitions within the city. Whether this is simple shamelessness, or whether Alcibiades' claims are somehow justified, is a question that concerns the evaluation of Athenian imperialism and the proper place of a statesman within the city. The career of Alcibiades presents these issues for Thucydides in their most difficult and most illuminating light.

Before we can determine whether Alcibiades' claims and aspirations are fitting, we must determine what they are. This is something of a difficulty in itself: the Athenians were wary of Alcibiades out of uncertainty concerning his real intentions. Alcibiades seems to have the greatest possible ambitions, ambitions that, like those of imperial Athens at her height, accept no traditional notions of restraint. To uncover those ambitions will be a political revelation as important as uncovering the ambitions of imperial Athens.

2

The Speeches of Alcibiades
and Alcibiades' Political Views

ALCIBIADES participates in all the problems that surround the theme of Athenian imperialism in Thucydides. He is its most unflinching proponent, more unflinching in the end than the city itself. Other problems, peculiar to Alcibiades, have to do with such themes as the character and role of great individuals or great statesmen in Thucydides' work. Yet even these are distinctly Athenian. Athens is the city that has devoted itself most fully to the liberation of human capacities and talents; by the middle of the Peloponnesian War Alcibiades has emerged as the most uninhibited of the uninhibited Athenians. Against the background of the Athenian experiment, as I have called it, one of the questions thus posed by Alcibiades is whether he must be understood as an archetype of liberated individualism as such. In particular, since Alcibiades is a man of the most uninhibited political ambition and the most exceptional political talents, we must wonder whether he is not the image of political ambition in its purest or most perfect form.

One of the most striking—or shocking—characteristics of Alcibiades is his ability to serve on all sides in the war with equal facility. Alcibiades' ambition and talent have liberated themselves from any ordinary attachment to city; his behavior in fact poses a grave question about the relation of political genius or ambition to the community. Alcibiades raises this issue most forcefully, but he is not the first to bring it to light in Thucydides—Themistocles is the one whom Thucydides uses to introduce the problem. Thucydides' presentation of Themistocles is noteworthy in two ways: he praises Themistocles more highly for natural political genius than anyone else in the History; and Themistocles also demonstrates amply that his talents could serve one state as well as another (1.137–38).

Thucydides inserts his longest discussion of Themistocles rather gratuitously into the narrative of Book One as a counterpart to the drama of the Spartan commander Pausanias (cf. 1.135 with 138–9). The parallel portraits of Pausanias and Themistocles demonstrate that Athenian genius, grounded in nature or natural talent, does not lose its force when operating apart from the city, whereas Spartan virtue, grounded in conventional discipline, does. Yet since both men at one time or another offer to work for the Persians, this difference has the consequence that, while Pausanias' foreign intrigue is incompetent and doomed to failure, Themistocles' is not. Themistocles, to be sure, never carries out his apparent promise to the Persians to betray the Greeks, but the fact remains that his powers are neither so dependent on his city as to lose all their force when separated from it nor so devoted to the city as to refuse unconditionally all service outside of it. Thucydides, who describes Themistocles' attributes and talents in detail, does not refer to him as "virtuous." The theme of his eulogy instead is Themistocles' rich natural endowment (esp. 1.138.3). And in his catalogue of Themistocles' specifically political talents or excellences, Thucydides does not include patriotism. Themistocles was most brilliant at discerning the better and worse courses of action and explaining them to others (1.138.3). The omissions from this account become conspicuous especially when we compare Pericles' famous list of his own political virtues, which combines these two qualities with patriotism and "superiority to money" (2.60.5–6).

Pericles, flanked by Themistocles on one side and Alcibiades on the other, seems in this as in other respects to represent more an exception than the rule. If the history of the greatest Athenian statesmen leads us to conclude that natural political genius is not only serviceable to all sides but inherently devoid of political attachments, this would represent not only a grave political problem but a profound paradox. We would be forced to wonder whether such genius can fairly be considered the peak of political leadership, since it makes sense to say that leadership should be evaluated from the perspective of the communities that make use of it. It is this common perspective that inclines to the equally common opinion that Pericles represents the peak of Athenian states-manship in Thucydides. But the paradox is heightened if we regard both Themistocles and Alcibiades as men of natural gifts superior to those of Pericles, as I believe Thucydides' presentation leads us to do. Alci-biades, who receives more exposure than Themistocles and who certainly articulates his position more, is the real focus of Thucydides' treatment of this paradox. Alcibiades refuses to submit to the narrow perspective of the particular political community, and he openly defends that refusal. The question is whether that gives him any allegience, indeed any goal, outside his own self-interest.

Alcibiades, for all his kinship to Themistocles, is actually more extreme than his predecessor in a number of ways. He goes through with his plan to aid Athens' enemies, though there is the important fact that Alcibiades was exiled from his city at a much earlier age than Themis-tocles, before he had made an immortal name for himself—Themistocles had secured his place in history by the time of his exile. It is the extreme and uncompromising way Alcibiades pursues his ambition within the city, and the vision of politics, both domestic and international, that he elaborates in speech and acts upon in deed, that makes Alcibiades truly unique in the History. His vision, as articulated in his speeches, revolves almost entirely around the phenomenon of great political ambition. Alcibiades emphasizes the great and beneficial accomplishments men of such ambition can bring to the community; this in his view amply exonerates him of narrow selfishness. Corollary to this, though, is a truly expansive view of the rights of great statesmen. If those rights are vi-olated, claims Alcibiades, the statesman is entitled to find his own rem-edies. His views thus involve some dramatic revisions in the traditional understanding of the structure of the city and of the very principle of political community. They are in fact novel enough to raise the question whether they are compatible with the integrity of the political community.

The problems that surround Alcibiades' politics are sufficiently grave to have made him a positively diabolical figure in the eyes of many, from his own day to this. In Thucydides' presentation, one of the causes of Athens' demise is the importation of the Athenian thesis on justice and rule into the domestic politics of the city, and the civil strife that resulted.

Alcibiades, who places great emphasis on the rights of the stronger, understood in a certain way, and on their title to rule within the city, might look like one of the prime agents of that corruption. On the other hand, as we shall see, there are also grounds for thinking that Alcibiades' political vision, his peculiar version of the Athenian thesis, if that is what it is, was the only thing that might have saved the city from destruction. Thucydides says that it was Alcibiades' absence, not his presence, that destroyed Athens (6.15.4).

Alcibiades' speeches are unusually helpful in ascertaining his views as well as in illuminating both his character and his actions, for one of the respects in which Alcibiades is a true Athenian is in his unabashed frankness of speech. And Alcibiades always speaks frankly about the most comprehensive issues, those we are most concerned with in our reading of Thucydides. This is true in part because Alcibiades is always surrounded by controversy, always compelled to explain or defend himself in his speeches—and always convinced that he can do so frankly, without deceit. Despite the controversy that surrounds him, Alcibiades' good conscience proves invincible. To all this we can add that Alcibiades is also very intelligent and sophisticated. He has clearly thought a great deal about the issues and questions that agitate his audiences (as befits after all a former associate of Socrates).[1] In spite of the fact that his two speeches in Thucydides, at Athens (6.16–18) and at Sparta (6.89–92), are necessarily ad hoc, they present a single, consistent, and very astute view of politics. They illuminate the case of Alcibiades quite well, which is also to say that they are important documents for the study of the character and place of great ambition in politics.

Alcibiades and the Peace of Nicias

Alcibiades' speech in favor of the Sicilian expedition is the first extended view of him provided by Thucydides, whose short introduction to that speech is the only explicit overview of Alcibiades' habits and career that

---

[1] On Alcibiades' connection with Socrates see Plutarch *Alcibiades* 4–7; Plato *Symposium*, *Alcibiades I* [*II*], *Protagoras*; Xenophon *Memorabilia* I.ii. Thucydides never indicates that he is aware of Socrates, and I do not intend to make anything of the connection between Socrates and Alcibiades. In this regard, the most one can say about Thucydides' Alcibiades is that he is clearly alive to the many sophisticated currents of thought developing in Athens before and during the war.

71

he offers (6.15). Alcibiades first appears in the History somewhat earlier, however, at a moment that seems to have been selected in part for the illuminating vignette that it provides of Alcibiades and his political manner.[2] The moment is early in the so-called Peace of Nicias; disputes have arisen concerning the fulfillment of some of the articles of that peace. These disputes, says Thucydides, emboldened some in Athens who opposed the treaty to press their views, in particular Alcibiades the son of Cleinias, a man who would be considered young in another city, but who was honored at Athens on account of his ancestry (5.43). Many of those who opposed the treaty, including Alcibiades, thought that Athens should conclude an alliance with Argos, a traditional enemy of the Spartans. Such an alliance would strengthen both cities against the Spartans but would undermine the peace.

Thucydides vouches that Alcibiades genuinely thought it better to accept the Argive alliance, but he was opposed to the Peace of Nicias on personal grounds as well. The Spartans, with whom he had been trying to reestablish his hereditary tie,[3] had overlooked him on account of his youth and had negotiated the treaty through Nicias and Laches instead. Believing himself slighted on all sides, Alcibiades took up the cause of the Argive alliance. He argued that the Spartans intended, under cover of the negotiated peace, to destroy Argos and thus isolate Athens. Therefore, when the first disputes under the treaty arose, Alcibiades sent privately to Argos, telling them to send envoys to Athens on the matter of an alliance. His plan was to induce the Athenians to negotiate with these envoys after they have arrived.

The first thing that strikes the observer about Alcibiades' behavior is the personal or private interest involved in his political calculations. His mixture, if not confusion, of public and private would strike ordinary or traditional political sensibilities as questionable, to say the least. Thucydides, like every moderately astute political observer, knows that some private motivation is present in all politics. Even so, this first Alcibidean episode seems to mark an epoch in the History, one with disquieting implications for the future. Its novelty is reflected even in the style of

[2]This is noted also by F. M. Cornford, *Thucydides Mythistoricus*, (London: Edward Arnold, 1907), pp. 191–92.

[3]The hereditary tie was that of *proxenos*; the title had been renounced by Alcibiades' grandfather. *Proxenoi* were men who, somewhat like permanent ambassadors (which did not otherwise exist), represented the interests of a foreign city in their native land.

Thucydides' presentation of Alcibiades, which unlike his presentation of other major figures, includes systematic comment on his private life and motivations.[4] Thucydides here describes him as filled with pride and love of victory (5.43.2). In spite of his youth (he is about thirty), Alcibiades does not hesitate to claim for himself a conspicuous position in the city; when he considers himself slighted, he acts to enforce that claim. The Spartans negotiated their treaty with Nicias, so Alcibiades' ambition leads him to oppose the peace. The fact that Sparta of all cities could be most expected to consider his youth an obstacle does not, in Alcibiades' eyes, excuse their implicit contempt of him. It looks as if his attempt to revive his hereditary ties with the Spartans was made in order to avail himself of it personally in his political machinations. When the moment seems ripe for negotiating the counteralliance with the Argives instead, Alcibiades sends privately to them for envoys. This "privately" casts long shadows forward in the History.

The use Alcibiades makes of the Argive envoys is worthy of the way they were summoned. With them hidden in the wings, as it were, Alcibiades orchestrates an elaborate drama at Athens to ensure their success. The Spartans, alarmed by the prospect of an Athenian–Argive alliance, send envoys of their own with full powers to resolve the disputes under the treaty; Alcibiades gets the Spartan envoys to deny before the assembly that they have come with full powers—deceiving them, deceiving Nicias who supports their cause, and deceiving the Athenians themselves. Through Alcibiades' machinations, the Athenians fly into a rage against supposed Spartan duplicity, turn their backs on the Spartans, and become favorably disposed to the Argives.[5] An alliance would have

---

[4]Others have noted that the inclusion of private details is characteristic of Thucydides' presentation of Alcibiades because in his case they are uniquely relevant. Thucydides' presentations of almost all other major figures are striking for their reticence about details of private life. Pausanias might be a revealing, if partial, exception. See H. D. Westlake, *Individuals in Thucydides* (Cambridge: Cambridge University Press, 1968), p. 212; John H. Finley, Jr., *Thucydides* (1942; rpt. Ann Arbor: University of Michigan Press, 1963), p. 218; J. B. Bury, *The Ancient Greek Historians* (London: Macmillan, 1909), p. 120; Robin Seager, "Alcibiades and the Charge of Aiming at Tyranny," *Historia* 16 (1967).

[5]There is controversy concerning the historical facts in this episode. Jean Hatzfeld, *Alcibiade* (Paris: Presses Universitaires de France, 1951), pp. 89–93, argues that the Spartans had not in fact come with full powers to negotiate, and Alcibiades only unmasked their deception. He supports this interpretation by pointing to the fact that Nicias himself travels to Sparta immediately afterward to negotiate and is forced to return empty-handed (5.46). Moreover, the Spartan Endius, one of the envoys Alcibiades apparently betrayed,

been approved on the spot had not an earthquake caused the assembly's adjournment (5.45.4)—even the gods seem to be disgusted with Alcibiades' mode of proceeding. But the Argive alliance, after some additional delay, is concluded by Athens.

On the basis of Thucydides' exposition it seems scarcely an exaggeration to say that this entire affair, from the summoning of the envoys to the conclusion of the alliance, is nothing but a personal intrigue of Alcibiades. This impression is strengthened in the sequel, in which all the initiatives undertaken pursuant to the Argive alliance are as much Alcibiades' as they are Athens' or even Argos' for that matter. It hardly needs saying that Alcibiades' means of bringing about the alliance are at odds with the ordinary functioning of politics, especially democratic politics.[6] They seem to owe more to manipulation than to persuasion. Yet there is the redeeming fact, which Thucydides notes at the outset, that Alcibiades pursued this course of action because he believed it to be best both for the city and for himself. And Alcibiades is a man whose political judgment is not to be scorned. Without his elaborate deception, the city might have chosen a bad course, in Alcibiades' eyes. Alcibiades acts, in other words, on what he believes to be a convergence of interest

becomes Alcibiades' closest ally later when he goes over to the Spartan side (8.6, 12). The discrepancy can perhaps be attributed in part to a disagreement between the Spartans and Athenians as to what "full powers" would imply for these purposes. As for Endius, it is possible that he formed part of the war party at Sparta at this time (5.36.1) and was quite content to see the negotiations fail, by fair means or foul. In any event, it is unmistakable in Thucydides' presentation that Alcibiades orchestrates the whole affair at Athens, including inducing the Spartans to change their public position, so as to produce the desired result.

[6]Jacqueline de Romilly tersely remarks that Alcibiades' procedure represents a violation of the conditions of public deliberation (*Thucydides and Athenian Imperialism*, trans. P. Thody [1947; rpt., New York: Barnes & Noble, 1963], p. 197n). This as we shall see is a problem more generally with Alcibiades' politics. Romilly concludes that Thucydides condemns Alcibiades' means and his ends here, although she thinks the Argive policy itself had its uses (pp. 196–200; see her review of some of the literature at p. 197n3). The question whether Thucydides favors the Argive policy would be an involved one, tied among other things to his final verdict and on the war generally. Much can be said for Westlake's suggestion (*Individuals*, pp. 217–19) that Thucydides was largely indifferent to it, that he includes the history of the Argive connection as much to reveal something of Alcibiades as to record events important for the war. Thucydides' judgment on Alcibiades' actions at this point are deliberately withheld, I think; it will depend on his comprehensive evaluation of Alcibiades' politics. As we have seen, the greatest Athenian statesmen all seem to acknowledge the need for at least some deception in dealing with the *demos* (see chap. 1).

between himself and the city. Whether his judgment as to the public good is tainted, here or elsewhere, by his conspicuous concern with his own interests, is one of the crucial questions that surround him. Thucydides is notoriously opaque concerning his own judgment on the advisability of this alliance and even of such pivotal undertakings as the Sicilian expedition. But assuming that the interests of Alcibiades and Athens do converge in this instance, the question still arises what Alcibiades would do in a case where their interests diverge.

This question takes us beyond the episode at hand. Not too far beyond, however: in typical fashion, Alcibiades raises this issue himself in the first speech he delivers in Thucydides. Typically too, he resolves it in essence by insisting that the problem does not arise, because it is impossible for the interests of Athens and Alcibiades to diverge. He will hold to this view, paradoxically, even when he and Athens seem to have become bitterest enemies.

Alcibiades' First Speech

The occasion of Alcibiades' first speech in Thucydides is the debate at Athens over the launching of the Sicilian expedition, a debate which in fact ranges over a whole series of issues, pitting Alcibiades against Nicias in a true struggle of opposites. Nicias speaks first. In his attempt to get the Athenians to reconsider the expedition, Nicias attacks its proponent, Alcibiades, in the broadest possible way, though not by name. He insinuates that "someone" is present who is too young properly to have a command in the expedition, but who advocates it solely out of regard to his personal interest, thinking to profit by it and thus support his horse-racing and other lavish and expensive forms of display (6.12.2). Nicias does not maintain that a statesman—or any citizen for that matter—must act in politics without any thought of his personal interests. He opens his speech with the assertion that the citizen who has concern for his own safety and prosperity will be led thereby to care most for the city (9.2). Alcibiades, however, consults "only" his own interest in counseling the Sicilian expedition. Thus, in addition to wasting his own property by profligacy, Alcibiades commits an "injustice" against the city as a whole (12.2).

Before recording Alcibiades' reply, Thucydides gives us a brief statement of his own, which constitutes his only explicit comment on the career of Alcibiades (6.15). He begins by corroborating, if not magnifying, everything Nicias says. Alcibiades came forward to defend the Sicilian project, says Thucydides, wishing to contradict Nicias, both because of their general political opposition and because Nicias had slanderously mentioned him in his speech. But most of all, he wished to have the generalship, to take Sicily and Carthage, and in the event of success personally to profit from it in wealth as well as in glory. For, Thucydides says, being made much of in the city, Alcibiades spent beyond his means in horse-raising and other things.

Thus far, Thucydides' introduction alludes obliquely at best to the fact that Alcibiades hopes to benefit himself only by benefiting the city—that is, if further conquests are indeed benefits. His private motivations meanwhile—a desire for wealth and glory and a highly personal rivalry with Nicias—are quite conspicuous. Concerning Alcibiades' personal extravagance, Thucydides' formulation seems to suggest that he indulged himself in this way only because he believed it to be fitting for men in positions of great esteem. Alcibiades takes this position in his speech. The issue of personal extravagance is much larger than this, however. Thucydides continues: it was the extravagant demeanor of Alcibiades that later became a prime cause of Athens' downfall. The extravagance of his "lawless" (*paranomon*) self-indulgence, together with the sheer extent of his designs, as revealed in everything he undertook, led the Athenians to suspect him of desiring a tyranny. They thus became hostile to him and entrusted their affairs to others, a course of action which "not long afterward" brought the city to ruin (6.15.4). For despite the Athenians' private jealousy of Alcibiades, or their jealousy against him on account of his private habits,[7] Alcibiades was best at directing the affairs of the city in the war.

The tone of this Thucydidean introduction to Alcibiades' manners and career is one of studied ambiguity. It seems at first to adopt the Nician perspective, then to move away from it; and it is not possible to say whether Thucydides blames Alcibiades for his habits or the Athenians for a self-destructive overreaction to them when he says that Alcibiades'

---

[7]These two formulations reflect the ambiguity of *idia* (private) here, an ambiguity alluded to earlier (chap. 1, n. 29). The context of this passage suggests the second reading, while the Harmodius and Aristogeiton passage, which I argued earlier is a parallel to the Athenians' jealousy toward Alcibiades, favors the first.

extravagance brought the city down. In fact, the passage as a whole appears intended not to answer questions, but to raise them; perhaps, more comprehensively, it could be said to introduce Alcibiades as a question.[8] But this is already something; the very ambiguity of the passage indicates that the judgment of Nicias, for example, is inadequate. And the passage begins to show us what the important or fundamental questions are—never a small achievement. We are led to ask whether Athens, or any political community, could under any circumstances be reconciled to the presence of a man like Alcibiades; we are forced to wonder whether personal extravagance is the natural concomitant of an ambition like Alcibiades', and indeed to wonder what the ambition of a man like Alcibiades is. Since Alcibiades was in Thucydides' estimation the only man who could have saved the Sicilian expedition and the city, it is obviously not a question of his extravagance or self-interest rendering him unfit for command in any literal sense. Whether the city is bound

---

[8]The wide disagreements in the literature about the interpretation of this passage are due in part to this fact. Disagreements are found on all levels, beginning with the purely textual—whether, for example, Thucydides refers in this passage to the final ruin of the city or merely to its defeat in Sicily (Dover, in Gomme, A. W. Andrewes, and K. J. Dover, *A Historical Commentary on Thucydides*, 5 vols. [Oxford: Clarendon, 1945–81], 4:242–45; F. E. Adcock, *Thucydides and His History* [Cambridge: Cambridge University Press, 1963], 132–35). What Thucydides says is that the Athenians resented Alcibiades, turned to others, and "not long afterward" brought the city to ruin, which is taken by Hatzfeld (*Alcibiade*, p. 201n) to refer only to the Sicilian defeat. He argues that the aorist *diathenti* must refer only to Alcibiades' excellence in organizing the Sicilian project. Aorists, however, may also be used to make the most sweeping generalizations. Indeed, since Alcibiades' expertise was scarcely seen in the Sicilian campaign, and since the rest of this passage takes the most general perspective, it seems that that is precisely what the aorist in this case signifies. Moreover, the strong verbs used here to describe the city's fate (*katheilon*, "pull down"; *sphallō*, "otherthrow"), which are applied to the whole city, seem to refer to more than the Sicilian defeat. A parallel passage in the eulogy of Pericles, which clearly refers to the city's final demise (2.65.10–13), seems to indicate likewise (Edouard Delebecque, *Thucydide et Alcibiade* [Aix-en-Provence: Centre d'Etudes et de Recherches Helleniques, 1965], p. 205).

On a more general level, G. B. Grundy argues that the tone of this whole introduction is negative toward Alcibiades (*Thucydides and the History of His Age*, 2 vols. [Oxford: Blackwell, 1951], 2:178; Werner Jaeger, *Paideia: The Ideals of Greek Culture*, vol. 1., trans. G. Highet (Oxford: Oxford University Press, 1939), p. 405; Finley, *Thucydides*, p. 229). Again, I believe Thucydides' presentation reserves judgment and only poses the proper questions. That he is posing them as questions, however, and not as answers, shows how deliberately he is moving us away from the ordinary moral-political perspective that Grundy's reaction (as well as Nicias') presupposes. On the fundamental ambiguity of this passage, see Peter R. Pouncey, p. 105, and chap. 4 below.

to give him authority on the grounds not only of prudence but of justice, whether in other words Alcibiades has a title to rule proper, is one of the questions left unanswered. We do not yet know what position Alcibiades claims for himself.

Concerning Alcibiades' claims, we are not long left in doubt. He opens his speech to the Athenians with a statement that fairly begs to be quoted out of context. "It is proper for me more than for others to rule," he says, "and at the same time I believe I am worthy of it" (6.16.1). The subject is command of the Sicilian expedition, but Alcibiades speaks sweepingly of "rule" (*archē*) rather than "generalship" (*stratēgia*; cf. 6.15.2). The first part of his speech in fact deals with his position in the city in the broadest possible terms. Alcibiades' amazing frankness is evident throughout.[9] He does not deny that he hopes to profit personally from the expedition and from his command. Instead, he openly flaunts his private extravagance, even claiming it is beneficial to the city: the very things for which I am so loudly blamed, he says, bring advantage to Athens (16.1). Alcibiades went to the Olympic games, entered seven chariots in the chariot races, and won first, second, and fourth places. Entering large numbers of chariots at the Olympic games, it should be noted, was a hallmark of tyrants, whose wealth, by reason of their despotism, was essentially no less than the wealth of their cities. As Alcibiades says, no "private individual" had ever made so splendid a showing before (16.2). As a result of his private splendor, he asserts, other Greeks conceived an inflated opinion of Athens' power, just when they had been thinking that the war was wearing the city down.

In fact, Alcibiades says, all his extravagance and display within the

---

[9]Westlake refers to Alcibiades' speech at Athens as the most "remarkable and brilliant" of Thucydides' speeches (*Individuals*, p. 225). Alcibiades' frankness makes this speech as much a character sketch as a statement of policy (p. 220). Cornford goes so far as to suggest that the first part of the speech is a fabrication by Thucydides for the sole purpose of delineating character: "It seems very unlikely that Alcibiades at such a moment would use language so offensively boastful" (*Mythistoricus*, p. 212). But such behavior is precisely in accord with Alcibiades' character and helps explain the Athenian reaction to him. Thucydides' remark at the beginning of the History that the speeches were composed by him according to *ta deonta* (the necessary or appropriate) as it would have confronted the speaker in each situation (1.22.1) would if anything have led him to suppress the first part of Alcibiades' speech, according to Cornford's dictum. My view is that the speech is perhaps polished so as to make every phrase deliberate and significant, but that we have no reason to doubt its essential fidelity. I believe the same is true of Alcibiades' speech at Sparta.

city, in the outfitting of choruses and so on, contributes to the city's image abroad (16.3). His display of wealth is an image to outsiders of the wealth and power of Athens as a whole. Accomplishments such as these, he says, bring honor in accordance with convention, and from them a supposition of power is made (16.2). Alcibiades' claim, quite remarkably, is that his personal extravagance is in effect a measure of public policy. This is an undeniable mixture of public and private, but, one wholly beneficial to the public. His personal profligacy creates an appearance of power in the city, which by itself increases the effective power of the city. The appearance becomes the reality, whether by intimidating Athenian enemies and subjects, or in some other way.

This part of Alcibiades' argument, explicitly designed to reassure those who are alarmed by his private extravagance, is in fact a brilliant resolution, in speech at least, of some of the most difficult problems we have identified in his politics. The view he outlines here, for example, makes his interest and the public interest coincide, even in the case of his lavish expenditures. That coincidence is inevitable, moreover, precisely because of the scale of Alcibiades' extravagance, which is so vast as to influence outsiders' estimation of the city as a whole. Athens might even be said to bask in the reflected light of Alcibiades' splendor. In this curious reversal, whatever enhances Alcibiades' private standing necessarily benefits the city; and his private activity is in fact doubly beneficial, since the public is benefited without public cost. As Alcibiades says, it is no "useless folly" when one, by private expense, benefits not only himself but the city as well (16.3). And even if it is true, as both Nicias and Thucydides have pointed out, that the burden of this expense is more than Alcibiades' (considerable) personal fortune can bear, we note that he seeks to increase his wealth at the expense not of his fellow citizens, like a tyrant, but of Sicily.

Alcibiades' wholehearted dedication to his own interests is beneficial to the city in effect because his private life is wholly public. He defends his apparently private activities, which so offend men like Nicias, as part of his public or political career. In that respect Alcibiades claims (as he makes clear in the next section of his speech) that he is only doing what all great statesmen and men of honor have done. Honor traditionally links the self-interest of the statesman with the public good of the community, allowing their interests to coincide: the statesman reaps honor for actions that benefit the city. Alcibiades seems to be the first to take this uncompromisingly into the realm of private life, making his private life part of his public project and his quest for honor. It is true, as he would remind us, that sponsorship of Olympic efforts, dramatic choruses, and so on, were time-honored (and sometimes compulsory) parts of the life of prominent citizens at Athens. Alcibiades, however, does it all so systematically, and on such a scale, as to make of it something new. He takes traditionally ancillary parts of the life of prominent public men and makes them central to his own attempt to live that life in the fullest way. In the process, he exaggerates them beyond precedent. But this dramatic scale is vital to the new role that Alcibiades wants this traditional path to honor and prestige to play. He desires to turn it into a real political force with international impact, one that will help him to rise to a position of the utmost preeminence in the city and even beyond. Alcibiades' understanding of the politics of personal display and lavishness significantly alters the relationship between the statesman and the city, even to some extent reversing their roles. Athens derives glory indirectly from Alcibiades, rather than the other way around.

This reversal is the very thing that ensures the compatibility, if not the identity, of interests between Alcibiades and the city: whatever contributes to Alcibiades' reputation contributes to Athens' power. We should not dismiss this view as completely beyond the pale of political discourse or experience; it does reflect to some extent the relationship that exists between the very greatest statesmen and their communities. As an argument for allowing the statesman to pursue not just honor but his own self-interest more narrowly conceived, however, Alcibiades' position is much more questionable. It is questionable not because it no longer promises the convergence of interests between statesman and city—Alcibiades' argument covers that case—but because the reversal of positions under these conditions has other political ramifications. We can best understand these ramifications in the following way. Nicias in his speech outlined the ordinary understanding of the legitimate role of private interest in politics when he said that concern for one's personal prosperity makes one a better citizen (and statesman) by giving one a stake in the prosperity of the city (6.9.2). Pericles made the same argument in his sober third speech (2.60.2–4). As this ordinary perspective has it, the citizen and the city are in the same boat—or the city is itself a boat, and the citizen, whether a pilot or a mere sailor, can prosper individually only so long as the boat fares well. Private prosperity is thus subordinate to and dependent on the general prosperity, the common good. Alcibiades does not deny the common good, but his own part is hardly subordinate. He comes close to maintaining that the city's prosperity is dependent on his.

The possibility that Alcibiades might conversely consider his own welfare independent from the city's is only one of the consequences of this argument that the Athenians might find troubling. Within the parameters defined by the speech on the Sicilian expedition, the argument works well to establish a common good between Alcibiades and his city. But Alcibiades' underlying view of the relationship between himself and the city menaces the community in a more fundamental way. Tyranny is abhorred by all cities in part because it destroys the community in the city or at least the specifically political character of that community. Alcibiades' near reversal of his stature and that of the city, in which he seems to engross all of the honor, indeed of the public life, of the city, suggests a state of affairs that in the Athenians' eyes may not differ much from tyranny. In any event, it is safe to assume that the attitude Alcibiades takes in the opening segment of his speech is precisely the kind of thing that led the Athenians to suspect that his real ambition was to become tyrant. This issue remains as a subtext to the succeeding parts of Alcibiades' speech.

In the remarks that immediately follow his sweeping pronouncement on his position in the city, Alcibiades admits, or rather explains that he is aware of, the fact that his lavish way of life necessarily or "by nature" causes envy among his fellow citizens (16.3). He implicitly maintains, though, that they, not he, are responsible for this antagonism, inasmuch as his behavior and attitude are wholly justified. Concerning what is probably the most irksome aspect of Alcibiades' attitude toward his fellow coutrymen, Alcibiades says that it is "not unjust" for someone who has a high opinion of himself to look down on others and refuse to concede equality to them (16.4). Just as no one voluntarily stoops to share the fate of those who suffer misfortune, so ordinary men should submit to being looked down on by those at the peak of success, such as Alcibiades. The conclusion, which Alcibiades puts in the imperative, is almost chilling: let each one submit, he says, to the pride of such a man (16.4). This argument hints at the Greek belief that the unfortunate

81

are accursed and therefore to be avoided and abhorred, because good and bad fortune are divine allotments.[10] Alcibiades shows no signs, here or elsewhere, of believing that gods control human fortune; but as this remark makes clear, he believes good and bad fortune in the broad sense to be a measure of desert. More to the point, he seems to assume that great good fortune is a kind of personal gift, in the manner of those who are said to be beloved of the gods. The pride and impenetrable self-assurance, characteristic of Alcibiades' political attitude in general, more than hint at this. Alcibiades of course has no right to this attitude, if it indeed derives from the traditional Greek notion of the *eudaimōn*, the happy one beloved of the gods, but it does closely parallel the "optimism" of imperial Athens, which had its own grounding in an implicit attitude toward "theological" issues.

In the context, Alcibiades' argument about men of better and worse fortune prepares the way for a charge of hypocrisy against those in the city who begrudge him his haughtiness, since they too secretly shun those lower than themselves. But it also widens the gulf that has already opened between Alcibiades and his fellow citizens. The argument implicitly divides the city into a hierarchy of separate classes corresponding to different human fortunes, each demanding that the ones below it submit to its pride. Alcibiades radicalizes the divisions that ordinarily exist among men in a city in order to prepare for himself claims of the most complete preeminence. By the time he occupies the summit of this hierarchy and the city has ranged itself below him, however, we may justly wonder what kind of a city this is. Thucydides presented growing equality among citizens as a key development in the evolution of Greek cities (1.6.4)—Sparta, according to his account, was the first community in which the wealthy adopted this more measured attitude toward the many. This seems to have paved the way for the development of the other admirable aspects of Greek civilization (1.6.4–5). We subsequently learn that the Spartans were also the most inveterate enemies of tyranny among the Greeks (1.18.1). Political community in the Greek cities, which we may take to be the model for political community as such in the History, is based for Thucydides upon a certain spirit of equality. Alcibiades' craving for supreme distinction seems the very negation of this principle.

[10]See Dover, in Gomme, Andrewes, Dover, *Historical Commentary*, 4:247–48.

Yet it is at this point in his speech that Alcibiades makes his claim not only that the position he demands is in accordance with justice but that it is a position no greater than that which great statesmen have always been accorded. Such men, he says, have always aroused resentment in their fellow citizens—after all, as he said a moment ago, such resentment is only natural. Future generations, however, always admire such statesmen, calling them their own, men who have acted nobly, taking an even boasting pride in them (16.5). The example of these great and famous men, as described by Alcibiades, shows on the one hand that the resentment of contemporaries is always their lot, and on the other hand that that resentment is somehow always a mirage—fleeting, whereas their fame is permanent. Alcibiades' statement betrays both resignation to the inevitable resentment against him and a calculated refusal to take it seriously. Alcibiades as it were appeals in advance to the Athenians' descendents to prove that the Athenians themselves, in their heart of hearts, do not mean their resentment seriously.

The Athenians of course shortly give proof that their resentment is no mirage. But this does not in itself refute Alcibiades' contention—after all, the Athenians also exiled Themistocles, one of the statesmen Alcibiades obviously has in mind, and many others. On the other hand, we have seen that Alcibiades' claim that he deserves resentment no more than his illustrious predecessors did cannot be entirely sustained. He has taken traditional avenues to prominence—especially private extravagance—and pushed them to such extremes as to alter the political balance, and the community itself, in fundamental ways. It surely sheds light upon the nature of politics, and on the nature of the relationship between a political community and its leaders, that the differences of degree Alcibiades embodies or advocates can have such a revolutionary, or distorting, impact.

Contrasting examples illustrate how unprecedented is Alcibiades' activity, but they also give some support to his claims. Pericles made many concessions to the resentment Alcibiades speaks of; he was almost self-effacing. He is practically invisible in the Funeral Oration, a speech in which he praises virtually everything else about the city.[11] Yet Thucy-

---

[11]The one remark in the Funeral Oration that might be regarded as an oblique form of self-congratulation is Pericles' claim that in Athens men rise to prominence only on the basis of virtue (2.37.1). On the general characterization of Pericles' politics, see also Strauss, *The City and Man*, p. 195.

dides asserts that in Pericles' time Athens was a democracy in name only; and it is relevant also to recall that Pericles was partly ignorant of how crucial his presence was to the proper functioning of the regime. Pericles' claims thus might have been moderated partly out of ignorance. Aside from that, Pericles' self-effacing style, to the extent that it is a conscious concession to democratic envy, might legitimately be viewed as a kind of slavishness by someone like Alcibiades. It is not clear on the face of it why democratic regimes should have the right to demand that kind of charade from their leaders.

It is not simply that Alcibiades impetuously demands what he views as his proper prerogatives. He refuses to believe that the fulfillment of his ambitions requires any kind of self-effacement, and he refuses to be anything less than honest about his ambitions in the city. Alcibiades wishes to dominate the city, but frankly and openly, as it were. It is probably true that the great statesmen of the past, like Pericles himself, loom in the eyes of posterity as large as the cities they inhabited. In that sense, Alcibiades' ambition is only to join their number. But he is impatient: he desires the pageant of immortality to be enacted for him in the present, so to speak, immediately. Alcibiades' ambition leads him to take a long view that may neglect some of the exigencies most characteristic of the present.

If the Athenian or democratic view of politics scants the rights of statesmen, Alcibiades' view centers almost exclusively on statesmen's actions and prerogatives. This is perhaps the most important way he overturns the view outlined by Pericles. Alcibiades describes the point of view of the great statesman, the man of political genius; his vision caters almost exclusively to the statesman's desires and interests. In this regard Alcibiades' speech at Athens and Pericles' Funeral Oration are at opposite poles.[12] Pericles' vision, so far from fulfilling the craving for glory of an ambitious statesman, has difficulty satisfying the desire for reputation of the ordinary Athenian citizen—Pericles told his audience to believe that their own glory was to be found in the glory of the city

---

[12]See also Westlake, *Individuals*, p. 225. Pouncey, *Necessities of War*, p. 111, has the same kind of thing in mind when he says that Alcibiades "inverts" Pericles' argument about the relation of individual and city. We noted before that Pericles' vision does not provide for great or extraordinary individual ambition (chap. 1, n. 21, and text, above). Alcibiades in effect turns Pericles' vision on its head—and might accordingly experience the opposite problem.

at large (2.42.1–2), exhorting them to fall in love with this great and glorious totality. Alcibiades, on the other hand, finds and assumes the one position in Pericles' scheme that could satisfy him—not the one Pericles modestly assumed but the one he gave to the city itself. Alcibiades becomes in effect the repository of the city's glory, to be shared vicariously by his fellow citizens. Alcibiades is not necessarily asking the Athenians to fall in love with him, but one who implicitly presumes the love of gods may not hesitate to presume the affections of lesser beings.

It is almost as if, for Alcibiades, the city is a stage for the performance of glorious deeds by great men of honor or for their Herculean rivalries (cf. 16.5). It would be difficult to overlook the histrionic elements in Alcibiades' own politics. His grand poses as the Olympic victor, as the man of extravagant gestures, are part of his political persona, and they play an even more deliberate and systematic role in Alcibiades' politics than we are yet in a position to recognize. We can already see, though, that they impart to him a light, paradoxically playful manner in the face of the gravity of the themes. Alcibiades' political attitude has an element almost of irony about it. But he does not reduce politics to frivolity or mere play. Immortal glory, for the man of political genius, is the greatest of stakes. And we must never forget that his talent brings immense advantages for his city, a fact that plays a large role in Alcibiades' argument.

Recalling the beginning of Alcibiades' speech, we see in fact that his self-proclaimed title to rule is based entirely on the benefits that he claims his apparently selfish activities bring to the city. Alcibiades' supreme usefulness to the city was emphasized in Thucydides' preface to this speech; now, after defending his private actions and ambitions, Alcibiades returns to this theme. Turning from private to public matters, he tells his Athenian audience, consider whether anyone is better at managing them than I: I brought together the greatest cities in the Peloponnesus without great danger or expense to Athens, and in one day at Mantineia forced the Spartans to stake everything on a fight (16.6). Though the Spartans won that battle, Alcibiades asserts that they have not yet regained their full confidence. The public service Alcibiades is talking about here is his activity on the Peloponnesus in connection with the Argive league, which culminated in the Battle of Mantineia. What we should notice in the first place though is the distinction between "public" and "private" activities with which Alcibiades introduces this—

it seems to correspond roughly to the city's distinction between "foreign politics" and "domestic politics." Alcibiades' "private" activities are the activities that have led him to dominate the domestic politics of the city and even to project a certain image of the city to outsiders. What Alcibiades says about his "public" successes on the Peloponnesus are equally revealing of his conception of his diplomatic activities and talents. His brief statement on the subject is quite dense and in some respects difficult to decipher, but the general sense of it is as follows. My youth, he says, and my seemingly (or reputedly) unnatural folly thus coped with the power of the Peloponnesians with fitting words and persuaded by means of a passion that inspired faith (17.1). He tells the Athenians therefore not to be afraid of it (his youth and his folly, or his youthful folly, the subject of the preceding sentence), but while it is still at its peak within him, to make the utmost use of it. He goes on to suggest that the Athenians also make use of Nicias' reputed (or seeming) good luck and put both of them at the head of the expedition to Sicily.

This part of Alcibiades' speech is permeated with a kind of good-humored irony as he plays upon popular opinions of himself and Nicias. A kernel of truth seems to lurk behind this characterization of Nicias' role in the expedition; and Alcibiades adopts an apparently critical popular view of himself—his phrase "youthful folly" no doubt represents a popular caricature or criticism of him—and makes it into a great virtue. "Folly" (*anoia* 16.3, 17.1) becomes in Alcibiades' mouth the name of the talent that allowed him to supervise so effectively the affairs of the anti-Spartan Peloponnesian alliance. The accomplishments of this "folly," if Alcibiades' account is to be believed, are impressive indeed. He brought into being and directed a power on the Peloponnesus that jeopardized Sparta's very existence, doing so, moreover, using little of Athens' resources, by the unaided application of his own personal gifts. Alcibiades speaks of persuasion, fitting words, and of a passion or ardor (*orgē*) in him that carries men along with it. Alcibiades' folly, with these tools, can make something of nothing. Or perhaps we should say that it can alter or direct forces in the political world simply by applying personal, spiritual forces. Alcibiades made one earlier reference to his "folly," saying it was no useless folly for him to increase the power of the city by the mere spectacle of his own private splendor (16.3). Alcibiades advances this folly seriously as part of his title to rule because it refers to some of his key political talents and the unprecedented ways that those talents allow him to accomplish what he desires in the political world. The terminology also refers, playfully, to the fact that these talents are perhaps misunderstood and suspected in the city at large.

"*Folly*," as used here, refers to Alcibiades' tendency to rush madly into the most audacious enterprises, apparently without the necessary backing, and then bring them to fruition. This however is nothing other than a form of that most typical of Athenian traits, "daring." That the Athenians should mock and ultimately dread this quality in Alcibiades indicates his true extremism (6.15.4). Alcibiades is too daring even for the daring Athenians, although they are about to embark together on the attempted conquest of Sicily. One of the attributes of Athenian daring, we recall, is its ability to augment or even supplant conventional power, simply by dint of audacity.[13] It even replaces the brute force characteristic of the old politics and especially the old land-powers with versatility and guile. But Alcibiades in his "youthful folly" goes even further than the city itself.[14] This may be in part because a talented individual can ply such devices with greater facility than is possible for a city. It is also true that an individual, especially one who is led to act independently of the city, is forced to rely more on such devices and less on conventional power. We shall return to this theme later. For now, we must confess that Alcibiades, in his "youthful folly," looks very much like a culmination of the Athenian project, a more perfect one than the city itself. This would seem to bolster his argument that this "folly" gives him a just title to precedence in the city of Athens.

Having completed his unorthodox defense of his own public and private activity, Alcibiades proceeds to his argument concerning the advisability of the Sicilian expedition. What he says here is of interest to us not only for its strategic significance, but again because of its pertinence to some of the themes already mentioned. Alcibiades argues

[13]See 1.144.4 and the discussion of this point in chap. 1 above.

[14]One way Alcibiades goes beyond Athenian tradition here, as a number of commentators have pointed out, is by turning his ambitions to land, even marching an army into the Peloponnesus itself. Alcibiades' daring goes beyond the time-honored daring of Athenian naval strategy. See Hatzfeld, *Alcibiade*, p. 100; Romilly, *Athenian Imperialism*, p. 69; cf. Plutarch *Alcibiades* 15. Athens did dabble in land empire when opportunity offered, advancing into Boeotia in an ill-fated adventure during the period of the *Pentekontaetia* (1.108, 113), and again during the war, prior to Athens' defeat at Delium (4.94–101), but such enterprises were relatively rare and no part of general Athenian strategy.

that no one should shrink from approving the expedition on the grounds that the Sicilian cities are likely to prove formidable foes. They are not, because these cities are scarcely cities: they have little internal cohesion or dedication to the common good. Each of the Sicilian cities, according to Alcibiades, is merely a motley collection of human beings, a "mob" (*ochlos* 17.2) of ever-changing form.[15] As a result, private interest triumphs over public. No man among them considers the city to be his own fatherland, but each is ready to plunder the community if he can, using rhetoric or faction, with the thought that he can simply leave the city if he fails (17.3). Hence, Alcibiades claims, one only has to speak to his pleasure to induce each man to betray his city—particularly since the cities are reported to be in civil strife (17.2–5).

Whether or not Alcibiades is correct in his estimation of the current condition of the Sicilian cities (note Nicias' snide reply, 20.2, but also the factious debate in Syracuse, 6.33–41), his almost contemptuous assertion of their feebleness, and of the reasons for that feebleness, might almost sound like hypocrisy to those in his audience left wondering after the first part of his speech what great attachment he has for his city— or indeed what grounds he offers to his fellow citizens to devote themselves to an Athens built on Alcibiades' model. It is tempting to see Athens' future factional strife, and even Alcibiades' part in it, in his description of the incohesiveness of the Sicilian cities. Since Alcibiades' point, however, is that Athens is a strong city compared to those of Sicily, the problem becomes what in Alcibiades' mind is the real bond of community in his vision of Athens, the thing that induces Athenians resolutely to put the public good ahead of their own interests. Alcibiades' elaborate presentation of the point of view of the ambitious statesman has all but dissolved the community. He argues for a kind of division of spoils, in which the statesman gets honor, while the city receives advantage or benefit. This is the sort of arrangement that has always brought statesmen and cities together, but Alcibiades in his extremism makes the division so complete as almost to strip his fellow Athenians of their citizenship, that is, their place in the public life of the city.

---

[15]We should note that there is a textual variant at this point in the manuscripts, which has Alcibiades saying that the Sicilian cities easily undergo either changes in their populations or changes in their form of government (*politōn* or *politeiōn*, 6.17.2). Either of these readings will comport with my interpretation of the passage.

Alcibiades seems to envision a city composed of one or more public men who vie for and receive public honors and others, the majority, who benefit from this activity in more mundane ways. The man or men of honor look down on the others, whose submission is compensated for by the advantage they derive from it. Advantage, however, would seem to be the only thing they derive: they are in danger of being relegated to a subpolitical role, losing in effect their status as citizens. For citizenship would seem to require at least some degree of participation in the public life of the city, and at least some share of its honors (cf. Aristotle *Politics* 1281a30–33). These men might be said to participate in the public life of the city inasmuch as they confer honor and perhaps appreciate its reflected glow, but it is questionable whether that is enough to make them citizens and to make their community a city.

But Alcibiades is not without a vision of community in the city. Perhaps the most important thing he identifies as a weakness of the Sicilian cities, to which must correspond an Athenian strength, is an inability to deliberate and act in common. Alcibiades infers this about the Sicilian cities on the basis of their instability and their citizens' concern for private over public interest. It is not likely, he says, that such a mass would either hearken to counsel with one mind or turn to action in common (17.4). A city that is more than just a "mob" must be able habitually to take counsel and find a common purpose, in order for the public good to triumph over private good. Its strength, and even its community, will derive from this. On the basis of this as well as his earlier remarks, we conclude that Alcibiades has in mind a city counseled by a great leader. His implicit view is that the cohesiveness, the strength, and the community in a city come from its finding its center in one or more great statesmen. It is this center that holds the whole together, conferring on it the wisdom of leadership and bringing it advantage. Alcibiades described these central men earlier; in his eyes, contrary to the questions we raised about their role, they hold their positions not in spite of the city's need for cohesion and community but because of it.

Alcibiades' analysis of the Sicilian cities helps make comprehensible the final parts of his speech, which are concerned with the strength and unity of Athens. The desperate Nicias was forced in his speech to appeal to the older men in the city against the younger in his attempt to forestall the expedition (13.1). Alcibiades in his conclusion poses emphatically as the advocate not only of Athenian tradition, but of Athenian unity. He exhorts old and young to deliberate in common, as he has just argued a viable city must do and as the Athenians did in the past to make the city's power great (6.18.6). Without this unity, Alcibiades says, nothing can be accomplished; but the city is strongest when the dull, the middling, and the very sharp are all combined. Alcibiades' view still puts these three types in a strict hierarchy—the words he uses to identify them here are openly judgmental—but they still belong to the city as significant, and contributing, parts.

Alcibiades' remarks about the Sicilian cities, together with his exhortation to old and young to deliberate together, indicate, contrary to our initial impression, that he sees an important role for public, even democratic deliberation in the city. We do not yet know exactly how he understands that deliberation to operate, given the views he expressed earlier, and especially given his behavior during the deliberations over the Argive alliance. But Alcibiades clearly relishes the public forum of the democratic assembly and would not want to do away with it. That assembly remains one of the premier platforms for the kind of great political activity he describes in the first part of his speech. It would be in the assembly first and foremost that the Alcibidean statesman collects his accolades and receives the deference of his fellow citizens. In any event, when Alcibiades presents the capacity to deliberate as a vital part of the health of the city, he does in some sense reenfranchise those members of the city, the "dull" and the "mediocre," who were virtually left out of account earlier. Alcibiades knows that deliberation of the type that he envisages, and that he says is lacking from the Sicilian cities, requires some kind of community.

This enfranchisement of the lesser members of the city is motivated not only by Alcibiades' desire to hear them acclaim him. Alcibiades speaks of the need for deliberation among all the classes in the city in part from an awareness that the power and dynamism of Athens has always depended on the participation of the *demos*. Alcibiades allows at the very end of his speech that Athens' current institutions and habits might be considered less than perfect, but he says that it is both necessary and desireable to continue with them (6.18.7). It is necessary because Athens, having become an imperial power, must remain continually active to preserve herself, and the current regime and habits are best suited to that. Alcibiades, in anticipation of Machiavelli, maintains that

90

an imperial power cannot remain static but must always expand to forestall the potential attack.[16] To await rather than to preempt the attack of powerful outsiders like the Syracusans is suicidal for an imperial power; as a corollary, the imperial power must accept as allies or subjects all those weaker states that present themselves (18.2). On the domestic side, Alcibiades argues that the democratic regime not only allows but requires such activity; without it, the parts of the city, which should be kept in harmony, will wear or grind themselves down (*tripesthai* 6.18.6), coming to harm due to internal friction. The city will also lose the sharpness of constant practice.

The self-interest Alcibiades has in making these arguments should not blind us to the acuity of his analysis here. Alcibiades has a very sophisticated understanding of the Athenian situation, both internally and externally, and he argues the advisability of the Sicilian expedition based on that understanding. This is Alcibiades' most direct or pertinent rebuttal of Pericles' notion that it is safe and possible for the city to keep quiet during the war. Pericles believed that the city could rally temporarily at least around an essentially static vision of its power. Alcibiades, however, argues that without continual movement outward the city will begin to disintegrate; it will begin to attack itself. Pericles believed that the city could be at once restrained and held together by a combination of the Athenians' native decency and restraint, and he appeals to eros, hoping to tie it temporarily at least to his reserved policy for the war. Alcibiades rejects the notion that the city can safely embrace inactivity, even temporarily. But adventurism is not enough in and of itself to preserve Athens. Alcibiades' view relies more than Pericles' does on the stewardship of a great leader to cement Athens' political community. We have seen already that the slighting of this element is a problem in Pericles' view. The course of Athenian history as presented by Thucydides seems to corroborate Alcibiades' view of the pivotal role of statesmen in the city. The movement from Pericles, to Cleon, to Alcibiades, to Nicias, and finally to an apparent anarchy of demagogues, involves

[16]6.18.3. See Machiavelli, *The Prince*, chap. 3, and his *Discourses* I.1; cf. also Aristotle *Politics* 1334a7–10. Machiavelli also argued that a republic, that is, a regime in which the people play some political role, is the only regime that can develop enough power to carry out this imperial strategy properly, even though it might result in some domestic turmoil (see, e.g., *Discourses* I.5,6). We will examine Alcibiades' understanding of the strengths and weaknesses of democracy more closely in his second speech.

91

a change in the regime and the character of the city at each point. The city takes on the character of its leaders. This is to be expected in Alcibiades' view but would be almost incomprehensible on the basis of the argument of the Funeral Oration.

Whatever the strengths or weaknesses of Alcibiades' analysis of the Athenian regime, the analysis is typically Alcibidean at least in its establishment of a perfect harmony between the needs and interests of the city and the ambitions and interests of Alcibiades himself. The peculiar form of political community Alcibiades describes in Athens is explosively powerful but unstable. It needs constant motion; because of this need, and because of other aspects of its internal constitution, this Athenian polity is also in constant need of great leadership, to hold it together and to lead it on far-flung exploits of political expansion. As long as some such exploit is always in contemplation or underway, there is a perfect harmony of interests between statesman and city.

This view of things allows Alcibiades simultaneously to enhance his own glory and preeminence and to embrace the city in his political vision. The vital role he sees for the *demos* in the city represents perhaps the most important counterargument to those who believe Alcibiades aspires to a tyranny. Alcibiades knows that a tyranny—the consolidation of one man's power in the city and his rule over the others by force—would only sap the real power of the city. Tyranny, at least to the Athenian way of thinking, is characterized as rule for the advantage of the tyrant rather than the city, and rule by force, not by consent.[17] Alcibiades argues forcefully and elaborately that his self-interest furthers the interests of the city—even if we doubt the validity of some of his arguments, their sincerity seems unassailable. Alcibiades genuinely does not believe that he is pursuing his own interests at the expense of the city, nor does he desire or intend to. Nor does he desire or intend to do away with public deliberation, rule by persuasion and consent, by honor and acclaim. Alcibiades' outline of his apparently outrageous public claims is nothing more than a fair attempt to persuade the Athe-

---

[17]Aristotle establishes the first condition as the definition of tyranny (*Politics* 1279b6; cf. 1279a17–20), but he also characterizes it as "irresponsible" or "unaccountable" rule (*anupeuthunos* 1295a21). Men cannot be presumed to consent to another's ruling for his own advantage. On the other hand, consent may not always be forthcoming for the man who truly deserves to rule, a problem to some extent sidestepped in the *Politics* but very pertinent to the case of Alcibiades.

nians, by open public arguments, to accede to his demands. Even his imperative "let each one submit" is scolding perhaps, or chiding, but not threatening. What Alcibiades craves is voluntary and conscious recognition of his superiority, not tyrannical imposition of his will. He is much too astute to make the tyrannical mistake of thinking that what he wants from the city can be obtained by force—if anything, he is too optimistic about the power of persuasion to bring about what he wants, given the record of Athenian maltreatment of leaders. If Alcibiades believes that "fitting words," persuasive passion, and his other talents allowed him to control events on the Peloponnesus, he believes *a fortiori* that persuasion will avail him within the city.

The fact that Alcibiades does not consciously seek a tyranny, however, does not settle all the issues involved. His vision of his place in the city could still amount to something alarmingly close to tyranny, without his intending or even being aware of it. This is the credible form of the charge that Alcibiades' ambition is tyrannical. It also comes closest to implying that all truly great political ambition is tyrannical. We cannot dispose of this issue here, but we can refine our understanding of it. One way of approaching it is to consider exactly what room is left for public deliberation once Alcibiades has the position he asks for in the city, and exactly what that deliberation consists of in Alcibiades' mind or what passes for persuasion in his view. The occasion of Alcibiades' first appearance in Thucydides, his orchestration of events before the assembly so as to predispose the Athenians to the Argive league, presents most vividly the extent to which Alcibiades' "persuasion" approaches manipulation. This episode suggests that Alcibiades has conditional faith at best in the city's power of deliberation, or a very minimal interpretation of its requirements indeed. His enfranchisement of the lower ranks in the city does not go as far as some, including the purest advocates of democracy, would deem proper.

Alcibiades' position as revealed in the early episode would be justified on the assumption that although some form of majority deliberation is necessary for Athens, it is not necessarily to be trusted on its own terms. There is some merit to this suggestion: all the Athenian statesmen who address the question in the History concur with it to some degree, as does Thucydides himself. But Alcibiades' tactics in overcoming the defects of democratic deliberation go further than those of his predecessors. His view might be that democratic deliberation can properly pronounce on policies of a general nature but should not descend too much to matters of detail and administration.[18] In practice this might lead to little more than acclaiming the ascendency of a great man, like Alcibiades, or perhaps a great undertaking like the Sicilian expedition, entrusting its execution to an Alcibiades. After all, once we presume the presence of a wise and talented counselor, the Alcibidean argument might be that it makes little sense for the city to retain the formal right to decide for itself, and therefore perhaps wrongly, on affairs of the first importance. It is not clear that it would be the duty of a public-spirited statesman, when persuasion does not suffice, to stand by and watch that happen. Alcibiades' speech and actions together indicate a strong belief in the importance of democratic deliberation in Athens, but it is a belief that can be and has been overridden by his conviction that his own political judgment is correct even when it comes into conflict with the democratic institution.

Regardless of any defense that can be made of this position, however, democracy must reject it in principle. Democracy cannot allow Alcibiades, or any individual, simply to substitute his own good judgment for that of the assembly. Such a view is simply not democratic. If there is a legitimate sense, therefore, in which Alcibiades adheres to democracy, there is also an undeniable gap between them. And whether Alcibiades has left enough room for the *demos* and democracy to suffice even for his own purposes is still an open question. Alcibiades wants it both ways. He desires an active and participating populace to support and carry out the most ambitious schemes and to grant him the accolades he desires. But his own ambition is so voracious and his self-assurance so domineering as to draw virtually all the honors and all the decisions to himself. The more serious version of the tyranny charge then holds that what Alcibiades wants would, literally in spite of himself, result in damage to the political community similar to that tyranny imposes, sapping the city's vital force. The full realization of Alcibiades' ambition

---

[18]This can be illustrated by an anecdote from Plutarch, who says that Alcibiades once wondered aloud as Pericles was preparing to give his accounts to the people, whether it would not be better to consider how to avoid presenting such accounts altogether (*Alcibiades* 7). The remark seems to contemplate tyranny, and certainly would have been interpreted so by Alcibiades' enemies, but it could equally well reflect simple chagrin at the minute or meddling oversight of leaders characteristic of the democracy of Athens.

might in practice look more like Caesarism than Alcibiades believes. Yet it remains true, as Alcibiades says, that all he wants is what statesmen have always wanted—only more so.

Not long after the delivery of Alcibiades' speech at Athens, Athenian resentment and suspicion, nurtured by demagogues in his absence, overcome attachment to his leadership. He escapes from Sicily into exile and is condemned to death in absentia. It is to explain Athenian suspicion toward Alcibiades and others that Thucydides provides his digression on Harmodius and Aristogeiton. In view of the foregoing discussion of Alcibiades' position, one new observation deriving from that digression should be made. The digression illustrates the excess and irrationality of Harmodius and Aristogeiton, and by implication of the Athenians their admirers, but it indicates the wrongheadedness of Hipparchus as well. Hipparchus unnecessarily provoked the lovers by using the public power of his family to affront them in their private lives. Alcibiades' own conflation of public and private might also be held to affront his fellow citizens "privately," to an extent not seen since the time of Hipparchus. He certainly does his share to provoke the Athenian reaction against him. Unfortunately, the reaction itself, and especially Alcibiades' exile, is ill-conceived from the point of view of the city's interests. The Athenians want it both ways as much as does Alcibiades: they want expansive imperialism but cannot brook the vigorous leadership it requires; they want complete freedom and resent even having to take counsel from others. Alcibiades seems correct in his view that real cohesion comes to Athens only under the stewardship of a great leader.[19] Conflict and tension as well as community are inevitable in the relations between statesman and polity. In this case, the conflict reaches the pitch that it does precisely because the leader and the *demos* are so similar in character, both in their ambitions and in their intolerance of restraint. Alcibiades is a true son of the Athenian regime, but the city is not big enough for the both of them.

[19]As Finley remarks, democracy has greater need for leadership and the cohesion it brings than do other forms of government (*Thucydides*, p. 306; cf. Adcock, *Thucydides*, p. 51). He therefore argues that Thucydides laments the end of Pericles' ascendancy at the failure of anyone to fill his position. This of course is true as far as it goes, but if we see Pericles' leadership as flawed and even doomed to ultimate failure, as I have argued that we must, we are left in a much more ambiguous intellectual realm, where the estimation of someone like Alcibiades inevitably rises.

Alcibiades' Second Speech

It is necessary to keep in mind that Alcibiades is condemned in absentia, in a move engineered, according to Thucydides, by personal enemies who waited until Alcibiades had left the city before beginning their agitations (6.29.3). Because the resentment against him is so conspicuous, and his exile in retrospect seems so inevitable, we need to remind ourselves that, so long as Alcibiades is present in the city, his ability to persuade the Athenian *demos* is formidable. Thucydides in fact never shows Alcibiades failing to persuade an Athenian audience of anything. As to his vulnerability outside of the city, Alcibiades is fully aware that the charges against him are much more likely to prevail in his absence than if he were allowed to confront them in person. He tries to prevent the charges from being postponed until after his departure; and Thucydides reports in indirect speech some remarks he made in that connection, remarks that, curiously enough, contain the only use of the word *moderation* attributed to Alcibiades in the History. As I remarked earlier, this word is rarely used by or applied to any Athenian in the History.[20] Alcibiades' use of it is significant: Thucydides reports him as arguing that it would be "more moderate" (or prudent) for the Athenians to allow him to stand trial immediately, rather than sending him out on an enterprise like the Sicilian expedition with a cloud hanging over him (6.29.2). It is more prudent for the Athenians not to send a commander out while his credibility or his title to command is tarnished, but Alcibiades' remark seems also to embody a more general awareness that the maintenence of his title and his position requires a kind of moderation or deference on the part of the city. It is the Athenians' "immoderation" in this respect, their jealousy of all rank and authority, that might play into the hands of Alcibiades' enemies. That of course is exactly what happens. According to an earlier indication of Thucydides, after the exile of Alcibiades the city gave itself over to demagogues who pandered merely to its pleasure.[21]

[20]See chap. 1, n. 51, above, on the use of *moderation*.

[21]2.65.10–12: this indication is given in the eulogy of Pericles, when Thucydides is describing the reasons for the failure of the Sicilian expedition. The interpretation of this passage and of the place Alcibiades is supposed to occupy in it is rather complicated and will be discussed in chap. 4. I believe the point made in the text, however, may be established by a simple comparison of 2.65.10–12 with 6.15.

Alcibiades responds to the Athenians' actions against him by fleeing to the Spartans, an action not calculated to persuade the Athenians that they were mistaken in their suspicions. But the speech that Alcibiades delivers at Sparta is the only one in which he explicitly claims always to have been an opponent of tyranny and a supporter and ally of the *demos* at Athens (6.89.3–4). Alcibiades does not repent before the Spartans of either of these things, or of anything he has said or done, either explicitly or implicitly. His fundamental view of the city and of his relation to it remains unchanged, in spite of his drastic change of circumstance. Nor, even more surprisingly, does he change his manner. Alcibiades' astonishing frankness is if anything more conspicuous in his Spartan speech, betraying not only continuing good conscience but an abiding belief in his great power of persuasion among men. His change in circumstances, as well as the special concerns of the Spartans or what Alcibiades believes their special concerns to be, lead him only to emphasize different parts of his understanding of politics.

The first part of Alcibiades' speech is devoted to an explanation of his previous actions as an Athenian statesman, particularly his advocacy of the Argive league and his campaigns on the Peloponnesus, actions on account of which he presumes the Spartans to be angry with him. Next, he discusses the strategy the Spartans should follow in order to damage most seriously the expedition in Sicily and Athenian interests generally. Only after divulging these secrets, as he claims, concerning what the Athenians dread most (6.90.2, 91.6, 92.5), turning openly against his homeland, does Alcibiades take up the issue perhaps of greater concern to the Spartans from the start—namely, how Alcibiades can betray his city in this way.[22] The way Alcibiades begins his speech is paradoxical because the fact that Alcibiades was opposed to Sparta when he was acting as an Athenian statesman would seem to require no explanation at all. Alcibiades' mode of proceeding implies that he does not consider it sufficient to say that he was simply serving his city's interests as he saw them; and in fact he never advances that argument in his speech.

---

[22]Consider for example the fact that the Mytilenaeans, when they appeal to the Spartans in preparation for their revolt from Athens, feel compelled to begin their speech with a very lengthy apology for the rebellion. Yet theirs is a much less extreme case of betrayal than Alcibiades' (3.9–12). An argument has been made by some commentators that Alcibiades' actions here would be seen by the Greeks as requiring no apology, but that I believe is unjustified. For a more thorough discussion of this point, see n. 27, below.

He begins by explaining why he harmed the Spartan interests at Athens just as he finishes by explaining why he harms the Athenians at Sparta, as though all his political actions required explanations independent of his connection to any particular city.

In the first part of his speech, the issue is complicated by the fact that Alcibiades is attempting to explain why he took a much more anti-Spartan line than that of official policy at Athens during the Peace of Nicias, and why he personally was the most vocal and active member of the anti-Spartan war party when the city was officially at peace. Alcibiades might have made the claim—which Thucydides himself partly vouches for, and which the Spartans could surely understand—that he was simply acting in accordance with his own best estimate of the Athenian public interest (5.43.2). What Alcibiades says instead serves indeed as a defense of his actions, but one whose premises only aggravate the problem created by the way the speech begins. He speaks exclusively of his own private motivations. He tells the Spartans that they deserved the harm he did them during the peace because, in spite of his attempt to reestablish his hereditary ties with them and in spite of his assiduously serving their interests in the Pylos affair, they passed him over in negotiating the peace. They dealt instead with his enemies in the city (especially Nicias), increasing their power and bringing dishonor, he says, upon himself. The Spartans may have had their minds set simply on negotiating a peace with the city of Athens as a whole, but their action was sorely misconceived. Alcibiades' view, in conformity with his first speech to the Athenians, resolves the city, at the level of leadership, into individual political actors. It may be a common enough necessity in interstate politics to have to cultivate a number of significant individuals in the cities or states one is dealing with, but Alcibiades goes beyond that, considering himself an actor not only of great significance *within* the city but virtually of equal significance *with* the city. It is for this reason that he does not consider it unseemly to proclaim that the slight he says he received was the provocation for his actions. That is, it was the provocation, we must strain to remember, for Alcibiades pursuing a course of action that brought a military alliance into the field which jeopardized the Spartans' very existence at Mantineia. Alcibiades now makes bold to tell the Spartans that they "justly" suffered this, for ignoring him when they negotiated their peace (6.89.3). He acknowledges that some of them might have been angry at him for this at the time, but he trusts they will drop any grudges they may bear him for it, now that his reasons have been explained.

We can only imagine an assembly full of gaping Spartans as Alcibiades completes this rhetorical tour de force. We must be careful, nevertheless, not to make Alcibiades' argument more brazen than it actually is. Alcibiades speaks of justice here, but even he presumably would not maintain that the Spartans deserved to perish collectively for slighting him in the matter of the negotiations. Alcibiades did not deliberately set out to wreak revenge upon the Spartans as a consequence of this slight. Rather, the Spartan action left no outlet for Alcibiades' ambition in the context of the resulting peace, which, together with the implicit slight, released him from any independent duty to respect their interests as allies of Nicias. If the only remaining outlet for his ambition led him to the Peloponnesus, and from there to a direct attack on Spartan interests, the Spartans have only themselves to blame.

Underlying this argument is of course the view that the statesman is an independent actor, one whose ambitions carry their own justification. Alcibiades has defined politics as the arena in which these men and these ambitions have their play, and he understands and justifies his own political actions in that fashion. To say, as Alcibiades said at Athens, that these ambitions are necessarily beneficial to the city to which the statesman is attached, or rather allied, is enough. It is the alliance between statesman and city that becomes tenuous. Alcibiades' view places the burden of maintaining it at least as much on the fidelity of the city as of the statesman. This is the theme of the concluding part of his speech. With regard to the present passage, it is important to see that Alcibiades' opposition to the Spartans was primarily motivated not by anger or vengefulness, but purely by ambition, an important distinction to grasp if one would understand his case. Hence it is fair for him now to ask the Spartans not to be angry with him in turn. Hence also, there is no obstacle to his coming to the aid of the Spartans. Indeed, given his view of things, and given the turn of events at Athens, that move is entirely logical for him.

The second part of Alcibiades' speech addresses the prejudice against him that he believes to have come from his domestic activities at Athens, specifically what he calls his support for the *demos* or the popular cause (89.3–6). Once again, Alcibiades declines to attribute his activity to ordinary patriotism or loyalty to the Athenian regime. Instead, he makes of it mostly a prudential political choice: he supported the regime because it was in place and because it would have been dangerous to attempt a change in the midst of war. He also indicates, almost in passing, that it had some legitimate claim to allegiance because the city had grown so great under it. At the same time, however, he seems to deliver a devastating condemnation of democracy as such, for, as he says, he is in a better position than most to know its defects (89.6). This part of Alcibiades' argument requires close scrutiny. His position is not inconsistent or incoherent, but it does depend upon redefining certain categories to fit Alcibiades' view of things. The passage is consistent given a particular view of good and bad in democratic politics, a view that follows from what Alcibiades said earlier in the History.

Alcibiades' argument is characterized by the use of two different but related words when speaking of the Athenian polity, namely, *demos* and "*democracy*." It is easy to get the impression that Alcibiades is using them interchangeably, which would indeed make his argument inconsistent, but that is not the case.[23] The word "*democracy*" is used only negatively in this passage. Alcibiades uses *demos*, on the other hand, when speaking of the serious reasons for his support for the people or for the status quo at Athens. Alcibiades begins his argument with the assertion that he (like the Spartans: 1.18.1) has always been an unqualified opponent of tyranny: this has put him and his family[24] on the popular side. For everything that is opposed to arbitrary power, says Alcibiades, is called *demos* (89.4). Democracy of course is opposed to tyranny, but it is not the only regime so opposed. The word *demos* is usually taken to refer to the popular party, the party of the radical democracy, but its strict meaning is broader than that, including every citizen, rich or poor, noble or base.[25] Democracy as a regime heavily favors the poor and low-born

[23]This misimpression is shared by most translators (an exception is Richard Crawley), who often make Alcibiades look inconsistent, or worse. Cf. Grundy, *Thucydides*, 2:184–85; Finley, *Thucydides*, p. 230; Leo Strauss, *The City and Man* (Chicago: University of Chicago Press, 1977), p. 168. Alcibiades uses *democracy* and *demos* each twice here (*demos* 89.3, 4; "democracy" 89.4, 6).

[24]Alcibiades does not refer to his family explicitly but simply uses the first person plural, "we." Alcibiades' family on the distaff side, the Alcmeonidae, were in fact traditional supporters of the popular cause and included Pericles in their number.

[25]Finley (*Thucydides*, p. 162) draws attention to the ambiguity in the word *demos*, hence in the understanding of democracy (citing also Aristotle *Politics* 1291b30–40, 1293a1–10), and points out quite rightly that the different interpretations of it are crucial to any argument concerning democracy (see also Lowell Edmunds, *Chance and Intelligence in Thucydides* [Cambridge: Harvard University Press, 1975], p. 48n). He also mentions

and is not immune from the abuse of power. Thus Alcibiades is entitled to take the position that while he and his family were always supporters of the Athenian *demos* in principle, his own support of the democracy as a regime was purely prudential. In a remark that must seem an affront to the good sense of his audience, Alcibiades proceeds to say that, after all, the democracy at Athens was always somewhat too unrestrained for himself and his kinsmen, although they did their best to make it more measured politically (89.5). The notion that Alcibiades should pose as the spirit of restraint at Athens is paradoxical to say the least: but his meaning is revealed when he says that there were others, both now and in the past, who misled the mob into worse things; it was such men who had Alcibiades himself exiled (89.5). Alcibiades and his family, unlike these corrupt leaders, stood over "the whole" and considered it only just to preserve the form under which the city had become greatest and most free, and in which it came into their hands (89.6).

When Alcibiades speaks of "the whole" of the city in connection with the proper way of organizing things at Athens, he is necessarily thinking of the broadest sense of the word *demos* used earlier, the sense in which it includes all in the city. It is reminiscent of the conclusion of his speech at Athens, in favor of the unity of the classes in the city. "Standing over the whole," if it is not unambiguously democratic, certainly champions the cause of the *demos* in the broad sense; in that sense, it can probably be equated with "serving the common good." It is the opposite of tyranny or arbitrary power and also, according to Alcibiades, of misleading the mob (6.89.5). In this passage, Alcibiades uses the word *ochlos* (mob) in connection with the phenomenon of bad leadership, that is, a particular abuse of democracy. The allusion is highly reminiscent of his earlier characterization of the Sicilian cities as "mixed mobs" (6.17). Here, "moblikeness" is similarly associated with faction, with politicians who mislead the city, catering to a part of it rather than to the whole, but also and particularly with the exiling of men like Alcibiades. These things seem a fair description of what Alcibiades must mean by the lack of restraint that sometimes prevailed in the city and that he and his family strove to rein in. It is also in perfect harmony with his one reported use of the word "*moderation*", discussed above. The absence of such

---

in passing Alcibiades' use of this ambiguity in the speech at Sparta. My argument is that it forms the real basis of Alcibiades' argument in this passage.

figures as himself at the head of the city results in political indiscipline and factionalism. It is an undeniable defect of democracy as a regime that it is rather too prone to the influence of leaders who turn it, moblike, to the bad. This is the true basis of Alcibiades' indictment of "democracy" here, and to that extent it is a valid indictment. Even so, it would be an exaggeration to say that his repudiation of democracy on these grounds is complete. His last word on the vices of democracy is that as a regime it is universally recognized as folly. This is undoubtedly the verdict of Spartan opinion, and of aristocratic and oligarchic opinion throughout Greece. We are compelled to note however that "folly" (*anoia*) is precisely the quality Alcibiades prided himself on in his speech before the Athenian assembly (6.17.1). Such folly can amount to an explosive and daunting political power; and Alcibiades has already taken care to point out that it was under the sway of this folly that Athens became "greatest and most free," and that the regime had some just claim to his, and his family's, allegience on those grounds (89.6). In fact, on this understanding, "folly" is what Alcibiades and democratic Athens have, or had, most in common. Alcibiades will discover soon enough that the sober and undemocratic Spartans are not quite so hospitable as the Athenians to his political style, nor quite so serviceable to his ambitions. Alcibiades' criticism of democracy must be understood to be qualified finally by the consideration that in all probability no other regime allows one to address "the whole" of the city so directly and to stand over it so immediately. Few other regimes are so well suited to accommodate even the ambiguous forms of public deliberation and public enfranchisement that Alcibiades' view of the city envisages.

Alcibiades' attitude toward democracy in the end is ambivalent. It is ambivalent not because it is wavering—Alcibiades wavers on no issue—but because democracy both is and is not hospitable to his own view of the proper constitution of a city. This ambivalence is captured in his partial distinction between *demos* and "democracy." Alcibiades wants a regime that incorporates the *demos* and that allows him to embrace and stand over it as a whole, but democracy is often recalcitrant and prone to internal "indiscipline" and faction. The distinction between these two things is enough to make Alcibiades' argument on the subject consistent, but in practice it may reflect once again his desire to have it both ways.

A further consequence of Alcibiades' political understanding becomes visible here that is crucial to understanding the later course of his career. Alcibiades' view stands in an ambivalent relation to democracy, but in a deeper sense it stands in an ambivalent relation to any regime. Alcibiades' view is built entirely around the phenomenon of the exceptional political man, considering his abilities and requirements first and foremost. Such a role can never be "institutionalized"; but a regime is by definition a conventional, institutional, arrangement. It cannot be the business of any regime to produce such men, since their appearance cannot be engineered. But neither can their appearance, when it does occur, be ignored. Their practices necessarily circumvent the conventional political arrangements out of which regimes are built and move in the direction of Alcibidean politics. Such men tend necessarily to overwhelm regimes in the states in which they arise and to monopolize the political life of the community. Even the ascendency of the staid and unassuming Pericles amounted, according to Thucydides, to a suspension of the democracy (2.65.9). More brilliant politicians will make this suspension more conspicuous, if not more complete, by their activity. This is precisely what happened in the case of Alcibiades. The resulting situation was described succinctly by Aristophanes, who wrote of the relations between Alcibiades and Athens late in the war, and of the more general problems that they point to. In the *Frogs* he makes Aeschylus, who later wins the prize for wise counsel, say, "It is best not to rear a lion in the city / But if one is reared, the city must submit to its ways." (1431–32)

The city's attitude, according to Aristophanes, is paradoxical or ambivalent: it longs for Alcibiades and hates him, yet wants him back (1425). Alcibiades may prefer a democratic city for prudential reasons, but he is in a still more profound way indifferent to regimes. This, later, is the conclusion the oligarchical conspirators at Athens reach about Alcibiades, a conclusion that Thucydides endorses (8.48.4). The oligarchs use it as a reproach, for it means that Alcibiades is not and cannot be truly attached to their cause. This is the same doubt the democrats have. Alcibiades' ambivalent remarks about democracy in his speech at Sparta would not still the doubts on either side.

Alcibiades turns in the central section of his speech to a discussion of strategy proper. Having stilled the enmities he thinks the Spartans might harbor against him for his activities at Athens, Alcibiades tells them how they may most effectively advance their own interests and harm the

Athenians. The results bear out his advice amply. A few things should be noted about his advice. First, Alcibiades maintains vigorously that, in spite of his departure, the Athenian commanders left on the scene in Sicily will continue with the plan of conquest, and he asserts that that plan includes designs on Italy and Carthage as well as Sicily. According to Thucydides, these were indeed Alcibiades' ambitions for the project, but we note that even he shrank from openly proposing them in Athens (cf. 6.15.2 with the omission of this from his speech at Athens as a whole). An irony in this passage stems from the fact that Alcibiades' speech at Sparta is almost immediately preceded in Thucydides' narrative by Euphemus' speech at Camarina, which sincerely denies even an ambition to conquer Sicily. Whether Alcibiades is puposely exaggerating Athenian aims in order to stir the Spartans, or, somewhat anachronistically by now, attributing his own imperial ambitions to the Athenians, is not clear. In either case, it is certainly true that even without Alcibiades in the Athenian command, the Sicilians are in great jeopardy.

The actual proposals Alcibiades makes to the Spartans for pressing the conflict with the Athenians are noteworthy partly for their distinctively "Alcibidean" approach to strategic problems. Alcibiades emphasizes the psychological impact of his proposed initiatives, relying to some extent on the power inherent in mere appearances. The fortification of Deceleia, aside from being a devastating blow to Athenian interests, will also harm the Athenians by making their allies more restive and less inclined to pay their tribute. The bare fact of Spartan initiative will change the entire psychological complexion of the conflict in ways that will have real strategic results. Alcibiades also recommends that the Spartans send a small armed contingent to Syracuse, and, more importantly, that they send a Spartan to command and organize the Syracusan forces (6.91.4). The mere appearance of such a figure, Alcibiades suggests, will alter the balance of forces in Sicily, inspire discipline in the Syracusans, and heighten their morale. The arrival of Gylippus at Syracuse does in fact prove to be the turning point in the Sicilian campaign (7.1.2). We must imagine that Alcibiades, with his appreciation for the psychological elements of politics and warfare, relishes this opportunity to make use of the potent mythology surrounding the Spartans and the Spartan character as an element in his politics of appearances. Just as he formerly played on the appearance of extravagant wealth as an element of Athenian power, he makes use of the legend of Spartan invinceability while in Sparta.

The brilliance of Alcibiades' advice, however, will do no good if it is not heeded by the Spartans. In the third part of his speech, therefore, Alcibiades returns to the subject of Spartan prejudices against him that may prevent their taking him seriously as an advisor. He tells the Spartans once again that they should not think worse of him on account of his actions—referring this time to his seeming treason against Athens. He responds to this problem by outlining his understanding of patriotism, which turns patriotism utterly on its head while of course justifying everything he has done. This part of his speech is justly the most famous or notorious, though in fact it is only the natural conclusion to be drawn from his previously elaborated understanding of the city.

Before addressing the problem of his apparent treason directly, Alcibiades takes up a related matter that prepares the way for his discussion of patriotism. The Spartans should not suspect his advice, he says, as proceeding from an exile's zeal. Alcibiades is speaking of the tendency of exiles to flee to the enemy where, by dint of false reports and overly bold estimations, and motivated largely by the desire for party revenge, they attempt to seduce their new hosts into lending support to their faction at home. Alcibiades dismisses this suspicion in his case with one captious remark. The remark seems really more a pun than an argument (and a bad pun at that, according to Dover, from whom it draws a rare censure),[26] but it makes a serious point. What Alcibiades says, literally, is that, although he has been exiled by the wickedness of some, he is not exiled from benefiting the Spartans, if they will be persuaded by him. The Spartans are in all likelihood unamused by this rhetorical ploy, but the serious thought behind it is Alcibiades' claim that his exile has not affected him in the way exiles are usually affected. He implies first that he is not speaking as a member of any party at Athens, plotting to return with Sparta's aid to expel and punish some other party. He is not giving the Spartans tendentious and self-serving advice simply to serve that end. More significantly, Alcibiades is telling his audience that separation from his city has left him neither unable nor unwilling to be

---

[26]The remark constitutes, according to his commentary, "a sophistry which is obscure and lame" (Dover, in Gomme, Andrewes, Dover, *Historical Commentary*, 4:366).

of service to whomever he wishes. His judgment is not clouded by the passions that usually cloud exiles' minds; he can see beyond the narrow perspective of any party or even city. Alcibiades' expertise, now as before, objectively surveys the whole political scene. As pure expertise or political genius, it is not inherently bound to either side. For the deepest, and one might say the most chilling, meaning of Alcibiades' contrived pun is that his own expertise and his own genius, not to mention his own ambition, are fundamentally independent of any ordinary attachment to his native city. Alcibiades in this respect does represent the culmination of that theme in Thucydides which began with Themistocles, the Athenian statesman who, unlike the Spartan Pausanias, was capable of using his genius effectively outside the narrow confines of his city's discipline. Themistocles' genius, Thucydides emphasizes, was the genius of nature, not of convention (1.138); and the Athenian regime, of all regimes, might almost be said to be directed to the production of such men. Now, as Aristophanes' Aeschylus said, it has produced Alcibiades. Alcibiades as the quintessential Athenian seems to embody most fully the Athenian unveiling and liberation of nature; but in him the city, or perhaps simply nature, has produced something that cannot be held within the city's horizons.

Alcibiades denies that offering his services so impartially to his city's enemies means that he lacks patriotism. In fact, he redefines patriotism in such a way as to make himself not the worst, but in some respects the best lover of his city. His argument, though certainly unconventional, once again has some merit. The worst enemies of a city, Alcibiades says, are not those who oppose it openly, as the Spartans oppose the Athenians, but those who compel its friends to become foes (92.3). He seems to be assailing here not Athens as a whole, but the orators there who have misled the *demos* and caused his exile. He emphasizes somewhat more than before the "wickedness" of these men (*ponēria* 92.3). Accordingly, in the following argument, the argument about patriotism, Alcibiades appeals emphatically to justice. "Patriotism," he says, he does not have when he has suffered injustice, but when he is able to live in his city in safety. Indeed, Alcibiades argues, it is not his fatherland that he has now turned against, but a city no longer his own that he is striving to regain. For true patriots are not those who, being deprived unjustly of their city, fail to turn against it, but those who will stop at nothing in their yearning to get it back (92.4).

Though the final note Alcibiades strikes in this complicated passage is yearning for Athens, the harshness of his action speaks for itself. Once again, however, we must be careful not to see Alcibiades' argument as harsher than it actually is. He claims, and the weight of Thucydides' presentation supports him, that he has been done a grave injustice by the city of Athens. That of course does not justify service to the enemy in the ordinary understanding of things; such action would still be considered treasonous.[27] The reason for this in the ordinary understand-

[27]This is not universally agreed upon. It has been argued by some that Alcibiades' position on patriotism (*to philopoli*) represents in fact the typical Greek position. Grundy, for example, maintains that Alcibiades' argument and behavior seem reprehensible only to us, whereas real dedication to city was a rarity in Greece: men were party men first and citizens second; oligarchs felt no attachment to their cities when a democracy was in power; and so on (*Thucydides* 2:184). Edmunds (*Chance and Intelligence*, pp. 84–88) maintains similarly that Alcibiades is only returning here to the traditional attitude that Pericles, in his call for unqualified devotion to the city, had anomalously attempted to overcome (see David Grene, *Man in His Pride* [Chicago: University of Chicago Press, 1950], p. 31). He points quite appropriately to the traditionalist Theognis, whose fabled loyalty is transferred to the city exclusively on condition of its being ruled by the proper men. The most sustained argument to this effect, however, is made by Nathan Marsh Pusey, "Alcibiades and *to philopoli*," *Harvard Studies in Classical Philology* 51 (1940): 215; and Anton-Hermann Chroust, "Treason and Patriotism in Ancient Greece," *Journal of the History of Ideas* 15 (1954): 280, who review all of the many rivals for men's devotion in Greek culture, of which the city was only one, and, they argue, not the most important. Others were family, tribe, and political club (*hetaireia*). These rivalries of course are thematic in dramas such as Sophocles' *Antigone* or even the *Bacchae* of Euripides, and Fustel de Coulanges does as thorough a job as anyone of showing the powerful pre- or subpolitical ties that ancient piety created (*The Ancient City*, trans. Arnaldo Momigliano and S.C. Humphreys [Baltimore: Johns Hopkins University Press, 1980]).

Pusey, however, shows that Thucydides makes it equally clear that political disintegration was a result of the rigors of the harsh schoolmaster, war, and was precisely a violent overturning of the ordinary state of affairs and ways of thinking. The natural sources of stasis, that is to say its sources in human nature, are of great concern to Thucydides, but that concern itself, as well as the theme of the relation of public and private that pervades his work, make sense only from a point of view that takes the city as the primary association. That is undeniably Thucydides' point of view.

It is of the first importance for us to be aware of the conflicts with civic authority that were characteristic of ancient life and of political life generally. However, we must also not forget that the ideal of *eunomia* so universally and ardently sought after in Greece was a state of harmony and shared devotion to the city, of which Sparta was taken to be the exemplar (cf. 1.18.1). And Alcibiades is speaking here to a Spartan audience. As to Alcibiades' own views, he believes that the only worthwhile city is one in which unity and shared dedication to the common task, by all the orders of society, prevails. It is the Athenians' reneging on this that has made them subject to Alcibiades' "treason." Moreover, it is undeniable that Alcibiades, in his willingness to attach himself to different

107

ing is that cities, as communities, have greater weight in the scale of right or justice than do individual citizens. Cities and individuals are not commensurable: it might be the right of a good citizen to resist within the bounds of law, but failing that, it is his duty to submit even to a communal injustice against him. But Alcibiades has implicitly maintained, from the opening passage of his first speech, that he enjoys a privileged position, not only a commensurable but an equal one, vis-à-vis the city as a whole. This is the core of his argument here as well. Alcibiades is not subordinate to the city; justice applies between himself and the city more or less as between equals, and it is Athens that has broken faith with him, not the reverse.

It is important to recognize once again that the justice Alcibiades speaks of is not the justice of revenge. Alcibiades does not want to punish Athens or to destroy her in anger. (The one remark, at the very conclusion of the speech (92.5), that could be construed that way is discussed in its context.) Alcibiades' argument here is to some extent parallel to the argument he gave the Spartans about his attacks on them: in view of the injustice committed against him, he cannot be blamed for asserting his interests and defending his integrity or for seeking to slake his irrepressible thirst for great accomplishments elsewhere. When Alcibiades speaks, as he does here, of being "compelled" to become Athens' opponent (92.3), the only compulsion he can be thinking of is his own ambition. The argument from ambition seems to preclude malice, if only because malice would hamper Alcibiades' ability to change sides as freely as he does, and thereby it would limit the avenues to his ambition. Alcibiades asserts here his intention of regaining Athens and insists on his patriotism, and it is the character of that self-proclaimed patriotism as much as anything else that removes Alcibiades from the class of angry, vengeful exiles. Alcibiades argues that it is not in truth his homeland that he is going against; his actions are directed to re-

---

cities or empires without compunction, is supposed to be a revolutionary figure in Thucydides, and not, for example, a simple traditionalist or disciple of Theognis. Pusey himself concedes that Alcibiades is unique in that his dedication runs not even to party but apparently only to himself. Thucydides' treatment of public and private devotions as a problem is discussed in chaps. 1 and 3. Not to recognize the decline of Athenian public-spiritedness, or its demise in Greece at the time of the civil wars, as unwonted and alarming declines of the cities themselves and indeed of Greek civilization as a whole in Thucydides' view, is to miss much of the point of the History.

gaining the homeland that no longer exists. It is implied that when Athens expelled Alcibiades it ceased in effect to be itself. This view proceeds from arguments Alcibiades has already made. If Aristotle will maintain that a city's identity is constituted by its regime, a change of regime making it in effect a new city,[28] Alcibiades can maintain that his own presence or absence at the city's helm is of comparable importance. This is particularly so if the city's change of attitude toward Alcibiades is conditioned by the ascendency of "wicked" men in the city, the consequent prevalence of a kind of political license or immoderation, and ultimately the degeneration of the *demos* into a mob. Thus can Alcibiades speak sincerely not just of a loss, but of the disappearance, of his Athens. His desire is not to punish but to reconstitute his city.

We have had occasion more than once to notice Alcibiades' lack of malice in circumstances where others might be expected to be overcome with rage. In fact this general observation can be made, that Alcibiades' political attitude or style in the History is not characteristically an angry or irascible one. This is true paradoxically in spite of the fact that Alcibiades seems always and everywhere to be a member of the war party and shares responsibility for some of the greatest devastation of the Peloponnesian War. Alcibiades' overall manner, as we also noted before, savors more of levity than of gravity. His combination of consuming ambition with an almost ironic outlook is surely as remarkable a trait as anything else about him as a political man. It is also a most difficult trait to comprehend and to give a satisfactory account of. Not surprisingly, it is the source of much misunderstanding both among Alcibiades' contemporaries in the History, and in his posterity.

We might achieve greater clarity about this distinctive feature of Alcibidean politics by means of a comparison proposed by Plutarch. Alcibiades and the Roman commander Coriolanus both became enemies of their cities in time of war; both are famous for treason. Yet the spirit in which they turned on their cities, and the motives that led them to do so, are quite different. Plutarch at first says that both men were influenced by anger, though that does not seem to be true of Thucydides' Alcibiades. Plutarch goes on to say that Alcibiades gave up his anger when the city repented, and he claims that of the two men, Alcibiades and Coriolanus, Alcibiades was less blameworthy in his actions because

[28]Aristotle *Politics* 1276b1–5.

he was motivated less by outright rage and more by straightforward political ambition and love of victory.[29] Ambition and love of victory attain the very peak of intensity in Alcibiades, but he exhibits what must be a very rare kind of spiritedness which, for all its intensity, is without the consuming anger that is usually its obverse side. Coriolanus displays a much more common type of prideful ambition, which responds to obstacles, slights, and injustices with rage. Achilles is the poetic archetype of this. Alcibiades' uniqueness in this regard is connected to his sophistication and his remarkable political views. Those views have led him to the conviction that Athens exiled him in a kind of lapse rather than out of genuine bad intent. On the one hand, the city succumbed (temporarily) to entirely natural feelings of resentment toward him; on the other hand, it was misled by demagogues. No city in its right mind, after all, would expel an Alcibiades. Alcibiades does not display vindictiveness toward the city, or even toward his personal opponents, whom he identifies as the culprits here, although some of them do fear him greatly for it.[30]

Everything about Alcibiades' political understanding seems to militate against anger. Coriolanus regarded as abhorrent and degrading the necessity imposed upon him by the Roman regime to appeal to the people, and he believed the people's capacity for political judgment to be nil. Alcibiades, to the contrary, revels in the publicity of democratic politics, and if he believes that democracy as a regime is somewhat too prone to the influence of demagogues, he has what seems to be an unshakable faith in his own ability eventually to prevail in Athens, in spite of both that democratic vice and the Athenians' natural resentment against him. He only reserves the right—and he does take it to be a right—to pursue his own ambitions independently in the interim, wherever they may lead

---

[29]Plutarch *Comparison of Alcibiades and Coriolanus* 2, 3. I am inclined to believe that Plutarch's treatment of Alcibiades is of limited usefulness in elucidating Thucydides. Plutarch's judgment of Alcibiades, in part the judgment of a moralist, does not capture the nuances characteristic of Thucydides' presentation not only of Alcibiades but of the political world in general. This is evident in Plutarch's treatment of Alcibiades' motivations and his judgment on Alcibiades' treason in particular. Plutarch's *Life of Alcibiades* should be used with some degree of skepticism for that reason and one other: Alcibiades is precisely the kind of figure around whom an unusually large number of apocryphal and wrongheaded legends may have sprung up in the interval between his death and Plutarch's writing.

[30]This point will be further discussed in the next chapter.

him. Alcibiades is less prone to anger in part because he always has other alternatives and options, because he is less attached to his city, or to any city, than is Coriolanus. Coriolanus is more like one of those exiles Alcibiades alluded to earlier, whose mind is clouded and obsessed by an animus against his native city. Such passion gets in the way of one's flexible and effective operation—and Alcibiades is nothing if not an operator. The "levity" of his political style, of which his insusceptibility to anger is only a part, derives ultimately from the fact that his versatility, his ambitions, his entire cast of mind transcend the city. This puts Alcibiades beyond the limits not only of any particular city, but of city politics as such. It represents a gulf between him and all cities.

Alcibiades' view of politics, the statesman, and the city makes that gulf inevitable. Since the unambiguous center of the political world, in his view, is the statesman, or even the statesman's ambition distilled to its purest form, the world of politics looks quite different to Alcibiades than it does to the cities. The political arena looks more like a stage to him; politics is less a matter of "issues" and contests over issues (as it is for the city), more a matter of great accomplishments, honor, and contests for honor. Of course, honor can be gained only by championing some issue and thus serving some community; this is why the interests of statesman and city naturally tend to converge. Ambition itself, however, can, if circumstances so dictate, move from project to project, from issue to issue, and ultimately even from city to city.

Alcibiades is free from attachments to city in part because he is detached from some of the concerns that constitute the substance of city politics. Inasmuch as the "issues" in question are for the city ultimately life-and-death matters, and inasmuch as ordinary, unflinching patriotism is in the eyes of the city the most important virtue, this nonchalance and even irony on the part of a man like Alcibiades cannot but be alarming to the city. As a matter of fact, his attitude may indeed make Alcibiades insensitive to the sometimes devastating effects of his activity. It is not clear that Alcibiades really comprehends the hardship that sending Gylippus to Syracuse and fortifying Deceleia is likely to impose on the Athenians, just as it is not clear that Alcibiades appreciated what was really at stake when he told the Spartans he was largely responsible for their peril at Mantineia. The stakes for the city are quite different from the stakes as Alcibiades appears to perceive them. To a degree, he reminds us of those thoughtless Athenians who longed for the sights

111

and spectacles of Sicily but who did not consider the oppression that their gratification would cause to others. To this extent, Alcibiades' view is defective and his actions irresponsible. This would be one justifiable basis for the city's suspicions toward him.

The revolution in justice involved in Alcibiades' placing statesmanly ambition at the center of the political world is now familiar. Only a few words should be added on the relation between Alcibiades' view of the statesman's prerogatives and the Athenians' revolutionary view of prerogatives of the city. It is tempting to call Alcibiades' view a derivative of the Athenian one on imperial prerogatives and justice, though it is a derivative with significant alterations. The Athenians claim that they are blameless in pursuing an imperial policy traceable ultimately to certain "compulsions" of human nature. Alcibiades implicitly makes a parallel argument about the statesman, asserting his ambition to be a kind of exonerating compulsion (cf. *anankasantes* 6.92.3). For the city, those compulsions are fear, honor, and profit (1.75.3, 76.2), with fear and profit predominating in the long run. For Alcibiades, the motivation is clearly honor; the need for wealth is purely ancillary.[31] Alcibiades never makes the argument that he is driven to any of his actions by fear for his safety. This difference is crucial, I believe, in understanding why Alcibiades' ambition never degenerates into the quasi-Melian position of the tyrant, who settles for security and profit when honor proves to be beyond his reach (cf. 1.17). Alcibiades is too exclusively and too consistently dedicated to honor to fall into that trap. A city, of course, cannot be dedicated to honor to the exclusion of safety or advantage in the same sense.

Partly for these reasons, it seems, the Athenian argument was always limited to asserting that "compulsory" actions are "not unjust."[32] Alcibiades moves in the direction of asserting the statesman's positive title

---

[31]It is a question of some significance of course whether "*honor*" is ultimately the proper word for what Alcibiades wants, since honor is usually tied to a whole complex of gentlemanly virtues that Alcibiades does not have (e.g., moderation and patriotism of the ordinary variety). It may be that Alcibiades' goal could better be called simply "brilliance" or "illustriousness" (corresponding to *lamprotēs*, a conspicuous word in Thucydides' treatment of both Athens and Alcibiades). This point will be discussed in the last chapter.

[32]The parts of the early Athenian argument that go beyond this are separate from the argument about compulsions and do not survive the loss of the Athenian argument from honor on Melos. See chap. 1.

112

to justice, based on a "compulsion" of honor, but he never says anything that requires us to draw that conclusion. Alcibiades, as we have observed, is indulgent not only to his own ambitious impulses but also in some measure to those impulses of the city that lead it to resent, envy, and resist him, and even to the ambitions of others who oppose him. Moving to a higher level of generality, we might say that Alcibiades' view of these "compulsions" looks almost like Diodotus' view, expressed during the Mytilenaean debate, and his indulgence like the indulgence of Diodotus or of the Athenians themselves under the influence of Diodotus. The "scientific" view of the political world and of the forces at work in it gives Diodotus a perspective of almost Olympian detachment closer to universal compassion than to any kind of serious political engagement. Alcibiades mimics this position in his elevated political perspective and his partial irony toward the politics of the cities; and if he has precious little compassion for those less successful than himself, he has that measure of indulgence which quenches anger or spite. Alcibiades is no more a moralist than is Diodotus.

But none of these things serve to quench Alcibiades' ambition, as they apparently do for Diodotus and for Alcibiades' fellow exile Thucydides.[33] Diodotus portrays a world in which law or justice has a very tenuous existence, where real and permanent progress is impossible. Alcibiades, on the other hand, envisages the world of perpetually conflicting and irrepressible ambitions not in terms of futility but in terms of the greatest and most glorious undertakings. Crucial to this vision, of course, is his view that the greatest and most worthy men and ambitions ultimately

[33]See also chapter 1, n. 39, and text. The question of Thucydides himself I do not treat thematically. But something must be said here, because many scholars consider Thucydides to have been chafing at his exile and even to have colored his History under the influence of this passion. Westlake, for example (*Individuals*, p. 60), suggests that the historian's "bias" against Cleon (which he apparently finds otherwise unaccountable) stems from Cleon's possible connection with his exile (see also Finley, *Thucydides*, p. 32). Thucydides himself, however, seems remarkably dispassionate about the exile. In fact, in the only mention he makes of it (5.26.5), he indicates only that it allows him to collect information from the other side with greater facility. In other words, his project of writing and understanding seems ultimately of greater concern to him than command or exile. The parallel with Diodotus introduced in chapter 1 seems to provide a better clue to Thucydides' attitude than the passions of ordinary exiles (cf. Strauss, *The City and Man*, pp. 226–41). I deliberately mention the example of Thucydides in this context because it accentuates that of Alcibiades, who is also not stirred by ordinary exiles' passion, yet who for some reason holds to the most intense political ambition.

prevail; that the contest, for all its apparent chaos, is ultimately a fair or just one; and that glory is therefore genuinely worthy of esteem. Alcibiades' optimism on this score, particularly given the circumstances of his career, seems absolutely irrepressible. Diodotus argued that honor should be essentially banished from public life, since it is an inducement to orators to speak only to please the multitude (3.42.5–6). He openly asserted that in Athens at least it is impossible to do good without deception (3.43.3). Alcibiades' astonishing frankness, in Athens and everywhere else, breathes the opposite conviction.

It is by now obvious that Alcibiades contains within himself the most unusual, even paradoxical, combinations of political qualities. His vision of justice is without vindictiveness, his ambition without revenge, his spiritedness without anger. Alcibiades combines the fiercest love of victory with an exceptional levity of style, and a keen sense of irony toward the political world with an indomitable thirst for political engagement. The only way to describe Alcibiades' politics is by oxymoron. What these descriptions point to is a political ambition so free from every external constraint, free even from attachment to any goal outside itself, that it practically leaves politics behind. Paradoxically, this can nevertheless be called political ambition in its purest or most complete form. Therein lies one of the most significant lessons of Thucydides' Alcibiades. At the moment of his speech at Sparta, Alcibiades' unsated thirst for glory and accomplishment continues to drive him. We learn from non-Thucydidean sources that at a later juncture, after his return to Athens and some brilliant military successes in the East, Alcibiades did content himself with a kind of political retirement upon falling again into disfavor at Athens.[34] Thucydides' presentation makes this as comprehensible as Alcibiades' earlier frenetic activity.

Alcibiades sounds one final note of paradox, of a more immediate or practical kind, in the conclusion of his speech at Sparta. He had claimed earlier that, as a true patriot, his ultimate goal was to regain possession

[34]See Plutarch *Alcibiades* 36–39; Xenophon *Hellenica* 1.4–2.1. Plutarch does say that Alcibiades undertook some campaigns privately from his home in Thrace during this period (*Alcibiades* 36), but it is difficult to make anything of this. The most intriguing report about Alcibiades' activities during this time concerns his attempt to warn the Athenian fleet of impending disaster before the battle of Aegospotami (Plutarch *Alcibiades* 36–37). Alcibiades in his semi-retirement seems to harbor some independent good will toward Athens.

of his city by whatever means necessary. His concluding statement, on the other hand, holds out to the Spartans the prospect of pulling down the Athenian power, "both present and future," and securing for themselves the peaceful hegemony of all of Greece, if they will but follow his advice (6.92.4, 5). Alcibiades thus appears literally to take the viewpoint of each side in turn, to the point of appearing to contradict himself outright. This fact demonstrates his versatility once again, but it also shows how close his position can come to simple incoherency. The only resolution that this contradiction could have in practice would be the triumphant return of Alcibiades to Athens at the head of a Spartan army and a universal Spartan empire; but that does not seem to be what Alcibiades has in mind when he speaks of his "patriotism" toward Athens. "Universalism" is clearly the perspective that Alcibiades' ambition and conception lead him to, but the existence of the cities is a fact not fully digested in Alcibiades' outlook. Alcibiades is clearly attached to the political form of the polis and to its kind of political community, but his perspective and his ambition shatter the boundaries that make the polis what it is. Alcibiades does not want to play the part of Caesar, nor that of the Macedonians who came to Greece a century after this war. But his politics more than hints of both.

These difficulties in Alcibiades' political vision Thucydides does not leave to speculation. After his second speech Alcibiades begins the most active phase of his career in the History. His activity elaborates on and tests the practicality of both his comprehensive vision of international politics and his vision of the domestic affairs of the best city. It is not clear on the basis of his speeches whether Alcibiades' city is a possible city or whether his view of the politics between cities is ultimately viable. We are entitled, purely on the basis of the speeches, to some skepticism about this. On the other hand, Alcibiades' great talents are now known to us, and his politics, even if they fall short of his ideal, may be more effective or more salutary than the alternatives.

In Thucydides' narrative, Alcibiades more or less drops from sight after delivering his speech at Sparta, as the disastrous Sicilian campaign unfolds. It is after the Athenian defeat there, in Book Eight, that Alcibiades comes again to the fore.

3

Book Eight of
Thucydides' History

WERE it not for the existence of Book Eight, Thucydides' History could
have the appearance of an ordinary moral drama. The Athenians, goaded
on by Alcibiades and their own hubristic imperial ambitions, finally
embark upon the overweening project of conquering Sicily, and suffer
an awe-inspiring defeat there at the hands of their enemies. The drama
of Book Eight, coming directly after that defeat, shows to the contrary
a great resurgence on the part of the Athenians, one far beyond the
expectations of the other Greeks and even of the Athenians themselves
in their moment of defeat (8.1–2, 24.5). By the end of Book Eight,
which is also the end of Thucydides' History as we have it, the Athenians
are in a better position than they were at any time since the Sicilian
defeat—and they are reunited with Alcibiades. Athens' ability to recover
from that defeat to the extent that it does is as great a testament to its
strength and resilience as anything in Thucydides.

Still, in Book Eight we also witness the real breakdown of public
order in Athens, the effective dissolution of the city's political community, the establishment of a harsh oligarchy, and the triumph of
private over public interest. While the Sicilian defeat does not prove an
unqualified reproach to Athenian imperialism, the ambition of the city
proves to be its nemesis in a less direct way, as the imperial doctrine of
the blamelessness of self-aggrandizement is applied to domestic politics.

116

In Book Eight we see both the great strength and resilience of Athens and its great fragility. This complex drama also contains important lessons about the strength or fragility of the city as such; it is a key to the ongoing Athenian experiment in politics, as we have called it. Athens saves itself from the imminent threat of defeat at the hands of its numerous enemies, but the Athenians fall upon one another and bring the city close to internal collapse. Alcibiades plays an important role both in these developments and in the subsequent restoration of domestic harmony at Athens, acting first as an instigator of the oligarchic conspiracy, and then, after the oligarchy has run its course without him, becoming instrumental in bringing it down and paving the way for the best regime Athens has had in Thucydides' time.

Alcibiades is clearly the major character of Book Eight, which is a highly unusual book, the most chaotic and difficult in the History. The narrative is choppy, scenes change rapidly, and some of the grand themes of the work seem to be less in evidence.[1] Hence the common supposition that the book is unfinishd or unrevised. Yet the striking shift of presentation could also be dictated by the unique qualities of the period we are entering.[2] Thucydides' narrative becomes more chaotic as the war itself becomes more chaotic and desperate. The Greeks, particularly the Athenians, are no longer capable of mounting grand campaigns and controlling the course of events in the way that they have; they are reduced to skirmishing in response to threats as they arise. Cities and individuals are driven to extremes merely to survive. Alcibiades seems to be the one exception, the one figure who is not consumed or rent

[1]See Peter R. Pouncey, *The Necessities of War: A Study of Thucydides' Pessimism* (New York: Columbia University Press, 1980), p. x; W. Robert Connor, *Thucydides* (Princeton: Princeton University Press, 1984), p. 217; Jacqueline de Romilly, *Thucydides and Athenian Imperialism*, trans. P. Thody (New York: Barnes & Noble, 1963), pp. 3–54.

[2]The suggestion has occasionally been made that Book Eight is not as unpolished a piece of work as is usually supposed. See Pouncey, *Necessities of War*, pp. x-xi, chaps. 7–8; John H. Finley, *Thucydides* (Ann Arbor: University of Michigan Press, 1963), p. 246; F. E. Adcock *Thucydides and His History* (Cambridge: Cambridge University Press, 1963), pp. 35, 83; Connor, *Thucydides*, p. 217. I do not intend to argue that Book Eight is finished, or even that what we have of it is in the final form that Thucydides intended to give it. But I do believe that, given the character of the period it describes, close examination shows it to be quite polished so far as general organization and highlighting of themes are concerned. For a thorough overview of this issue, see Andrewes, "Indications of Incompleteness," in A. W. Gomme, A. Andrewes, and Dover, *A Historical Commentary on Thucydides*, 5 vols. (Oxford: Clarendon, 1945–81), 5:361–83.

by the new circumstances of the war, but who actually thrives in it.³ It has even been suggested that the principle of organization of much of Book Eight is in fact nothing but the career of Alcibiades himself.⁴ Whether or not that is true, the career of Alcibiades is the thread that we shall be following. It is certainly true that Alcibiades is the only figure whose activity parallels the new course of the war. He moves not only from theater to theater but from camp to camp, and his movements are to a remarkable degree responsible for the varying fortunes of the different parties in the war. Everywhere he goes his political style, if not his immediate political goals, remains constant. We have already seen that Alcibiades holds to the same views in speeches both at Athens and at Sparta; his political activity likewise involves a consistent attempt to implement this vision of politics, wherever he finds himself. The question we have posed to ourselves as observers is whether that vision is ultimately a workable one.

Book Eight, and the History as we have it, closes with the happy image of Athens recovering from her worst internal and external wounds, victorious at sea, blessed with the best regime that the city has had in Thucydides' lifetime (8.97.2), and reconciled with her greatest commander, Alcibiades. The rosiness of this image is tarnished by the problem that its two constituent elements—the sober regime of the Five Thousand and the recall of Alcibiades—are not clearly compatible. The recall of Alcibiades by Athens represents the (temporary) salvation of the city in the war, but it seems to suggest or prefigure the triumph of Alcibiades' political vision in the city as well, that is to say, the acquiescence of the city in his political claims. This impression is heightened by the fact that Alcibiades' return is prepared by certain significant, even traumatic, changes in the city of Athens itself.

The first time that Alcibiades and the city came together was at the moment of the Sicilian expedition. The expedition was in some respects the culmination of decades of Athenian imperial expansion and is for Thucydides an epitome of the democratic, imperial project at Athens. Its core was an attempt to push unsupported or unapologetic human power to its furthest extent, an attempt of the utmost daring, which

³Cf. Pouncey, *Necessities of War*, p. 110.
⁴See Edouard Delebecque, *Thucydide et Alcibiade* (Aix-en-Provence: Centre d'Etudes et de Recherches Helleniques, 1965), pp. 92–95.

Thucydides characterizes as erotic daring. The Athenians' erotic passion for Sicily seems to hold out the promise of eternal and undreamed-of bliss. Almost immediately, however, they recoil from Alcibiades and advance Nicias; when the city goes to Sicily on these terms meets with unimaginable disaster, it appears to represent not a simple check to expansion but almost a dismantling of the entire Athenian project. In all of Book Eight, in spite of Athens' amazing recovery from the blows dealt it, its formerly most conspicuous trait is no longer visible. The city is no longer referred to as daring,[5] although such references abound in earlier parts of the History. Nor is eros alluded to.

Athenian daring was the very opposite of moderation. At the beginning of Book Eight, when the full extent of the Sicilian disaster is finally recognized, Thucydides notes that the Athenians, influenced by alarm and apprehension, introduce a certain moderation into their affairs.[6] This newfound moderation in extreme adversity is crucial to the recovery of the city but also the emblem of the city's desperate plight. It is this spirit that is instrumental in Athens' eventual reconciliation with Alcibiades. Alcibiades was always aware that a certain kind of moderation in the city was required to allow him to take the position he desired.[7] When the question of his recall is first broached in Athens in Book Eight, it is explicitly linked by the oligarchic conspirator who is urging it with the new need for moderation in the city (53.3). Indeed, consenting to strong leadership always calls for moderation of a certain kind from a democratic populace. The problem here, from Alcibiades' point of view as well as that of the city, is that the immoderation which found its expression in jealousy toward great men is intimately connected to the immoderation that produced Athenian power and empire. Demo-

---

[5]This fact might be considered of dubious significance if one supposes Book Eight to be only a rough and unrevised draft. In fact, however, Thucydides' use of other significant words is as careful in Book Eight as it is elsewhere. Considering the significance Thucydides has given to *tolma* in particular, its use or nonuse would likely be quite deliberate even in a final draft. Indeed, Book Eight contains one of the most important passages in the work on the contrasting character of Athens and Sparta and how they stand in relation to daring (8.96.5).

[6]8.1.3. The Athenians give greater authority to old men and decide to "moderate" expenses (*sōphronisai*). The use of the word, though in a somewhat incidental matter, is striking given Thucydides' previous refusal to apply it to Athens in any matter (see chap. 1, n. 51, above).

[7]See 6.29.2, and my discussion of this theme in chap. 2.

cratic jealousy, daring, and erotic passion are of a piece at Athens, as is also suggested by Thucydides' digression on Harmodius and Aristogeiton. Hence the moderation required for the city to accept Alcibiades might bring with it a relaxation of all the springs that had made the city most powerful. If there was not room in a single community for the old Athenian *demos* and a man like Alcibiades, the *demos* might now make room for Alcibiades at the expense of those traits that Alcibiades wants most to make use of in Athens. Book Eight is in part a test of whether the Athenian regime or anything like it can survive Alcibidean leadership.

Alcibiades' return is the salvation of the city at the end of Book Eight, but it is not clear how well it augurs for the ultimate restoration of the political community. The moderation that brings Alcibiades back after the episode of the oligarchy and establishes the regime of the Five Thousand represents indeed a new and salutary dedication to the common good in the city; but it is a dedication conditioned by extreme necessity, by fear for the city's very existence. It is predicated, that is, upon a very minimal understanding of the common good. We do not know if this return to sobriety and public-spiritedness is a reconstitution of the political community of the city on any higher plane, or whether it represents a real vindication of the solidity of the city—the city of Athens or the city as such. Our doubts on this score might be reinforced by another peculiar feature of Book Eight, its conspicuous lack of quoted speeches.

The lack of speeches in Book Eight is often adduced as proof of its unfinished character. But Thucydides might have had reasons for leaving it without speeches, depending upon the motives that led him to include speeches in the other books. Those speeches doubtless serve many purposes, but the most general one is surely to show the importance of speech as such to the life of the Greek cities, and thereby to help illustrate why the Greek cities should be considered peaks of the political form. Deliberative public speech is one of the greatest accomplishments of human culture as represented by the city. The speeches delivered during this war in particular are important parts of what makes it the greatest war.[8] Thucydides may include speeches in the History to indicate that

---

[8]It seems, as I argued in the introduction, that one thing that makes this war the greatest war for Thucydides is the fact that it was the most self-conscious war: the war

hearing the delivery of the speeches firsthand as it were, and experiencing in that way the essence of political life, is crucial to the understanding of Greek cities and of the war. To the extent that this is his motive, speeches may be excluded from Book Eight by design, to indicate that in this period the cities have been reduced to the most minimal concerns of the public good, especially as concerns political community at Athens.[9] Thucydides does partially quote one Athenian speech in Book Eight, a fragment of Peisander's speech urging moderation and the recall of Alcibiades (53.3). Alcibiades is eventually recalled and twice addresses the Athenian troops on Samos, but neither speech is quoted directly. These speeches, which Thucydides describes indirectly, represent the culmination in effect of Alcibiades' efforts to return to Athens, but they are hardly models of deliberative public rhetoric (8.81, 86). They are, on the other hand, strangely appropriate as models of Alcibiades' ambition to reign supreme in the city. Therein lies the parting dilemma in Thucydides' treatment of him.

The first place we are led to look for illumination on the problems of Alcibiades' practical politics in Book Eight is the account of his activities at Sparta. Sparta is the model of traditional political solidity, the place where political community or devotion to the public good is most secure. The record of Alcibiades' activities there sheds light on the character and instincts of traditional political community and on the practicality or impracticality of Alcibidean politics seen against that background.

Alcibiades at Sparta

From his speeches at Athens and Sparta, we were able to conclude that Alcibiades does not in principle distinguish cities according to regimes. Alcibiades is more or less indifferent to regimes because he places himself

---

in which the major combatants, their allies, and those caught simply in the middle of the conflict were all forced to think about the issues of war and peace, justice and might. This is seen most in its speeches. Marc Cogan, *The Human Thing*, (Chicago: University of Chicago Press, 1981), makes a similar point, though to somewhat different effect. Those interpreters who follow the so-called *logos–ergon* patterns in the History in a way take a parallel view.

[9]Cf. Cogan, *Human Thing*, pp. 112, 165; Finley, *Thucydides*, p. 246; Adcock, *Thucydides*, p. 35. The last two also address the question why most of Book Five contains no speeches.

implicitly beyond any regime; in every city he would stand over the whole and lead it directly, making it over so to speak in his own image. Alcibidean politics, dedicated as it is to brilliant deeds and great men, presumes a very active and ambitious city; the impetus required for this will come from the statesman himself if it is not already present in the city. Alcibiades' speech to the Spartans betrays an implicit belief that even they can fit this mold. The clearest single indication of this is the way Alcibiades concludes his speech. His final statement to the Spartans offers them the prospect, if they but heed his advice, of living in safety and securing the leadership of all of Greece, not by force but voluntarily, that is, by simple goodwill (6.92.5). In the context of the rest of the speech, the inclusion of this concluding scenario is rather gratuitous, and it strikes us as wildly optimistic to say the least, going far beyond the narrow strategems for the war presented in the speech itself. This unlooked-for and immensely attractive prospect, offering the Spartans nonoppressive and unhazardous hegemony over Greece, seems to represent Alcibiades' attempt to stir up in Sparta the kinds of ambitions for universal rule that were so characteristic of Athens. His formulation is almost reminiscent of Thucydides' description of the Athenian passion for Sicily, containing precisely the kind of vision that Athenian eroticism attached itself to so readily and so vehemently: it is flattering to the greatest ambitions, even strictly impossible ambitions, while at the same time it makes them seem safe and within the city's grasp. Alcibiades evidently believes that the same ambitions and passions are latent in the Spartans and that he will be able to bring them out. He is also evidently aware that he must bring out these passions and ambitions in order to be able to operate as he wants in Sparta.

After Alcibiades delivers his speech, the Spartans agree to follow his advice as regards the prosecution of the Sicilian war and the fortification of Deceleia in Attica—both things that they would not have done, or would not have done with such alacrity, otherwise (6.93)—but the effects of Alcibiades' deeper appeal to their ambitions is not immediately clear. For the remainder of Book Six and all of Book Seven Alcibiades drops from sight,[10] and the activities of the Spartans themselves, outside Sicily, are only occasionally alluded to. At the beginning of Book Eight, shortly before the relationship between Alcibiades and the Spartans is

[10]Alcibiades is alluded to once in Book Seven: 7.18.

taken up again, Thucydides assesses the general Spartan outlook. They were very heartened by the Athenian defeat in Sicily, he says, and were now in good hope of freeing themselves from the threat of the Athenians altogether and having safely the hegemony of all the Greeks to themselves (8.2.4). This description of the Spartan outlook both resembles and differs from that which Alcibiades would have hoped for at this juncture. Their hope for the undisputed hegemony of Greece seems to be the boldest they have allowed themselves yet (cf. 1.118.2). Thucydides' emphasis here, however, seems to be on their expectations of safety, ease, and brevity regarding the war: they hope to be delivered of it. Even hegemony seems to appeal to them primarily for the sake of the safety it will bring. Thucydides gives no hint, nor does the subsequent course of events indicate, that the Spartans have been fatally charmed in the Athenian manner, either by Alcibiades' words or by the possibilities that the new course of events has opened to them.[11]

This does nothing to inhibit Alcibiades. He persists in acting as though the Spartans were essentially assimilable to his model of politics, which only means that he himself continues to act according to his own principles of political action and seeks to gain the kind of position in Sparta that he sought for himself at Athens.[12] He is met there less by open resistance than by lethargy. To open the second phase of the war, the Spartans decide to support the revolt of the Chians and attack the Athenians in Ionia. The Spartan progress in this initiative is excruciatingly slow, in conformity with the Spartan manner we have become familiar with from the earlier parts of the History. They first meticulously confirm the Chian claims of strength, then decide to send a modest ten ships to aid them. When an earthquake occurs, they reduce the number of ships

[11]This is not to deny that Spartan ambitions described here might reflect the first stirrings of the hegemonism they display after their final victory over Athens. Yet even that revival of Spartan imperialism was quite halting and incomplete. See for example Plutarch *Lysander*; Xenophon *Hellenica*; and also the good discussion of A. Andrewes, "Spartan Imperialism?" in P. D. A. Garnsey and C. R. Whittaker, eds., *Imperialism in the Ancient World* (Cambridge: Cambridge University Press, 1978).

[12]Plutarch makes much of the fact that Alcibiades while at Sparta conformed himself to the austerity of Spartan manners in a way that would previously have been thought impossible. There is no particular indication of this in Thucydides. Even if Alcibiades' outward manners changed, it did not affect his politics. Plutarch's story of Alcibiades' seduction of King Agis' wife suggests that even his private restraint was not so great as it might seem. Plutarch *Alcibiades* 23.

to five and change commanders (8.6.4–5). When the ships finally set out, they are met and contained by a small Athenian squadron directly off the Peloponnesus. The Spartans, immediately discouraged, consider abandoning the enterprise altogether (11.2–3), and Alcibiades must exert himself to inject some non-Spartan vigor and daring into their policy. He goes about this task in characteristically Alcibidean fashion.

According to Thucydides, it was due largely to Alcibiades' influence that the Spartans decided to go to Ionia and aid the Chians rather than proceeding to the Hellespont or Euboea first (8.6). Thucydides pauses to explain that Alcibiades was acting as a friend and ally of the ephor Endius in this, since other prominent Spartans were advocating aid to one of the other two places. Alcibiades, Thucydides notes, had hereditary ties with Endius; he has evidently turned these ties into a private political alliance. From here Alcibiades begins to develop a genuine politics of personal intrigue at Sparta. When the Spartans become discouraged at their first setback, Alcibiades pushes them to send five ships to Ionia anyway, including himself in the party, so that they might persuade the cities there to revolt before news of their first defeat arrives. In connection with this, Thucydides says, Alcibiades argued to Endius "privately" that by this strategem Endius would gain honor along with Alcibiades, and that together they would thus prevent the revolt from being a prize that King Agis could garner (12). When Alcibiades subsequently arrives in Ionia he proceeds with great skill and success to detach cities from the Athenian empire, securing almost immediately the revolt of Chios and Miletus. Thucydides mentions once again that Alcibiades wanted to induce as many cities as possible to revolt before the rest of the Peloponnesians arrived, so as to secure the greatest prize for himself and those in Sparta connected with him (17.2). Almost at a stroke, Alcibiades has created a faction around himself at Sparta; he does not even shrink from rivaling the king.

It would scarcely be too much to say about the subsequent campaigns in Ionia, that Alcibiades is singlehandedly responsible for the prosperous beginning of the Peloponnesian and Spartan campaign in the East during this phase of the war. He achieves this success with private honor as his goad and goal. If anything, there is less pretense of serving the city of Sparta, per se, than there was of serving Athens earlier. Yet the Spartans are very well served, so far as successes in Ionia are concerned. The whole series of episodes shows clearly the great benefits that can accrue to a city by giving Alcibiades free rein. It also shows how his activity depends upon, in fact demands, a specific kind of politics within the city. Alcibiades' presence in Sparta begins indeed to reshape the city in his own image. It goes without saying that this was not previously the Spartan way in politics. But Alcibidean politics does not sort well with even a limited monarchy like the Spartans'; Alcibiades eventually gets into considerable trouble by acting as a rival even to Agis.[13]

Alcibiades' politics is one of men who stand out against the backdrop of the city and who can in principle engage in the greatest rivalries among themselves. Yet the Corinthians struck a genuine note of contrast in their speech to the Spartans before the war began, when they said that while Athens was indeed a city in which individual citizens became independent political agents in their own right, Sparta was virtually the opposite (1.70). The Corinthians, like Alcibiades, were attempting to stir the Spartans to action, but they had a much greater sense of the obstacles to such a course. Sparta, whose citizens are not independent like the Athenians, does not have the same kind of daring or power at its disposal. What the Corinthians did not make clear in their argument was the extent to which this is fundamental to the Spartan polity and, more importantly, the fact that their polity is one source of the kind of power that the Spartans do have.[14] The Spartans are highly suspicious of individualism and individual initiative, among commanders almost as much as among ordinary citizens. Brasidas is the only Spartan in Thucydides who has real success acting independently of the city. Yet he comes to be regarded with suspicion at the very height of his fortune, in large part because of his success. Thucydides says that Brasidas favored war for the sake of his own particular honor (5.16.1), at a time when the Spartans as a whole were desirous of peace. His great desire for honor, his ability to speak well, his ingenuity as a commander, and finally the very triumphs that these things brought him, inevitably detached Brasidas from the traditionally seamless and monochrome community of the Spartans, something that the Spartans necessarily look askance at.

[13]Cf. 8.12.3, 45.1, and n. 12, above.

[14]This is one of the themes of Archidamus' reply to the Corinthians in the debate at Sparta before the war (1.84–85). See also Finley, *Thucydides*, pp. 91–92, who speaks of this virtue in the Spartans but concludes, with the Corinthians, that the Spartan way is simply outmoded at this period.

Individual ambitions of this kind are somehow illicit among the Spartans. This is true despite the fact that Sparta, as a city, could be said to be dedicated to honor or glory more than other cities are (cf.1.84.6; 6.11.6). The political community there holds to an implicit dictum that no one among them shall distinguish himself too conspicuously, even in the city's service. The Spartans implicitly recognize that emulation for personal or private honors is subversive of their community when carried too far. They are also aware that the temptation to such honors is a powerfully corrupting influence for individuals. The Spartan ideal has to do rather with adherence to the law and to the virtue prescribed by law, giving the regime a sober, stolid solidity. Even honor in effect is held communally in this regime; the Spartans are loath either to praise or to blame any individual overmuch.[15] Thucydides remarks that Brasidas was the first—and so far as we know the only—man to receive signal honors from the Spartans for individual valor during the war (2.25.2); Agis was the first Spartan king to suffer the indignity of having overseers follow him into the field by way of censure for a previous mistake (5.63.4). The Spartans, who owe their virtues quite strictly to their regime and their laws, differentiate less among themselves on the score of virtue than other cities do. One might almost say that they hold not only great honor, but great virtue, in suspicion, seeing it as a menace to the solidity of their community.

We can begin to understand on the basis of these considerations how much dissonance is involved in Alcibiades' activity at Sparta. Not that the Spartans when left to themselves succeed always in following the ideal just laid out—Thucydides informs us occasionally of more or less significant splits in the Spartan community that disturb the normal appearance of uniformity and unanimity. For example, in the midst of the Peace of Nicias, he speaks of factions in Sparta for and against the peace, somewhat like those at Athens, the party opposed even attempting to

---

[15]The Spartan regime might seem in this respect like the Athens of the Funeral Oration, whose citizens are exhorted by Pericles to find their glory in serving the most glorious city, Athens. Pericles, however, was attempting with his appeals to common glory to satisfy individuals who were anything but self-effacing. Perhaps more important, Pericles' common glory was cut off from piety and many of the moral ideals that traditionally make the city an honorable enterprise and the city's glory an honorable prize. The Spartans are in a peculiar sense more resolutely egalitarian than the Athenians. Their regime shows the close connection between political community and some kind of equality. See 1.6.4 and the discussion of this point in chap. 1.

subvert the treaty after it is formally ratified (5.36, 38.3, 39.3). There were also significant disagreements among the Spartans as to whether the city should go to war in the first place (1.80–88). Indeed, the fact that the Spartans have now explicitly invited Alcibiades, an outsider, to collaborate with them is something of a departure (6.88.9). But whatever they know of Alcibiades, they cannot have foreseen the profoundly distorting effect that his presence and his activity will have on their city. Alcibiades takes the largely suppressed divisions of interest and rivalries in the city and systematically plays upon them to build a politics of personal honor and prestige. He injects the animus that would be necessary to make Sparta a vigorous and dynamic power, but he threatens thereby to shake the very pillars of the Spartan polity. In the long run, the Spartan reaction to this can only be one of alarm, even abhorrence.

Indeed, after a period of activity in Ionia in his own inimitable style, Alcibiades is repudiated by the Spartans and condemned to death. The Spartans take this action, according to Thucydides, because Alcibiades had become an enemy of King Agis and in general seemed "untrustworthy" (*apistos* 8.45.1). It is doubtless a sign of Alcibiades' versatility that he thus becomes the only man to be condemned to death by both sides in the war. The charge of untrustworthiness, which haunts Alcibiades at Sparta and Athens both (8.51.3), is connected in fact to his versatility. What the charge represents is doubt as to where Alcibiades' allegiances really lie. The cities suspect, understandably enough, that they lie with Alcibiades only, on account of his extreme devotion to his own honor or prestige. The difference between Alcibiades' devotion to his personal honor, on the one hand, and narrow self-interest, on the other, is admittedly a subtle one. Alcibiades' quest for personal distinction will confer the greatest benefits on any city he serves, but it makes him willing and able to serve any city he chooses. And he will serve only so long as a city tolerates his terms. If it does not, he will consider himself free to pursue his ambition elsewhere. Sparta, of all cities, is least likely to tolerate Alcibiades' mode of proceeding, and the Spartans are least likely to see any difference between Alcibiades' love of honor and narrow selfishness. The love of honor, which traditionally links the interests of the statesman to those of the city, is nevertheless capable of detaching a statesman from the city or of dividing the community by rivalry. The Spartans, however, are devoted first and foremost to the integrity of the city as a community. The Athenians, who are devoted

127

more to political individualism, do not enjoy unqualified success as a community in Book Eight.

The Spartan regime of course has defects of its own, which put the Spartans at a distinct disadvantage when Alcibiades begins to work against them. After his eviction from the Spartan camp, Alcibiades flees to Tissaphernes, the Persian satrap, and proceeds to prey on Spartan weaknesses with great success. The notorious corruptibility of Spartan commanders away from home is one consequence of their dependence upon the community; Alcibiades, in his capacity as advisor to Tissaphernes, turns to bribing the Spartan commander Astyochus. Astyochus' complicity with Alcibiades and Tissaphernes for the sake of gain has the effect of virtually paralyzing the Peloponnesian effort in the East (8.45.3, 50.3, 83.3). Alcibiades also persuades Tissaphernes to slacken his support for the Peloponnesian navy on the grounds that he should not allow either side the upper hand in the war. By these measures, as well as by promising the Peloponnesians the aid of the Phoenician fleet without ever delivering it, Alcibiades and Tissaphernes succeed in sapping almost entirely what vigor and enterprise the Peloponnesian navy had begun to show (46.5). Vigor and enterprise are the qualities the Spartans need to make gains in the East but defensive caution and even lethargy are their characteristic traits, and they prove all but defenseless against the kinds of stratagems Alcibiades uses against them.

Alcibiades himself is now working unequivocally to bring about his recall to Athens. Thucydides announces near the beginning of Alcibiades' partnership with Tissaphernes that this is his goal in damaging the Spartan cause: so long as Athens is not destroyed, Alcibiades knows he will be able to secure his recall to the city, "by persuasion" (47.1). His first advice to Tissaphernes, to allow neither side the upper hand in the war, may well be the most pro-Athenian advice that he could have given on the occasion: Alcibiades tells Tissaphernes to leave the Athenians in control of the sea and to share dominion with them rather than with the Spartans (46).[16] This fact deserves attention particularly because the

[16]The immediate effect of this advice would be to weaken the Spartan position drastically. Given the fact that Tissaphernes was already allied to the Peloponnesians, Alcibiades probably could not have pried him further away from them than he does here. It might also be noted that when Alcibiades was still with the Spartans, his advice to attack Athenian interests at Chios rather than in Euboea, where King Agis wanted to proceed, was itself the most sparing of Athenian interests. The loss of Euboea would have been

advice to play the Athenians and the Spartans against one another, taken too much to heart perhaps by Tissaphernes, subsequently proves a great stumbling-block to Alcibiades' attempt to bring Tissaphernes whole-heartedly into the Athenian camp.[17]

Alcibiades begins his actual attempt to return to Athens, which opens the next phase in Thucydides' narrative, by suggesting privately to some in Athens that the democracy which exiled him be overthrown in favor of an oligarchy (47.2). It might look from this as though Alcibiades' experience at Sparta has taught him something new about the significance of regimes. But Alcibiades was always aware that democracy had vices, and that those vices had been responsible for his exile from Athens. This did not prevent him from displaying a certain affinity for democracy even in his speech at Sparta. It may be closer to the truth to say that Alcibiades' move here is dictated by the fact that inspiring a change of regime was simply the ordinary way in the Greek cities to bring about a recall of exiles. It is in connection with Alcibiades' attempts in this regard that Thucydides endorses the opinion of the Athenian commander Phrynichus that Alcibiades does not really care about the regime that prevails in the city, so long as he is allowed to return (48.4). Once back in the city, it is safe to say, Alcibiades' activity would fall into the pattern it has always followed, tending to bring the political life of the city as a whole under its spell.

It does not seem then that Alcibiades' apparently newfound preference for an oligarchy in Athens is dictated by any real change in political views. As a matter of fact, Alcibiades does not learn anything in the course of Thucydides' History about the importance of regimes. This must be considered something of a defect, in the light especially of his

---

an incalculably greater threat to Athens than the loss of more remote possessions in the East.

[17]See even Xenophon *Hellenica* 1.5, where this problem persists for Alcibiades and the Athenians. It may be that Alcibiades gave this "even-handed" advice in part to hold out on the Athenians until they should actually recall him; he uses Tissaphernes' alleged willingness to help as a bargaining chip with Athens. The fact remains though that Tissaphernes becomes too attached to the idea of a war of attrition for either Alcibiades' or Athens' good. G. B. Grundy, *Thucydides and the History of His Age*, 2 vols. (Oxford: Blackwell, 1948), 2:84, thinks that the one tactical mistake of Alcibiades' career was his failure to side with Lamachus on the question of the strategy for Sicily (6.47–49). I am more inclined to think that this piece of advice to Tissaphernes might take that title. Cf. H. D. Westlake, *Individuals in Thucydides* (Cambridge: Cambridge University Press, 1968), p. 260n. The subject will also be discussed in chapter 4.

129

experiences at Sparta. The defect has its roots in his own very strong view of politics, which essentially circumvents the question of regime. This perspective nevertheless has its justifications. Alcibiades does not learn on this subject, but he teaches others who do not know, that overwhelming pride along with overwhelming ability form a combination that is capable in effect of suspending many regimes.

Alcibiades and Phrynichus

Thucydides makes the drama of Alcibiades' struggles to return from exile center in its early phases around the contest between Alcibiades and the Athenian commander Phrynichus. Phrynichus is an otherwise obscure historical figure whom Thucydides elevates to a role of some importance in this part of the History.[18] His career follows a striking pattern. He begins by opposing the oligarchic plot and the recall of Alcibiades, both in the name of the public good, but in the end becomes one of the most hardened members of the oppressive oligarchy itself.

Phrynichus is sent to Ionia as a commander shortly before Alcibiades begins his intrigues there; he quickly shows himself to be a good and loyal commander. He contributes to a great and unwonted victory over the Persians and the Peloponnesians at Miletus, then prudently orders a withdrawal to prevent his force from falling into enemy hands (8.25, 27). When Alcibiades makes his first overtures to the leading men in the army concerning an oligarchical coup, Phrynichus opposes him vehemently, on unimpeachably patriotic grounds. He mistrusts Alcibiades, correctly believing that Alcibiades cares nothing for any regime but only desires to return to Athens; he expresses concern above all that the Athenians not, under the present circumstances especially, become factious (8.48.4). When the plot and the movement for recall appear to be succeeding nonetheless, Phrynichus feels compelled to take drastic steps against them. But his motives are no longer so pure. In order to avoid the personal retribution that he believes would come with Alci-

---

[18]There has been some scholarly comment on the great exposure given to Phrynichus by Thucydides. Westlake thinks that Thucydides is simply exaggerating the importance of Phrynichus, in part in order to develop some contrasts with Alcibiades (*Individuals*, pp. 421–47, 315). I believe the Phrynichus affair is an example of the Thucydidean device of putting unusual emphasis on an episode in order to develop a theme associated with it.

biades' return (on account of his initial opposition to it), Phrynichus proceeds to betray the conspiracy even though that might scuttle the city's hopes for Persian aid (50.1–3). When Alcibiades and the oligarchs subsequently fall out, Phrynichus joins the oligarchic party himself in a rapid about-face, motivated once again by fear of Alcibiades (cf. 68.3). He remains with the oligarchy even through its moments of greatest violence and excess, and he is finally murdered by anti-oligarchical conspirators (90, 92.2). Thucydides, in his brief synopsis of the men who formed the oligarchy, says that Phrynichus was of all the oligarchs the most zealous for the whole undertaking, due to his fear of Alcibiades (68.3).

The initial conclusion that the reader is tempted to draw from Thucydides' presentation of the course of Phrynichus' career is that Phrynichus, a perfectly serviceable and even exceptional commander, was more or less driven to treason by the insidious influence of Alcibiades, or Alcibidean politics. Phrynichus acted under the strong impression that he had to fear the worst reprisals if Alcibiades were allowed to return, in spite of the fact that his original opposition to Alcibiades was entirely public-spirited. Phrynichus' fear is obviously based on his observation of Alcibiades' highly personal political style and his opposition to such men as Nicias on clearly personal grounds; to that extent, his action appears reasonable and the entire episode appears to be a serious indictment of Alcibiades. Alcibiades seems to play the same jealous and corrupting role toward his rivals that the Athenian *demos* played toward some of Athens' greatest statesmen in the past, forcing them into actions detrimental to the public good in order to save themselves. However, Phrynichus' fear of Alcibiades is unwarranted: Alcibiades' personal politics are not vindictive and certainly not physically dangerous to his opponents.[19] One can understand Phrynichus' fear to some extent, and Alcibiades must share some of the blame for its effects. The whole affair does establish a certain link between Alcibiades' politics and the weakening of the city's cohesion, on account of the intense rivalries that he

---

[19]See chap. 2. It is true that once Phrynichus has begun to betray the Athenian cause, influenced by his opinion of Alcibiades' vindictiveness, Alcibiades attempts to have him put to death (50.4). One need not be vindictive, however, to see a need to get rid of political enemies who are also betraying the city. There is no other political opponent in the History against whom Alcibiades makes such a move, not even those responsible for his exile from Athens.

creates. The example of Phrynichus to that extent represents a vindication of the Spartans' insight: Alcibiades' politics is corrosive to the city. But this judgment ignores the fact that the dialectic of self-interest which reaches a peak in the oligarchy of the Four Hundred, has been developing independently at Athens for some time already. Alcibiades, Phrynichus, and the oligarchs are also actors in this larger Athenian drama. The provisional judgment on this episode also abstracts from the fact that Alcibiades' self-interest is different from that of others, particularly that of the oligarchs. Alcibiades' alone is capacious enough to encompass the public good and to be the salvation of the city. Both of these qualifications are crucial in understanding Thucydides' treatment of this part of the war.

Phrynichus reminds us initially of the earlier Athenian general Demosthenes. He is both very clever and very devoted to the good of the city. At Miletus, like Demosthenes during the Sicilian campaign, he advises withdrawing from a fight rather than risking a serious defeat for Athens. Phrynichus, like Demosthenes, advises this course of action fully aware of the displeasure such actions always arouse in the Athenians (8.27; cf. 7.47.3, 48.3–4). Demosthenes' advice, which is overruled by Nicias with disastrous results, was governed by a recognition of the extremely precarious situation that the Athenians were in after the failure of his night assault on Syracusan positions (7.43–44). Phrynichus in Book Eight, working within the new and very threatening balance of forces created by the debacle in Sicily, refuses to risk his fleet at Miletus in an attack on a Peloponnesian fleet the size of which he does not know. In spite of the fact that he, unlike Demosthenes, has just won a victory, Phrynichus refuses to consider anything before the preservation of the fleet, which represents Athens' only hope in the war (8.27). Thucydides seems to praise Phrynichus for this action, and even to praise him in advance for actions he will later take: on account of his present and subsequent actions both, Thucydides says, in this and in other situations, Phrynichus won the reputation of being "not unintelligent" (*ouk axunetos* 8.27.5). His action here is well advised indeed: the Persians and Peloponnesians, on Alcibiades' advice, were preparing to defend Miletus at all costs (26.3). Phrynichus withdraws from Miletus to Samos and there establishes the base that becomes the secure center of Athenian operations in Ionia for the remainder of the History.

It is at Samos that Phrynichus becomes the most vocal early opponent of the oligarchic plot and of Alcibiades' return. Thucydides scrupulously details Phrynichus' reasons for opposing the plot, which reveal a lively concern for Athens' best interests as well as a high degree of political intelligence (48.4–7). We have already noted his concern about factionalism and his recognition that Alcibiades cares only about having himself recalled to Athens. For the rest, Phrynichus doubts that the Persians could ever be induced to support Athens, even under an oligarchy that included Alcibiades. He argues that Athens' subject cities will not become more loyal if their governments are changed to oligarchies to comport with the revolution in Athens; they will only be induced to strive for freedom outright, regardless of the regime that is offered them. In fact, Phrynichus professes to be certain that the subject cities believe the *demos* in Athens to be a moderating influence on the so-called "gentlemen" who would come to power in an oligarchy, and therefore that they prefer democracy in Athens over a potential oligarchy. Phrynichus even indicates his agreement with the allies on these points.[20] These arguments prove remarkably prescient.

Thucydides' presentation of Phrynichus in general is remarkable for its detailed explanations of the reasons and motivations for his actions.[21] The reason for this seems to be not only that Phrynichus is a very thoughtful and astute commander, but that over time his outlook develops in a way that parallels his unusual career. The development of Phrynichus' logic in fact sheds light on a number of important Thucydidean themes. Not only his actions but his thought is symptomatic of larger changes that are taking place at Athens. Alcibiades plays an important, but still only an auxiliary, role in all this.

The first time we see Phrynichus in action, and the first time we are told of his thoughts, is in connection with the action at Miletus. Thucydides summarizes Phrynichus' arguments to his fellow commanders as to why they should abandon Miletus and retreat rather than fighting (27). It would scarcely be permissible, given the problematic state of Athens' affairs, to risk a decisive battle even if their forces were fully prepared and the strength of the enemy known; but it is completely

<hr/>

[20]Phrynichus says that the allies have drawn their understanding from the facts themselves, indicating thereby that theirs is the true understanding (48.7).
[21]Cf. Westlake, *Individuals*, p. 242; Delebecque, *Thucydide et Alcibiade*, p. 95, makes a similar observation about this section of the History in general, suggesting the reason is that psychology is unusually important to understanding this part of the war.

inexcusable now to hazard the whole fleet in ignorance. The greater and more interesting part of Phrynichus' reasoning, however, is devoted to a defense of his action on the grounds of honor. After all, ordering a retreat after winning a victory would ordinarily be considered a great disgrace.

Phrynichus begins by declaring that in circumstances like the present, he would never give way to considerations of shame and run risks unreasonably (27.2). Phrynichus implicitly maintains a distinction between the shameful and the unreasonable: the desire to avoid shame or to defend honor can well lead to unreasonable—that is, suicidal—actions, and Phrynichus in his capacity as commander declares the reasonable more important. He does not leave it at that, however. Phrynichus proceeds in effect to redefine shamefulness and nobility, bringing them into line with reason, that is, self-preservation. It is not shameful, properly understood, to retreat—the most shameful thing in these circumstances would be to suffer a defeat that would bring the city not only shame but mortal danger as well (27.2–3). Concerning ordinary notions of honor or nobility, according to which honor must somehow transcend mere self-preservation, Phrynichus implies that he has the courage or fortitude to resist them. The language in which he rejects these old notions (he says that he refuses to "give way" to vulgar shame) even suggests a quasi-heroic act of will, a new kind of courage on Phrynichus' part.[22] His eyes clearly set on the preservation of the city itself, Phrynichus overrules his colleagues' rash sense of honor and commands the Athenian forces to withdraw.

To us, Phrynichus' arguments and actions may seem nothing more than the astute application of reason to the situation at hand. After all, it makes a great deal of sense to say that self-preservation and not honor is the primary goal of cities as opposed to individuals. Thucydides' own apparently favorable judgment of Phrynichus in this passage suggests the same. What is less clear in this context, though

---

[22]The word I am translating as "giving way" is *eikein*, which appears in Homer and the tragedians and is used among other things to describe the battles of heroes. Pericles uses this word in his first speech in Thucydides to warn the Athenians against "giving way" to the Spartans (1.141.1) and in his third speech as an exhortation against giving in to misfortune (2.64.3). Phrynichus' curious inversion, refusing to "give way" before shamefulness itself, is very striking in the context. It also suggests comparisons with Plato's Socrates, who uses the same and similar inversions.

perhaps more clear to Phrynichus' colleagues, are the consequences of discounting the claims of ordinary honor so thoroughly and on principle. The seemingly universal attachment of nations to an ideal of "national honor," even under the most difficult circumstances, seems to point to a problem that Phrynichus' impeccable logic may have slighted. The briefest way to understand this problem is to consider two parallel instances from earlier parts of the war, the case of Melos and the case of the Spartan soldiers at Pylos. The Melian episode reveals terribly the futility of insisting on honor in the most difficult circumstances. It also reveals the tenacity of that notion of honor even in the face of such circumstances. Honor does not in itself provide for compromises of honor in duress, even when necessary for survival's sake; nor does it like to distinguish between individuals and cities on this score. Traditional honor, in cases of real duress, is more likely to retreat into pious hopes for divine aid, which are its ordinary supports. Thus while it is true, as the Athenians say to the Melians, that from the point of view of political necessity the Melians are simply fools, consideration of the strictures of honor tends to cast the Melian episode in a more tragic light. The Spartans, more men of the world perhaps, choose the expedient rather than the strictly honorable route when confronted with a lesser dilemma of the same kind. A number of their best men are trapped on the island of Sphactereia by an attacking Athenian force. The Spartans cut a rather comical figure: when communicating with the men trapped on the island they prove utterly unable or unwilling to advise them whether to fight valiantly to the death or to capitulate, in spite of the fact that the loss of so many hoplites would be a severe blow to the strength of the city. The Spartans' paralysis forces the men on the island to choose for themselves; they opt for survival (4.38.2–3). The paralysis itself, though, is testimony to the difficulty of the dilemma from the point of view of a city like Sparta: necessity itself is a very problematic excuse for doing the apparently dishonorable.[23] This dilemma haunts

---

[23]Xenophon reports the later case of the Spartan commander Callicratidas, who, in a situation more like that of Phrynichus, categorically refuses to retreat (*Hellenica* 1.6.32). He leads the Peloponnesians in their defeat at Arginusae.

This issue is connected to a very broad theme in Thucydides' work. Thucydides' discussion of the causes of the war in Book One, for example, revolves partially around this dilemma, particularly as it relates to the Spartans. The Spartans feel "compelled" to

the Spartans even after the fact: the men recovered from Sphactereia are later temporarily deprived of their political rights, out of fear that the dishonor they were presumed to have incurred might spur them to some subversive action (5.34.2).

Presented objectively with the choice between honor and survival, especially for the city, it is difficult to fault a preference for survival; nevertheless, we can imagine that this Spartan action is the kind of thing that the Athenians on Melos have in mind when they say that the Spartans above all others consider the pleasant to be honorable and the expedient just (5.105.3). Honor and expediency are not the same thing, and the Melian case shows that every viable city must occasionally prefer expediency over honor. That being the case, it seems that the question only remains whether this is done by means of some kind of hypocrisy, as the Athenians accuse the Spartans, or by a more consistent, outright rejection of honor as ordinarily understood. It is a credit to Phrynichus' sophistication that he sees the implications of the conflict between honor and survival at its extreme and that he makes the uncompromising argument he does. His intelligence in this respect is also of course Athenian intelligence, since the Athenians have argued from the beginning of the History that necessity or expediency is the ruling force of politics among cities, a force that negates the moral imperatives commonly thought to have a place there. The Athenians have traditionally applied this argument against others, their imperial subjects or prospective subjects like the Melians, and now Phrynichus applies it, in the matter of honor and self-preservation, to the Athenians themselves. He continues in this way the admirable Athenian tradition of intellectual honesty or consistency, though perhaps with some unanticipated consequences.

The consistency can be seen by comparing the logic of Phrynichus to the logic of the Athenians on Melos. The latter maintain that it is foolish to stand by a pretense of honor unless one has the power to defend it (5.107, 111.3). Honor is a seductive thing, requiring intelligence and fortitude to resist it (111.3), though the Athenians give contrary indications as to whether relinquishing honor for necessity in this way is

___

go to war to protect themselves from Athenian power (1.23.6); yet they do not consider such a reason, based merely on necessity or interest, publicly defensible as a reason for breaking their treaty with Athens. This is part of the reason why this "truest cause" should have been broached "least in speech." The dilemma thus pointed to is part of Thucydides' subject in his famous discussions of true causes versus pretexts for the war.

itself a disgrace (111.3, 4). All the major points of Phrynichus' argument are here. One argument that the Melians attempt to level at the Athenian position is that some day the tables may be turned: the Athenians may become the weaker and be confronted with harsh necessity themselves (90). The desperate situation of Athens in Book Eight is to some extent a fulfillment of that warning; and Phrynichus does not hesitate to apply the Athenian logic with consistency. He withdraws from Miletus with victory half-accomplished, in spite of the fact that on Melos the Athenians boasted that their city had never lifted a seige for fear of an enemy (5.111.1). Demosthenes' advice at Syracuse anticipates Phrynichus in this, but Phrynichus provides or applies the argument that makes this kind of action possible systematically and in principle. The result in the circumstances is a much-needed liberation of prudence from the constraints of the old understanding of honor, such that the city's preservation can now be served completely and unabashedly. This is perhaps the last of the old, traditional constraints on the behavior of the city that Athens has not yet given up.

Phrynichus, however, after the retreat from Miletus and the arguments connected with it, after his subsequent resistance to the oligarchic plot and the recall of Alcibiades, all on the most public-spirited grounds, quickly begins to go bad. He eventually proves prime material for the oligarchy himself. At each stage he gives carefully reasoned arguments for his actions, all of which claim that necessity has compelled him to prefer his own interest. If one of the objects of Thucydides' History is to show how the Athenian logic of justice and necessity inexorably destroyed the city from within, and how the "compulsions" of profit and self-interest destroyed that of honor in the Athenian thesis on empire, the career of Phrynichus is one of the vehicles for that theme.

Phrynichus' first betrayal of the city is connected to his opposition to the recall of Alcibiades. In spite of his outspoken opposition, an oligarchic conspiracy is formed among the Athenians at Samos, and they resolve to get Alcibiades back. Phrynichus thereupon attempts to prevent at least the recall by secretly informing the Spartan commander Astyochus of the plan, denouncing Alcibiades to his erstwhile allies the Spartans. Thucydides does not speak any longer of a desire on the part of Phrynichus to prevent the oligarchy as such, since the plot seems to be succeeding; he is motivated exclusively so far as we know by fear of

Alcibiades' vindictiveness (50.1). The secret message to Astyochus bears an explanation from Phrynichus to the effect that it is excusable for him to harm a personal enemy of his even at the cost of some harm to his own city (50.2). Phrynichus is aware that he is betraying Athenian interests; he openly admits that he is acting not for the city's good in denouncing Alcibiades but for his own good. When this letter, which Astyochus passes to Alcibiades, causes Alcibiades to denounce Phrynichus to the conspirators and urge that he be put to death, Phrynichus is moved to write a second letter to Astyochus, this time offering to betray the entire Athenian fleet to the enemy. Once again, he includes a defense of his action, claiming that it is excusable for him to do this, or anything else, rather than perish himself at the hands of his worst enemies.[24]

These arguments and actions are extraordinary enough in themselves, particularly given Phrynichus' earlier record. But in Thucydides' narrative the description of Phrynichus' public-spirited opposition to the recall of Alcibiades (48) and the episode in which he displays willingness to betray the whole Athenian cause to save himself (50) come so close together as practically to shock the reader. This appears to be a case of the Thucydidean device of paradoxical but thought-provoking narrative juxtaposition. The abrupt about-face is caused—and excused according to Phrynichus—by his fear of reprisal from Alcibiades, an argument which as we noted has a certain plausibility to it. There is also, however, a striking affinity between Phrynichus' logic in the episode of Miletus and that which he offers in his letters to Astyochus. Phrynichus began

[24]8.50.5. There are a number of different interpretations of these episodes. Jean Hatzfeld suggests that the supposed letters of Phrynichus to Astyochus might have been pure fabrications of Alcibiades, designed to incriminate his opponent (*Alcibiade* [Paris: Presses Universitaires de France, 1951], p. 236). He gives no real evidence for this, however. Delebecque (*Thucydide et Alcibiade*, p. 87) argues that Phrynichus' second letter, written in the knowledge that Astyochus is a creature of Tissaphernes, is part of an elaborate plot by him to discredit Alcibiades by making it appear later, when Alcibiades sends a second denunciation, that he is simply attempting to slander Phrynichus. That is in fact what happens (8.51, 68.3); Phrynichus in any case turns things to his own advantage before the second denunciation arrives, making him the only person in the History to outsmart Alcibiades. That the second letter should be merely feigned treason seems to me unlikely, because of the astonishing argument that Phrynichus appends to it to excuse his treason, an argument that he later shows he takes fully to heart. Cf. Pouncey, *Necessities of War*, pp. 133–34; Malcolm F. McGregor, "The Genius of Alcibiades," *Phoenix* 19 (1965):27–46.

by replacing the demands of ordinary honor, in the case of the city itself, with the consideration of mere survival. This is precisely what ordinary, less clever and less enlightened cities and statesmen shrink from doing. We find him arguing not much later that his own self-preservation justifies his betrayal of the city. Phrynichus' public-spiritedness, as great as it at first appears to be, dies in him rather easily, and the reason seems to be that it was slightly too clever all along. Alcibiades' political style appears to put Phrynichus in a rather difficult situation, but he already has half the argument ready that will allow him to prefer his own good to that of the city, in need.

The case of Phrynichus suggests that once the city's actions are bereft of honor in principle, or once the city's honor is explicitly subordinated to expediency—once the city ceases to be a noble enterprise in that specific sense of the word and directs itself self-consciously to mere survival—it begins to give up the pretense that its survival is higher or more important than that of any individual, a pretension that obviously lies at the heart of any viable patriotism. In the case of Phrynichus at least, the heritage of Athenian imperialism leads to this result by a double route, both by preparing the argument that expediency is higher than honor and by creating the desperate situation, that of Book Eight, in which that argument must be developed and applied in all its rigor. The Spartan and Melian attitudes toward the honor of the city, by contrast, embodying respectively perhaps its comic and tragic extremes, reflect an important political truth as well as a difficult political dilemma. We as observers can distinguish between the requirement that individuals rate honor above their lives and the sense in which cities cannot do so; but it seems that honor itself is not so subtle a thing. The subtle Athenians are exasperated by the Melians' refusal to relinquish their honor, but behind that exasperation is a failure to understand something about politics.[25] That defect of understanding, and all that it implies, is the single greatest reproach to Athenian sophistication in Thucydides. The argumentation of Phrynichus is its first indication. The career of the oligarchy, which represents the culmination or degeneration of Athenian logic on self-interest and rule, explores this theme to the fullest.

---

[25]Cf. Connor, *Thucydides*, p. 154.

*The Regime of the Four Hundred and the
Internal Decay of the City*

The story of Phrynichus is the prelude to the moral saga of the Four
Hundred, but Alcibiades is the first mover of the oligarchic plot as
Thucydides recounts it. The question of Alcibiades' relation to the rise
of the oligarchy begins with much the same ambiguity that the question
of his relation to the corruption of Phrynichus did. The first that we
hear of the oligarchical conspiracy in Thucydides is that it is a proposal
of Alcibiades; but Thucydides points out immediately that even more
significant for the development of the plot was the fact that the most
powerful Athenians at Samos were already leaning to the overthrow of
the democracy (47.2). Alcibiades' overture solidifies this movement perhaps, but he does not bring it into being or give it its primary impetus.
Once the plot is under way, Alcibiades and the conspirators part ways
rather quickly. The history of the oligarchy in fact suggests that Alcibiades caused its corruption even less than he caused the corruption of
Phrynichus. On the other hand, the initial concord between Alcibiades
and the oligarchs does reflect some kinship. When Alcibiades supplants
the failed oligarchy later, it represents in some respects only the fulfillment of the promises and the hopes that the oligarchic movement was
originally based upon.

With regard to the oligarchic plot and the oligarchy itself, we could
choose to believe that, like Phrynichus, it began its career with some
genuine public-spiritedness.[26] Thucydides says that the conspirators'
original hope was both to bring the direction of the city's affairs into
their own hands and to prevail over the enemy (48.1). There were
grounds enough for doubt that the democracy could prevail in the war,
given its previous record and the new and more precarious circumstances
after the disaster in Sicily. Alcibiades' initial argument in favor of the
plot, one the conspirators also use, is that the aid of the Persian king
and of Alcibiades can be reasonably hoped for only if the city gives up
its fickle and untrustworthy regime (48.1, 53.3). The oligarchy is urged

[26]Ibid., pp. 221, 224. Connor argues that Thucydides presents the oligarchy as a
corrupt sham from the start. I believe Thucydides' presentation of it is somewhat more
ambivalent in the beginning at least, if only because of the real public needs the oligarchy
responds to. Thucydides implies later that the oligarchy was to some extent defensible:
see 8.68 and my discussion of that passage, below.

in the name of moderation and steadfastness, for the sake of survival; the crucial rhetoric of Peisander, which finally persuades the Athenians to accept the oligarchy, centers precisely on these arguments. The part of his speech counseling "moderation" is the only instance of directly quoted speech in Book Eight (53.3). Peisander argues that the establishment and support of an oligarchy are essential to the public interest and required by public-spiritedness. The Athenians, in what is incontestably a great display of public spirit, relinquish the democracy and accept the oligarchy.[27] But none of this is meant to deny that the oligarchy itself, once established, degenerates markedly and rapidly from its concern from the public good. That it did degenerate is certainly a fact, and not even a surprising fact.

Alcibiades and the oligarchs part company when Alcibiades proves unable to bring them Persian support. Thucydides remarks at this point that the oligarchs' aim is still to bring Athens to victory in the war, though with a somewhat greater tincture of self-interest: their zeal is now said to be fortified by the thought that their labors in Athens and the war are undertaken for none but themselves (63.4). After the successful establishment of the oligarchic regime in the city, their rule becomes ever harsher and more lawless; and they also become increasingly perfidious to Athenian interests in the war, making secret overtures to the Spartans for peace (70.2, 71). The harshness of their rule soon begins to threaten their hold over the city. The army stationed at Samos overthrows the oligarchic party there, elects to remain staunchly democratic, and comes to look upon the oligarchy in the city as an enemy outright. When the army subsequently recalls Alcibiades of their own accord, the oligarchs, in a virtual panic, begin to contemplate the height of treason: they prepare to betray the city to the Spartans, if necessary, in order to save themselves. Thucydides says at this point that they still hope to preserve the oligarchy, the city, and the empire; failing that, they hope to maintain the independence of the city and their position in it; but if the need arises, they are willing to admit the Spartans into

---

[27]Thucydides says that the *demos* was "taught" by Peisander (and by their fear) of the necessity of submitting to the change, which they hoped it is true to undo later. This is in contrast to the soldiers at Samos, whose primary motivation in acquiescing to the oligarchic movement seems by Thucydides' account to have been the easier prospect of money from the Persians (48.3). The army at Samos proves to be more anti-oligarchic than the city itself throughout this episode.

the city itself rather than to suffer personally the revenge of a restored democracy (91.3). It is clear from Thucydides' account that Phrynichus is among those willing to carry things that far (92.1; cf. 68.3, 90.1). Others among the oligarchs were not; for the oligarchy itself had by then begun to disintegrate on the now familiar principle that private ambition and interest take precedence over public and even party loyalty.[28]

The combined stories of Phrynichus and of the Four Hundred, which thus end with the triumph of the most narrow individual interest over everything else, are the characteristic events of a certain phase of the war in Athens, but they represent as well a culmination of one of the major themes in Thucydides' History. Throughout his book, Thucydides explores the critical question of the relation between public and private in political life and the nature of the balance between them. Political life obviously depends upon bringing public and private together somehow, but Thucydides forces us to contemplate continually their natural tendency to break apart. We watch the complete triumph of private over public good in the civil wars at Corcyra and elsewhere and a similar process in the plague at Athens (3.81–83; 2.49–54). When we finally see the political community and the public interest effectively collapse at Athens during the period of the oligarchy, we are forced to wonder what the status and grounding of the political community and the public interest were to begin with. To the extent that we are possessed by doubts on this score, we might be more inclined to sympathize with the oligarchs, who were responding to the problems reflected in those doubts. The oligarchs, over the course of their career, take the Athenian thesis on self-interest and rule and apply it to the domestic politics of the city. One of the corollaries of that thesis is that there is no community among cities; power dictates the relations among them. If we conclude that community or public interest within the city are illusory, we must admit that the action of the Athenian oligarchs is justified on parallel grounds.

This is a possibility that all serious students of politics, and not only

---

[28]Cf. 8.89. This fact alone shows that it is not sufficient to interpret the episode of the oligarchy as a simple manifestation of Greek loyalty to party over city, as some have done, but as part of a larger moral drama typical only of the war and periods like it. Cf. chap. 2, n. 27, above.

students of Thucydides, must confront. The most striking indication he gives that it is a serious possibility is his praise of the oligarchs themselves. We have already noted his apparent praise of Phrynichus' intelligence (8.27). Thucydides inserts a chapter in the midst of his narration of the history of the oligarchy, a kind of digression, naming the major conspirators and describing briefly their qualities (8.68). The tone of the passage is somewhat surprising: the men Thucydides without exception describes as individuals of great natural gifts. It was hardly unaccountable, he says, that the oligarchic plot should have succeeded in spite of its great difficulty, being guided by such a wealth of intelligence (68.4). The most striking and most notorious part of this passage, though, is Thucydides' description of the oligarch Antiphon as a man second to none of the Athenians of his time in "virtue" (68.1). The case of Antiphon, on which Thucydides puts the greatest emphasis in this digression, is paradigmatic of certain larger themes brought out in this part of the History. Antiphon, according to Thucydides' description, was most able in conception and in his ability to explain what he had in mind. Although he was not the most conspicuous of the oligarchs, he was the one who put together the plan by which the conspiracy succeeded and who had been concerned for the longest time with it. In spite of his great intelligence and eloquence, Thucydides says, Antiphon had never undertaken a public career under the democracy and indeed had never willingly spoken in public at all. Thucydides suggests that the reason for this was that he was regarded with suspicion by the people, precisely on account of his reputation for skill and cleverness. We seem to see here a paradigmatic case of the suspicion of the Athenian *demos* toward men of talent or accomplishment. Antiphon chose never to expose himself to their jealousy, but he had apparently been contemplating establishing an oligarchy in the city for some time. We cannot say from Thucydides' description whether his motive in doing this was resentment at the democracy or simple desire to gain some control over the affairs of the city, whether it was to gratify his ambition or simply to improve on fickle democratic policy. We can say with certainty that the *demos* was partially responsible for driving him to this course of action.[29] Even after the fall of the oligarchy, according to Thucydides,

---

[29]Thus it is not enough to say that Antiphon, who has some of the talents of Pericles, is to be blamed for not following Pericles' path in politics (see Connor, *Thucydides*, p.

Antiphon did the best job, standing before the city on trial for his life, of defending the deeds of the oligarchy themselves.

One of the striking things about this portrait of Antiphon is the fact that Thucydides evidently does not consider his actions to impugn his "virtue." This suggests that Thucydides considers those actions to be somehow defensible, that Antiphon's defense was to some extent credible to intelligent people. Beyond that, praising Antiphon for virtue, very great virtue at that, implies a significant revision of what is ordinarily meant by virtue. The Greek word Thucydides employs here, *aretē*, can signify excellence of many kinds, but its general connotation is moral. In applying this word to Antiphon, Thucydides obviously has in mind his political skill and intelligence, or more generally what we might call his natural gifts. These things can all be forms of *aretē*, but the fact that Thucydides uses the word in an absolute sense produces a moral paradox that has drawn comment.[30] He creates the same kind of paradox by describing the Peisistratid tyrants of Athens as "virtuous" men (6.54.5).

These paradoxical formulations are not the products of haphazard composition on Thucydides' part; they are only the most striking examples of a general pattern that emerges in Thucydides' use of the word *"virtue"* in the History. Thucydides uses this word quite rarely in his own name.[31] The word itself appears frequently enough, for the most part in the mouths of Thucydidean speakers who use it in its conventional, moral sense. This usage predominates especially in the first several books of the History. Thucydides' own references to *virtue*, as opposed to those of his speakers, are always ambiguous or paradoxical, and that quality becomes controlling in the final books, where speakers tend to fall silent about it. That virtue should be less often appealed to or extolled in public reflects perhaps the weakening of social and political bonds in general later in the war. Thucydides himself, to judge from his usage,

---

225). That no one followed in Pericles' footsteps is not only due to the eclipse of conventional virtue on the side of the leaders. This is one of the primary themes of this passage I believe, and of the treatment of Alcibiades as well.

[30]David Grene, for example, emphasizes the moral inversion implied here (*Man in His Pride*, [Chicago: University of Chicago Press, 1950], pp. 80–83) and contends that for Thucydides the virtue of Antiphon, a statesman's virtue, is the ability to manage political events and bow ruthlessly to political necessities. See also Westlake, *Individuals*, p. 209, and J. T. Hooker, "*Charis* and *Aretē* in Thucydides," *Hermes* 102 (1974):164–69.

[31]According to Bétant's *Lexicon Thucydideum*, there are five such instances. In fact there are at least six: see 1.2.4; 2.51.5; 4.81.2; 6.54.5; 7.86.5; and 8.68.1.

is very ambivalent toward what he calls in the case of Nicias "law-bred virtue."[32]

Something of the character of Thucydides' ambivalence, and its bearing on the grounding of the political community, might be seen in the following. The reference to Antiphon's virtue is Thucydides' last use of the word in the History as we have it; its first appearance, which is also Thucydides' first use of it in his own name, occurs very early in the Archaeology of Book One, where Thucydides says that cities founded in fertile regions were early subject to attacks from without and sedition within because of the excess of wealth produced by "the virtue of the soil" (1.2.4). Both these Thucydidean references seem to treat virtue as a purely natural excellence, one moreover that is potentially dangerous to the integrity of the city. This in turn might suggest the following. Virtue of the sort that Antiphon typifies is a kind of rich human soil on which the city is built but whose own natural vocation is not clearly civic or political. The city is built on it as a kind of artifice, supported by it but not entirely in harmony with it. In the case of the actual soil, excessive fecundity destroyed cities by (among other things) fostering factious strife. Cities built in less fertile regions were more often spared that fate. According to the Archaeology, Athens was one of the latter and enjoyed early, tranquil growth, while Sparta, built on fertile soil, was for a long time plagued by more sedition than any other city that Thucydides knows (1.18.1). The Spartans were finally given by law the stable regime for which they are famous; its stability depends on what

---

[32] 7.86.5. The epithet is *aretēn nenomismatēn*, which I translate loosely as "law-bred virtue," not meaning to minimize the complexities or the difficulties of the phrase. On some of the complexities see Dover, in Gomme, *Historical Commentary*, 4:461–64; Grene, *Man in His Pride*, pp. 71, 81; Westlake, *Individuals*, pp. 209–10; Leo Strauss, *The City and Man*, (Chicago: University of Chicago Press, 1977), pp. 150, 207–209; Connor, *Thucydides*, p. 205n.53.

A brief synopsis of the Thucydidean uses of *virtue* listed in n. 31 may help to give a sense of the ambivalence I detect in his attitude. (1) 1.2.4 refers to the virtue of the soil in fertile regions of Greece, which made those regions targets of conquest and centers of sedition in ancient times. I make some use of this in my discussion below. (2) At 2.51.5, Thucydides refers to the pretense of virtue that led some to care for plague victims at the cost of their lives. (3) 4.81.2 refers to the virtue and intelligence of Brasidas and represents probably the least problematic of Thucydides' uses of this word. (4) 6.54.5 refers to the virtue and intelligence of the Peisistratid tyrants of Athens, using the same phrase that was applied to Brasidas. (5) 7.86.5 refers to Nicias' "law-bred" virtue. (6) 8.68.1 refers to the virtue of Antiphon.

we might call a rigidly enforced domestication of human virtue, one of the goals of which is to produce in the citizens a certain uniformity of virtue itself. One might say metaphorically that the Spartans have rendered their human ground somewhat arid by design, for the sake of stability. Athens, by contrast, as Pericles proclaims most beautifully, has a regime that encourages the greatest possible human richness and brings forth the most luxuriant and diverse foliage. These robust and untethered plants eventually come into their own in the city. Antiphon is one of their number; Alcibiades is another.

This account conforms to the problem of Antiphon's virtue and his place in the Four Hundred, as well as to the larger problem of talent or virtue and political leadership as posed by Thucydides. Thucydides introduced this theme in his treatment of the natural genius of Themistocles. He ascribes to Antiphon some of the same natural perfections characteristic of Themistocles' leadership, namely, his ability to conceive courses of action and to expound them to others (1.138.3; 8.68.1).To these two qualities Pericles added patriotism and superiority to money (or bribery) to complete the profile of statesmanly virtue as ordinarily understood in the cities (2.60.5). Pericles' career comes closest to epitomizing this profile, but his example does not do away with the problem raised by other talented Athenian statesmen. Pericles is not praised as highly as is Themistocles for natural gifts, and he is not called virtuous as Antiphon is.[33] We can only conclude from this, and from the example of Alcibiades, that political genius is related only coincidentally to conventional virtue. If anything, judging from the totality of examples Thucydides gives us, there is a certain tension between them: virtue as genius

[33]Themistocles is not called virtuous by Thucydides either, although his talent would seem to fit most of all the definition of virtue suggested by Thucydides' praise of Antiphon. I made use of Thucydides' silence on the virtue of Themistocles earlier to develop the point that moral virtue and political talent are separate things for Thucydides (see chap. 2). I believe Thucydides calls Antiphon virtuous in Book Eight because he has been preparing the reader gradually for this otherwise scandalous revaluation. After all, to suggest that political expertise and conventional virtue are different is one thing, but to allow amoral genius or expertise to replace conventional morality as the core of virtue is quite another. Thucydides seems to develop a number of themes in this incremental fashion; I have argued that apparent discrepancies in Thucydidean terminology and thematic treatment, which have often fueled the controversy about the dating of various segments of the History, are to be explained in this way rather than as undigested changes in the Thucydides' outlook. On this point, see also Connor, *Thucydides*, pp. 10, 15–18; White, *Words*, p. 88 and n39.

146

resists narrow attachment to the place of its origin, and it even resists the kind of domestication that conventional morality represents. This tension is only heightened by the suspicion of the *demos*, which can drive a man like Antiphon to sedition. The existence of this natural tension, of course, also justifies some of the democratic suspicions. The dilemma formed on one side by the amorality of political talent and on the other by the partly justified and partly excessive suspicion of the popular mind, is the dilemma Thucydides indicates is central to evaluating Alcibiades (cf. 6.15).

This is not to deny that the lucky combination of qualities found in Pericles is the most politically viable one. Pericles' manner and his career represent a certain golden mean that commands our admiration. However, we must resist the temptation to exaggerate Pericles' greatness. The pleasing spectacle of Periclean Athens depends on a number of fortuitous elements. It occurs at that moment of Athenian history when the empire is at its height but the logic of imperialism has not yet seriously eroded public harmony at Athens. The city is fortunate enough to find in Pericles a leader with great natural gifts but also a dedication to traditional notions of public service, although those were notions that some of his own policies were indirectly working to undermine. The harmony created by this is indeed beautiful and desirable but it is also in an important way artificial or conventional. The question before us now is whether political talent, indeed natural human capacity as such, is essentially inhospitable to the city, whether man is in any sense a political animal; whether the political community has any secure grounding. The fact that Antiphon and the Peisistratid tyrants are the only rulers Thucydides refers to without qualification as "virtuous" raises the question forcefully, since they ruled by force or without consent, suspending in effect the political community of the city. Even Pericles' success, in Thucydides' view, was connected to the fact that his rule effectively suspended the regime in the city and imposed de facto rule of the first citizen (2.65.9).

Since this is one of the deepest questions that Thucydides' History presents us with, we must be certain to consider it in the broadest possible context. This question has two sides for Thucydides. The tensions between men of genius and the political community suggest that there is something unnatural about political community. This is one of the most important lessons to be learned from Thucydides' treatment of statesmanship in the History; but against it, and against the many indications in Thucydides that human nature and the political community are somehow at odds, must be weighed other lessons we learn just as surely from Thucydides. Thucydides unquestionably imparts to his readers an appreciation for civic harmony and a sense that the Greek cities, in their prime, represent a genuine peak of human accomplishment. The fact that Thucydides sees this as a peak implies that man does somehow attain his perfection in properly functioning political societies—that he is a political animal. Even the tensions between political community and the natural genius of leaders could never have come into being prior to the flourishing of the cities themselves, in the weak and barbarous times of the Archaeology, for example. Civilization and political community are thus the setting for human flourishing. But that flourishing produces the seeds of its own destruction. Perhaps nature itself is equivocal in the kinds of perfection it bids us to seek.

The paradoxically difficult relationship between individual political genius and the political community is one facet of this broader problem in Thucydides. Athens is of course the critical case, since it has liberated human nature to the greatest degree, at the level of leaders and citizens both. Or, in the idiom Thucydides has developed, Athens has liberated human eros. Pericles attempted to hold the city together by focusing this eros upon the city and the power of the city. When Athenian erotic passion reaches its peak at the time of the Sicilian expedition, however, two things become clear: not only does that passion incline heavily to the most extravagant imperial adventures, but it also seems to divide the Athenians as much as it unites them. According to Thucydides, the erotic longing for Sicily took three forms. For the older men it stemmed from the notions of conquest and the safety of the expedition; the young fell in love with the idea of faraway sights and spectacles; and the rest, the majority, fell in love with the prospect of eternal pay (6.24.3).

This trifurcation of erotic passion in the city, precisely at the moment of its greatest flowering, suggests that even if such passion can be focused upon a common object—the expedition to Sicily or the power of the city—erotic passion in itself is highly individual. Eros is private; at its peak at least it resists community. In a sense, therefore, to call a city erotic is a misnomer. Eroticism is not fundamentally political and cannot ultimately be domesticated for the purposes of the city, even by a statesman of Pericles' stature. The political domestication of human nature, along Spartan lines for example, requires the suppression of eroticism instead. To the extent that the democracy at Athens is erotic, its model is the eroticism of Harmodius and Aristogeiton, an essentially private and even selfish passion that entered the political realm and took on the appearance of public-spiritedness. To the extent that eroticism lies at the foundation of Athenian imperialism, the empire is ultimately devoted to the private gratification of each Athenian. Free human eros as exhibited at Athens settles in the end upon no higher object than that. This is precisely what Thucydides' description of the motives for sailing to Sicily indicates.[34]

The degeneration of Athenian imperialism into private aggrandizement is inevitable in part, therefore, because private gain stood behind that imperialism all along. Athenian imperialism itself had to degenerate, however, before it could finally infect the domestic politics of the city. The Athenian imperial argument, as it moves from the expansion of the city to the aggrandizement of the individual, itself degenerates as honor or nobility in the city decays. When the Athenian emissaries to Sparta first make the case for Athenian imperialism, before the war, they contend that the city's expansion is justified by the compulsions of honor, fear, and profit (1.75.3, 76.2). By the time of the Athenian action on Melos, honor has effectively been dropped from the Athenian account of the empire; the empire is maintained for the sake of profit and safety alone. This accounts for much of the new mean tone of the Athenians on Melos, but in retrospect the change is inevitable. The Athenians by the time of Melos have already been told, by Pericles and Cleon both, that their empire is a tyranny or is like a tyranny (2.63.2; 3.37.2). This is the only name that can honestly be given to rule imposed on others in disregard of justice, which is what the Athenians have always conceded their empire to be. Pericles believes honor and tyranny to be somehow compatible in the empire,[35] but the combination is tenuous to say the

---

[34]The "old men" are the only ones for whom this is not clear: their thoughts seem to revolve much more around the simple question of safety (6.24.3). The eros of "the young," or those in the prime of life, poses special problems because it seems to have the greatest element of generosity or disinterestedness in it. They long for faraway sights and spectacles (*opseis, theoriai*). This, however, only accentuates the private or apolitical character of their longing.

[35]Cf. 2.63.1, 2. Pericles' language is ambiguous as to whether the empire is a tyranny or like a tyranny, but I do not see that the difference is significant in this context. Perhaps

least, and he seems finally to resolve the honor he believes the Athenians will get from their tyranny into mere grandeur or brilliance (2.64.3, 5–6). Pericles is the last to defend this synthesis of honor and imperialism explicitly at Athens. When Thucydides describes the Athenian passion for Sicily, which by proximity is a complement of sorts to the Melian episode, love of honor plays no part in it. For the majority of the Athenians, the empire now represents profit and safety alone.[36] Not only are their motives for the expedition private rather than public-spirited, by and large they are base. The eroticism of the city as city (using the phrase advisedly again) even at its most brilliant peak, proves to be not only private but for the most part rather low. The Athenians overthrow the divine law, usurp the place of the gods, and even aspire implicitly to immortality, but in an all-too-human way. Most of them fall in love with the prospect of eternal pay. Much of the meanness and oppressiveness of the empire itself must be traced to this fact.

The Athenians began with the claim that honor is a primary goal and a prime justification of the empire, but two things conspired to make honor disappear from the groundwork of the empire. First, the Athenian *demos*, in its cupidity, proves not to be too concerned with honor; second, a fatal blow is delivered to the notion of honor when the pure right of the stronger is maintained against traditional divine law and public restraint. These things are related. It stands to reason that the city should cease to care about honor once the gods and the divine law, ordinarily the sources and supports of honor, have been overthrown. This fact, and the internal decay of Athens that it presages, might be called the true revenge of the Melians upon their Athenian oppressors. It is not, as the Melians suggest, that the Athenians may have need of the law of

---

the empire could only be "like" a tyranny because tyranny strictly speaking is the rule of one man over one city. See also Euphemus' comparison of Athens to a tyrant at 6.85.1.

[36]Romilly points out that since the empire was founded on the democracy, on the sailors and the poorer classes, its motivation was necessarily economic in significant part (*Athenian Imperialism*, pp. 74–75, citing pseudo-Xenophon *Constitution of Athens*). She says that Thucydides indicates this "in passing" in 6.24. Thus as she sees it the empire always had two simultaneous motivations: the Periclean love of honor and the cupidity of the "man in the street" (p. 79). She argues, as we have noted before, that this tension is present in the Athenians' speech at Sparta (pp. 255–57; see also my chap. 1, n. 46). I agree with the general point concerning the tension between divergent motives, but I think that the dialectic of honor and profit in the empire has to be investigated in greater detail than Romilly has done.

justice when they are at the mercy of some stronger city (5.90), but that they need it for the continued integrity of their own city. The unrestrained and unadorned rule of power represents the triumph not of honor but of self-interest.[37] The fantastic Athenian experiment, an attempt to tap the tremendous power and serve the aspirations of human beings released from practically every restraint, produces not a new race of gods but a merely human and rather fragile empire.

A word may be said in light of this about the alternative that we can call ordinary or conventional politics. That alternative may look comical next to Athens at the height of its powers, but it gains a certain luster from Athens' decline. The ordinary city lives with a whole series of muddling compromises that Athens disdains. One is the mixture of justice or honor and expediency in the city's international activities, veiled inevitably with some degree of hypocrisy. Similar compromises mark such a community's management of the tension between the public and private interest. These compromises and this hypocrisy though serve the function not only of maintaining the integrity of the community but paradoxically of giving it some elevation. The liberation of Athenian individuals from civic and moral restraints leads not only to a weakening of public-spiritedness but to debasement of the political motivations and concerns of most of those individuals. Most human beings, left to their own devices, do not it seems conceive particularly elevated passions or aspirations. The restraints, in particular the pious restraints, characteristic of regimes such as Sparta may thus be seen to serve an elevating—or perhaps an educative—function, not simply a repressive one. The Spartan compromise of the peaks of human virtue and talent at least prevents individuals, and the city as a whole, from sinking into certain kinds of debasement. The Spartan compromise between justice or honor and expediency, which sometimes offends consistency or even shocks decency, avoids at least the Athenians' outright rejection of justice, and the systematic unleashing of private interests within the city. The ordinary political mentality is best embodied in Athens by Nicias, who declares in his speech before the Sicilian expedition that in his under-

[37]Grene formulates this in an interesting way: the powerful imperial city at its peak attains to a kind of transcendence, but in the end the object of its transcendence is nothing but the city itself. The transcendence is therefore precarious (*Man in His Pride*, pp. 83–86). I argue that it is precarious precisely because the transcendence is not, and cannot be, complete. The city as city is too wedded to lower economic or material concerns.

standing, the best citizen is one who cares for honor certainly, but who also has a certain sober concern for his own preservation and his property in the city, and hence who is dedicated to the good of the city in part out of concern for his own good (6.9.2). This is a rough and imperfect combination of honor and expediency, public and private interest, but it has a certain solid respectability.[38] Both Nicias and the Spartans come under rather easy charges of hypocrisy when extreme circumstances force them to choose expediency for themselves over justice or noblility. The Athenians, however, come to grief and even to a certain repentence after rejecting that muddling way.

The Athenians' repentence, however, is not and probably cannot be complete. The Athenians can not go back in earnest to the old piety or the old understanding of honor. They have seen and known too much. After the sacrilege of the Hermae and the appearance of Euphemus, after the crushing defeat of the Sicilian force, which Nicias at least is inclined to interpret as punishment for Athenian hubris (7.77.3), they still resolve to retain their empire at all costs. This resolve opens Book Eight. The Athenians' astonishing recovery from the brink of disaster in Book Eight is not based upon any return to piety, although it is based upon significant political changes whose keystone is a newfound moderation or restraint. To that extent, the political form that evolves in Book Eight and reaches its culmination in the regime that recalls Alcibiades represents something new again from the ever-innovative Athenians. The oligarchy, and the Athenians' acceptance of it—out of moderation—may be seen as faltering steps toward this goal. This is not to say that the Athenians could do better, given the problems that

---

[38]Lowell Edmunds argues that Sparta and all ordinary cities are characterized by the primacy of self-interest and that it was the innovation of Periclean Athens that made the public interest primary (*Chance and Intelligence in Thucydides* [Cambridge: Harvard University Press, 1975], pp. 84–85, citing Strauss, *The City and Man*, p. 170). All cities, however, are characterized by more or less unstable combinations of public- and private-interestedness; the important thing, it seems to me, is to see with greater precision how the balance is struck in different cases. In the case of Athens, there is a wide variety of scholarly pronouncement (most of it alluded to already) on either the individualism or the selflessness of its citizens. This seems to reflect the difficulty of sorting this balance out in the case of Athens, as well as the different phases Athens goes through. In addition to Edmunds, see Grene, *Man in His Pride*, p. 31; Finley, *Thucydides*, pp. 146–49; Nathan Marsh Pusey, "Alcibiades and *to philopoli*," *Harvard Studies in Classical Philology* 51 (1940); Anton-Hermann Chroust, "Treason and Patriotism in Ancient Greece," *Journal of the History of Ideas* 15 (1954).

confront them. The oligarchy represents the low point of Athenian political cohesion and highlights all the questions concerning the naturalness of the city as such; it is not clear that the new restraint at Athens is the stuff out of which political community in the city can truly be reconstructed. Its most obvious blemish is the fact that it represents moderation in adversity, moderation that owes its birth only to the desperate circumstances that the Athenians find themselves in, and not to any independent discovery of the choiceworthiness of virtue.

The viability of this new Athenian solution, like that of the Periclean solution and even the traditional political solution, is tied up with the problem of the natural foundations of the city. We have become aware that human virtue, human erotic passion, and human nature itself stand in an ambiguous relation to political community. When Diodotus speaks of the recalcitrance of human nature, even when the laws attempt to restrain it, his argument is that at least its erotic character is fundamentally at odds with the city, both lawless and irrepressible (3.45). The very possibility of real moderation, which would in this context be an essential political virtue, is doubtful at best. The Spartan counterexample is anything but conclusive. The greatest praise that Thucydides gives the Spartans in Book Eight, in common with the Chians, who seem to have a similar regime, is that they are the only two cities of which he knows that are at once prosperous and moderate (8.24.4). He later reveals that the Spartans and Chians also have more slaves than any other city that he knows (8.40.2). The moderation of the Spartans and Chians is conditioned by the fact that they must keep constant vigil over huge populations of slaves; thus it is no more true moderation in prosperity than is that of the Athenians.[39] Since at Sparta the Helots are in fact peoples conquered in old, expansionist wars, they are the emblem of former Spartan imperialism. One might even read out of Thucydides a moral history of the Spartans, as follows: the Spartans indulged in imperialism until they reached the limit of their power, then they retreated into a kind of pious hypocrisy contrasting the imperialism of others with their own self-restraint, a hypocrisy all the more effective for being invisible to the Spartans themselves. Spartan moderation is

---

[39]On the necessity of dealing with the Helots as a fundamental determinant of the Spartan constitution see Grundy, *Thucydides*, vol. 1, chap. 8; 2:176; Finley, *Thucydides*, p. 122; Edmunds, *Chance and Intelligence*, p. 84.

thus "artificial" not only in the sense that it is produced within the city by a rigid set of conventions but also in the sense that it is a product of the oppressive necessity of maintaining their empire. Spartan reserve or timidity, their military prowess, their extreme dedication to the community of Spartiates, and even their pessimistic or diffident form of piety are all connected to this artificial constraint. The Spartan path to moderation and political cohesion thus is not entirely what it seems.

This is of some interest for the understanding of the Athenians, who by Book Eight seem to have reached the limits of their power or even exceeded it, but who do not retreat into the Spartan mold. In part they do not retreat because they have seen and known too much, in part because they are in too much trouble—timid moderation would be all but suicidal for them now. The Athenians have indeed felt the temptation to react in the Spartan manner to duress, demonstrating how natural a reflex that is for the city. There is the outpouring of pious sentiment after the sacrilege of the Hermae and the subsequent turn to Nicias; but such impulses can be seen almost as clearly in the speeches of both Cleon and Euphemus. Euphemus believes that Athens has met if not exceeded her limits as an imperial power, and he outlines a possible imperial policy that is genuinely defensive in intent and diffident in attitude. Cleon, whose career predates the desperate Athenian situation of Book Eight, nevertheless has a lively sense both of Athens' danger as the mistress of an empire and of the difficulty of controlling the democratic assembly at Athens. His speech at the time of the Mytilenaean affair in some respects compares to the speech of the Spartan king Archidamus as much as to any speech of Pericles, whom he is obviously trying to imitate.[40] Cleon argues that ignorance combined with moderation is better for a city than the Athenians' excessive sophistication and love of novelty. In effect he asks the Athenians to obey the laws without thinking too much about their merits or demerits, because such potentially subversive free thinking is a luxury the city can no longer afford: the precarious situation of the empire means any mistake or miscalculation of policy is potentially suicidal. Thus, with the subjects of Athens' imperial tyranny awaiting

---

[40]Speech of Archidamus, 1.80–85; Cleon, 3.37–40. This parallel has received some attention before, but there has not been the proper emphasis on the common political psychology it reveals. The more common comparison is obviously that between Cleon and Pericles.

only the opportunity to revolt, Cleon bids the Athenians in the case of Mytilene to think only of justice, by which he means the interests of the city according to the friends-versus-enemies perspective of the crudest civic consciousness. In this, Cleon resembles not even Archidamus but Sthenelaidas, who represents the cruder side of the Spartan mentality. All of Cleon's quasi-Spartan arguments can be traced to the peril he believes the city to be in. They shed interesting light on the case of Sparta as well as Athens, and indeed on key aspects of the conventional political consciousness as such.

The Athenians, however, do not follow Cleon; they do not, even under the most dire circumstances of Book Eight, retreat into a quasi-Spartan hypocrisy in foreign affairs. Even Cleon has the honesty to admit that the empire is a tyranny, though he clearly does not want to consider, and does not want the Athenians to consider, the implications of this fact for his argument about the justice of punishing the city's enemies. Athenian frankness does not desert them at that moment or at any moment up to the end of Thucydides' History. Nor do the Athenians develop within the city the kind of moderation or unquestioning obedience to laws that the Spartan community is based upon. But they do develop their own kind of moderation by the beginning of Book Eight, and a fresh dedication to the public good. In fact, public-spiritedness never completely dies at Athens, in spite of the forces that tend to overwhelm it. It dies in certain individuals or classes of individuals, and in the city it does seem, by Book Eight, to require more direct external threat to assert itself unambiguously, but at those critical moments it continues to rise to that level of impassioned dedication that Pericles describes, an intensity that even the Spartans cannot match.[41] This con-

---

[41]This is an important point in the comparison between Athens and Sparta, and it is shown by Thucydides in a number of ways, some of which are discussed in the text. An interesting paradigm is provided in an early naval battle between Phormio and a Peloponnesian naval contingent commanded by Brasidas, among others. In exhortations to their troops before the battle, the Spartans appeal in the final instance to the self-interest of each soldier, promising honor for valor but punishments for cowardice (2.87.9). Phormio, by contrast, tells his Athenians only to think that the welfare of the city depends on their success (89.10). The Athenian dedication to the city, when it exists, is immediate, in the sense of unmediated (see Strauss, *The City and Man*, p. 170; Edmunds, *Chance and Intelligence*, pp. 84–85). This seems to derive from the peculiar Athenian regime and continues to distinguish Athens from her opponents at least until the early parts of the Sicilian campaign (see, e.g., 6.69.3). The problem with this kind of devotion at Athens, as I have argued at length, is that it is not stable or reliable, particularly in times

tinues to hold true to the end of the History; and Book Eight, in which the tyranny of the Four Hundred is established, also paradoxically describes Athenian moderation and public-spiritedness under duress reaching new heights. The Athenians begin by introducing new moderation into the direction of the city's affairs, particularly in the matter of money (8.1; cf. 8.97), and deferring to the counsel of older men. They give over their habitual jealousy of prominent leaders, also in the name of moderation (8.53). The first fruit they reap from this patriotic restraint is the tyrannical oligarchy. The oligarchy is eventually overthrown, however, in an even greater display of public spirit, and the regime of the Five Thousand, the best Thucydides has seen at Athens in his lifetime, is established (8.92–97). The Athenians simultaneously vote to recall Alcibiades.

The Return of Alcibiades

The triumph and subsequent degeneration of the oligarchy of the Four Hundred, with all the questions it raises about the city's solidity, is only the penultimate episode in Thucydides' History as we have it. The establishment of a new, nontyrannical regime in the city, and the recall of Alcibiades, form its culmination. These developments seem to augur the city's salvation in the war and the healing of its political wounds. Whether this promise is actually fulfilled must be considered on both a practical and a theoretical level.

The moderation the Athenians display in Book Eight culminates paradoxically in the recall of Alcibiades, the most immoderate of men. This is evidently a moderation that acquiesces in the immoderation of Alcibiades, and also somehow in his political claims, well known to all in Athens. The moderation that recalls Alcibiades is in this sense the same as the moderation that acquiesced in the initial establishment of the oligarchy in the city. The oligarchy failed ultimately to preserve the interests of the city in even the most basic sense. Against this background, Alcibiades, recalled first as a general of the Athenian navy on Samos and then to the city itself, brings about once again the fulfillment of the public interest at Athens, at least in the basic sense. But he does not do

---

of prosperity—it has its own element of selfishness, one that in the long term is more virulent than any other.

this in the conventional way, by subordinating his private interest to the public interest of the city. He does it, we can fairly say, by encompassing the public within his private interest.

Alcibiades' unique ability to combine public and private might even be said to be the primary difference between him and the oligarchs. When he replaces them, he does not so much refute their logic or the logic of the Athenian past as embody it in such a way as to make his own and the public interest necessarily coincide. This is a dominant theme of Alcibiades' political rhetoric, but it is more than mere rhetoric, for his superiority in this regard is precisely one of speech or conception: Alcibiades is incapable of conceiving his interests, his ambitions, or his actions in terms more limited than those of an entire community. Unlike the oligarchs he is not a party man; his defect is if anything the opposite—he is unable to conceive his acitivities and interests in terms as narrow as those of a single city. And Alcibiades, unlike the oligarchs, is distinguished by his ability successfully to operate on this plane.

When Alcibiades returns to the Athenian side and revives the city's prospects, the promised reconstruction of the city cannot be along conventional lines. Alcibiades is a representative of what we have called "natural" or unconventional virtue in its most untamed but also probably its most brilliant form. He does what he does not by reshackling prudence to notions of selflessness and conventional virtue but by giving it freer play than ever, over a field no less restricted than the city or the war as a whole. Alcibiades is also a representative of self-interest, but not narrow self-interest. If honor traditionally links the self-interest of the statesman to the broader public interest, then Alcibiades' unique serviceability is connected to the fact that he, perhaps alone among political figures, is still concerned seriously with honor rather than simply with profit or safety—that is, if it is possible to speak of honor without reference to the virtues that traditionally define it. *Honor* may in Alcibiades' case refer to nothing more than the fact that his self-interest is capacious enough to contain the public interest within it. The question of Alcibiades' conception of honor, and thus of his ultimate usefulness to the city, must await consideration of the events leading to Alcibiades' recall to Athens and the recall itself. That story teaches us much about both Alcibiades' usefulness and the limits of his use, for politics.

When Alcibiades begins in earnest his attempt to return to Athens, Thucydides gives to Phrynichus the most thorough argument against recalling him. According to him Alcibiades cares neither for oligarchy nor democracy but merely wants to return to the city by whatever means possible; the Athenians should be concerned only that they do not, in these dire circumstances, fall into factions (8.48.4). Phrynichus treats Alcibiades' indifference to regimes as a reproach to his politics; he equates it with an indifference to the good of the city and with exclusive devotion to his own interest or to that of some party. Alcibiades' indifference to regime seems to make him a factious figure not only in the present circumstances but altogether. Phrynichus' initial opposition also involves a preference for democracy over oligarchy: in the present regime it is the *demos* that has restrained the so-called "gentlemen" from the worst excesses (48.6). Phrynichus seems here to envisage the oligarchy as a kind of untrammeled rule of the Athenian demagogues; he certainly does not distinguish Alcibiades from that crowd of politicians he thinks would come to power in an oligarchic coup. Yet that such a distinction must be made is clear; it is the very point of departure for understanding this part of the History. Thucydides himself implies as much when he says before Alcibiades' Sicilian speech that it is the city's turning to those other leaders that leads to Athens' final ruin (6.15). We must keep this remark in mind, especially here: insofar as it means that Alcibiades' leadership is the only hope the Athenians have of maintaining the city and prevailing in the war, it implies that the Athenians in their own most pressing interest must accept Alcibiades on his own terms. For his views and his political style are constants and indeed are connected to the services he offers to the city.

One problem presented by the final segment of the History is the fact that the relation between this imperative and what seems to be the other great hope for Athens at the conclusion of the History—the regime of the Five Thousand—is anything but clear. The virtue of the regime of the Five Thousand consists in its "measured" blend of the few and the many (8.97.2). Alcibiades in his speech at Athens argued that his political solution was the one that appropriately blends all the different parts of the city (6.18.6), but we were forced to conclude that it relied so much on the preeminence of someone like Alcibiades that it in fact bypassed the arrangements characteristic of "regimes." Alcibiades' effect on the regime of the Five Thousand, which we have to believe is a rather fragile flower, must in the long run be distorting or worse.[42] Yet Alcibiades' unique serviceability is connected precisely to his indifference to regimes and his consequent distorting effect on any that happen to be in place. Alcibiades embraces and advances the public interest, but he does so by making it his own, by almost appropriating the entire public realm to himself, by standing over and directing the whole without the mediation of institutions that regimes make use of. We can nevertheless give a number of reasons for the necessity, vouched for by Thucydides, of recalling Alcibiades. Some of them have to do with the present situation, but others are connected with the character and the needs of the Athenian polity itself. In its dire predicament the city has need of its greatest commander, but the democracy at Athens always had a certain need for authoritative direction outside the democratic principle.

The parallel between Thucydides' praise for Pericles and his praise for Alcibiades is illuminating in this respect. The prudent Pericles attained such a position that the city in his time became a democracy only in name (2.65.9). In the eulogy where Thucydides says this, he also gives us his first overview of the decline and eventual defeat of Athens; the most comprehensive reason he gives for it is that Pericles was freely accorded a preeminent position in the city while none of those who followed had the same authority (2.65.7–10). In the parallel passage concerning Alcibiades, Thucydides again alludes to the decline and destruction of Athens, attributing it to the city's rejection of Alcibiades (6.15). Athens always needs such a figure, one whose leadership is so strong as practically to usurp the authority of the democracy, in order to function successfully. The character of Alcibiades, however, and of Alcibiades' times, virtually redefine this necessity. Alcibiades as opposed to Pericles comes into his own at a time when the Athenian logic of self-interest has run its full course and the centrifugal forces of democratic individualism are much more in evidence. The solidity of the political

---

[42]It is difficult to know exactly what to make of Thucydides' praise of the Five Thousand, in part because its historical existence is so shadowy. It certainly had a short and fragile life. Aristotle's *Constitution of Athens*, for example, mentions it once in passing, then drops it entirely in the recapitulation (33–34, 41; cf. also Grundy, *Thucydides*, 2:20). Wettergreen, "On the End of Thucydides' Narrative, " *Interpretation* 9 (1979), argues that the existence of the Five Thousand, in effect the rule of the hoplites, was predicated not only on the absence of Alcibiades from the city but on that of the whole naval population, who were at Samos. The problem of the Five Thousand is discussed further below.

community is more in question than it ever was in Pericles' time. And during this period the city is in greater peril than it was at any moment in Pericles' career. These are the circumstances that lead to Alcibiades' recall. They also serve as a fair indication of why that recall is traumatic for Athens.

The novelty of this historical situation and of the new politics it requires is indicated both by the trauma it brings upon the city and by the fact that an intellegent man like Phrynichus, who in other respects is able to see what the new conditions require, is still opposed to Alcibiades, on grounds that are in a sense obsolete. Phrynichus is aware that the traditional notion of the honor of the city must be dispensed with, but he does not recognize that his opposition to Alcibiades on the grounds of regime has in effect also been overtaken by history. This is a point of some importance in understanding the behavior not only Athens of but of the other cities in Book Eight. Peisander ultimately convinces the Athenians to suppress the democracy and in principle to accept Alcibiades by arguing that the city must become moderate, which he bluntly explains to mean that it must concern itself less with questions of regime and think simply of its own salvation (53.3). The Athenians are persuaded. The grave danger that requires the subordination of honor, as Phrynichus argues, also forbids overly fastidious attention to questions of regime.

Nor does this harsh necessity affect only the Athenians in Book Eight. Phrynichus himself argues in opposing the oligarchic plot, that the Athenian allies have by now learned to consider the question of regime as secondary; they will prefer freedom over any regime, oligarchic or democratic, that the Athenians offer them (48.5). When Phrynichus is shown to be correct, Thucydides explains that the cities had acquired "moderation" and hence preferred freedom to the sham of "good laws" offered by the oligarchs.[43] Within the context of Book Eight—a desperate fight

---

[43]8.64.5. An interesting rendition of this passage has been proposed by Connor (*Thucydides*, p. 222), based upon the notion that *moderation* and *freedom* are slogans or euphemisms used by the oligarchic and the democratic factions in the cities respectively. The suggestion that Thucydides is playing ironically on the political rhetoric of the parties in this passage is well taken, though I think Thucydides' use of these terms here is more than just irony. Moderation of precisely the kind described is something Thucydides shows actually developing in Athens and in the other cities. Thucydides here speaks of this moderation being learned by whole cities and not just factions, although one might have expected him to speak only of the oligarchs in the cities under the reading proposed.

for independence and survival on all sides—moderation manifests itself as a refusal to attend to any but the most supreme and needful goals, independence and survival. This represents an enforced return to genuine concern with the interest of the city as a whole—that is, the public interest—but it is a diminished and a limited return, focusing on only the most pressing and most minimal concerns of public deliberation, those prior to the question of regime. This represents a real contraction of political life. The new moderation allows the city to pull itself together while essentially setting aside the divisive question of regime; but from the point of view of the political community indifference to regime is a severe curtailment of public life, of the scope of public deliberation, and of the human ends that it can serve.

This applies to Athens and to the subject cities both. The moderation the Athenians develop during the course of Book Eight is both an admirable quality and the emblem of Athens' distress and perhaps disfigurement. It is partly in this light that the recall of Alcibiades has to be considered. The Athenian moderation in duress has the flavor almost of martial discipline and makes the beleaguered city look increasingly like an armed camp, surrounded by the enemy. In fact, as Book Eight progresses, the city of Athens and the Athenian armed camp proper, the army stationed at Samos, increasingly resemble each other. Shortly after the establishment of the oligarchy in the city, the army revolts and retains its staunchly democratic constitution, in effect constituting itself as a city in its own right. Thucydides calls the meetings of the Athenian soldiers during this period *assemblies*.[44] It is not coincidental that the army, thus constituted, rather than the city, is the first to recall Alcibiades: an army is more amenable to the direction of one man, whose authority stems from expertise.[45] Alcibiades returns as a military com-

---

Hence the "immunity" (*adeia*) they have gained seems to come not from their newly oligarchic status but from the unsettled state of affairs at Athens. Connor appears to overemphasize the grammatical opposition between *moderation* and *freedom* here by reading *antikru* in place of the *antikrus* of the manuscripts. The passage is in any case a difficult and complicated one.

[44]*Ekklēsiai*, 8.76.2; 77; 81.1. See also *xunepoliteuon* 73.6.

[45]This point is complicated, but also corroborated, by the fact that the leading office in the city of Athens itself had, well prior to this, become the generalship. The generalship was assigned by election and not by lot, due to the expertise required (cf. pseudo-Xenophon, *Ath. Pol.* 1.3). In some respects this was a revealing happenstance, since it meant that real political leadership in the city always assumed the form and title of military rank.

mander at the head of a community that is more military than political. Although the city itself also recalls Alcibiades before the end of the History (8.97.3), we see him only in the role of general and advisor to the army. What we see is nevertheless a very revealing glimpse into the conditions and effects of the politics of Alcibiades triumphant.

The episode in which the Athenian soldiers on Samos seize their independence from the city, resolving to rely on themselves and chart their own course, is one of the most touching in Thucydides. Impelled by their loathing for the lawlessness of the oligarchy at Athens, of which they receive exaggerated reports, they declare their independence from the city. But independence from the city that is their home is a profoundly unsettling prospect for them. They hold an assembly to arrange their own affairs in which, as Thucydides describes it, men rise in their places to make reassuring speeches to each other (76). It was the city that rebelled and not they; they have ample resources to maintain themselves and are even better circumstanced than the city in that regard; in the worst event they can go anywhere and establish themselves; and the city by its revolution has become incompetent to provide them with good counsel, which is the only reason cities have control over armies. By holding out, they hope to bring the city back to democracy. They elect new generals and rulers and tell themselves that if they vote the recall of Alcibiades as well, he will secure them the aid of the Great King himself.

What makes this spectacle touching is the quiet courage almost of desperation that the Athenian soldiers display in their plight, as well as their patriotic devotion to a city that in their minds barely exists any more. Thrust out on their own practically against their will, they muster all the resolve that they can. They do somehow constitute an "assembly," but we cannot make too much of that fact. Their situation is an epitome of the harsh and disfiguring situation that cities find themselves in in Book Eight; the soldiers' assembly may serve as an epitome of what has become of public deliberation as well. The soldiers are concerned for their survival and deliberate only as a beleaguered army. Thucydides does not characterize their activity as deliberation but calls their speech in this first assembly mutual exhortation or encouragement (77). It is in this spirit that they look to the return of Alcibiades. In due course they vote his recall, and after he is brought back he addresses them himself.

Thucydides reports two speeches of Alcibiades to the soldiers on Samos (8.81–2, 86). They mark an epoch in the history of Book Eight and of Alcibiades' career, as his first addresses to an Athenian audience since his exile. They are also his last in the History as we have it—only glimpses of his reunion with Athens as an orator and a statesman rather than just a general or strategist. In certain respects this second coming together of Alcibiades and the city is more perfect than the first. It is certainly more enduring, and it is instrumental in healing the city's wounds.[46] More than that, Alcibiades' return to Samos and his speeches there, can be interpreted as paradigms of Alcibidean rhetoric and as the fulfillment of his declared ambition to have the firm directorship of a political society. The fact that Alcibiades attains this position in a society that is political only in a qualified or diminished way is not entirely accidental and in fact serves to accentuate the problems with his politics. Similarly, the speeches he delivers to the troops on Samos are immensely successful from a rhetorical point of view, but as pieces of deliberative public speech they are ultimately unsatisfying.

Both of these speeches are described in some detail by Thucydides, but neither is quoted directly. Thucydides' failure to report the speeches directly could be sufficiently accounted for by the postulate that the absence of direct speech in Book Eight reflects the decline of real public deliberation, and hence of political community, in the cities during this period. Alcibiades' first speech to the soldiers, in particular, is an extravagant rhetorical barrage for the purpose of exhorting and encouraging the army. The army is in great need of encouragement, but the speech as Thucydides describes it is little more than a harangue (8.81–2). Alcibiades claims that Tissaphernes has sworn to aid the Athenians, led by Alcibiades, to the utmost extent of his fortune—he would even sell his own bed for the purpose, if it should come to that. He has also promised, according to Alcibiades, to bring the Phoenician fleet to help the Athenian cause. Declaiming "excessively," even "boastfully" accord-

---

[46]This reunion is "more enduring" in that it lasted almost four years, until 407, although we do not learn this from Thucydides. This period was marked by brilliant military successes. If there is room for doubt whether the Sicilian expedition was good for the city, these extremely opportune victories are unambiguously to its advantage. If we consider that Alcibiades in his early career struggled on the sidelines of Athenian politics under the Peace of Nicias, and only gained center stage at the time of the Sicilian expedition, the first coming together of Alcibiades and the city was short-lived indeed.

ing to Thucydides, on these and other matters, Alcibiades successfully bolsters the morale of the navy; after his speech, the soldiers who were formerly on the brink of despair become so confident that they begin to despise their enemies in Ionia and even conceive the desire to sail immediately for the Peiraeus to attack the hated Four Hundred.

Alcibiades' speech might be seen as an overly effective, perhaps even dangerous piece of rhetoric, were it not for the fact that he can just as handily dissuade the army from their rashness (82). The extraordinary ease with which he accomplishes both these things is precisely what makes us feel the defectiveness of his performance here relative to the kind of deliberative public speech that Thucydides has elsewhere impressed his readers with. In the best case, such speeches, no matter how one-sided they are, attempt to persuade by a kind of disinterestedness and detachment, in that way enlisting the reason of their audiences. Alcibiades' speech, however, is marked by blatant exaggeration and boasting. The speech, for all its effectiveness, operates by a kind of deceit and manipulation rarely seen in the History even in exhortations to armies. This manipulative quality makes the long-awaited address of the recalled Alcibiades to the Athenians a disappointment to us. Alcibiades can move the Athenians in whatever direction he desires, but the character of his persuasion leaves us disappointed.

Alcibiades chooses an extravagant rhetorical approach in part because of dejection among the troops he is addressing. He tells them just what they crave to hear, and they respond to it enthusiastically. But Alcibiades earlier showed an inclination toward a manipulative or deceptive approach to public deliberation: his approach here is reminiscent of his behavior in his first appearance in the History, where he relied on deception to induce the Athenian assembly to follow the course of action he desired. Here on Samos, where Alcibiades occupies center stage unopposed, he is attempting to achieve many things simultaneously. According to Thucydides, his first speech to the soldiers is designed both to solidify his own position as general and to strike a pose, as it were, that will have an effect well beyond the limits of the camp, in Athens itself and even among the Spartans and the Persians (81.2). The combination of Alcibiades' ambitions and the desperate need of the Athenian soldiers on Samos essentially dictates the character of his relationship to his audience. It takes the desperate conditions of Book Eight to bring about Alcibiades' recall; these conditions, along with

Alcibiades' rhetorical skill, put his audience so thoroughly at his disposal that for all practical purposes they may be seen to have abdicated their judgment.

The results of this are not, at this moment in the History, entirely negative. When the second assembly that Alcibiades presides over on Samos decides how to respond to emissaries from the Four Hundred, Alcibiades adroitly curbs the violent rage of the soldiers, something Thucydides says no one else would have been capable of, and then decides completely on his own what message to send to the oligarchs (86.6–7). Thucydides' description of the incident emphasizes that Alcibiades' rhetoric successfully restrains those who are angered "privately" at the emissaries (86.5) and prevents a disastrous attempt to sail to Athens. The service he thus renders to the city, according to Thucydides, is unrivaled.[47] But then we encounter once more Alcibiades' tendency to substitute his own judgment for consultation. After calming the soldiers down, Alcibiades apparently does not even inform them what action he is taking vis-à-vis the city. This is perplexing especially since the message he sends to Athens is both moderate and conciliatory and is scrupulously attentive to the interests of the city as a whole. It is also a brilliant piece of strategy aimed at undermining the regime of the Four

---

[47]There is an important textual controversy at this point (8.86.4), based on the alternate reading *prōtos* or *prōton*, which signifies either that Alcibiades is now serving the city "preeminently," to an extraordinary degree, or is serving it now "for the first time," the first time in his career. I have adopted the first variant, attested by most manuscripts. Many editors and commentators prefer the second, on the grounds that it comes from one of the better manuscripts (*B*), that it is more idiomatic, and that it represents the preferable interpretation. Andrewes (in Gomme, Andrewes, and Dover, *Historical Commentary*, 5:286–87) prefers it on the grounds that the idiomatic reading should prevail in the absence of compelling evidence to the contrary. I, with different professional inclinations no doubt, put the substance of the matter in the controlling position. So far as that goes, it seems to me difficult to maintain that Alcibiades is benefiting the city "for the first time" here by preventing the soldiers from sailing on the Peiraeus, when Alcibiades has performed exactly the same service just four chapters earlier in Thucydides' narrative (8.82). Some suggest that Thucydides here conflates the two episodes, but Thucydides says nothing to indicate this. Many interpreters appear to prefer the reading of *B* simply because they believe Thucydides to be highly critical of Alcibiades, which I think is unjustified, or at least too simple. For the rest, it might be possible to maintain that these two incidents represent the first time in the History that Alcibiades has *unambiguously* served his city, since his earlier exploits were all connected with the adventurous policy of the Argive league or with the Sicilian expedition, but even this would hardly justify the reading of *B*.

Hundred in the city. It has precisely that effect (89.2), but it remains a purely personal initiative of Alcibiades. The spectacle of his extravagant first speech upon being recalled to Samos thus stands as the ironic paradigm for the consummation of Alcibiades' relationship with the community. His return provides us with a fair and only partially exaggerated picture of what the triumph of his ambition in the city would mean. We must wonder whether the event does not, in time, prove somewhat disappointing even to Alcibiades himself.[48]

The irony of these episodes on Samos is that the fulfillment of Alcibiades' political ambition not only turns out to be problematic for the integrity of the political community as such but also becomes self-defeating for Alcibiades himself. If Alcibiades is able to have his own way so completely, even if by persuasion and not by force, if his ability to persuade and his audience's deference to his judgment make them mere plastic in his hands, the city becomes an almost nonpolitical association, and Alcibiades' speech becomes monologue. Alcibiades in this case will scarcely be recognizable as a political leader, since in monopolizing political judgment and the political stage so completely, he destroys the specifically political character of the community he is leading. In the end, we must suspect that the recognition or esteem he might get from such a community would not be of the kind or quality he craves. Alcibiades' triumph will turn his community into something like an army, or perhaps a private household, but not a city.[49] Like Tantalus, he is doomed to see the object of his craving vanish even as he grasps it.

This drama holds the interest it does, for Thucydides and for us, in part because Alcibiades' dilemma is not simply a problem posed by his career but one always created or confronted by ambition or the love of honor. The career of Alcibiades only presents this problem in its most extreme form. Alcibiades represents perfectly unrestrained ambition, of the kind that could only arise in Athens, political genius free of all conventional ties and restraints, including restraints on its frankness or openness. Returning to the comparison of Alcibiades and Pericles, we

---

[48]See also Westlake's similar description of the return of Alcibiades (*Individuals*, pp. 250–52). Westlake says we get the sense that the rapprochement between Alcibiades and the army rests on brittle foundations; the soldiers are simply duped by Alcibiades. The soldiers are indeed duped, and that is a problem; the brittleness of this relationship, however, depends on how deft Alcibiades is at managing things this way.

[49]Cf. Aristotle *Politics* 1285b30–34, 1288a33–34.

can see why this must lead to the dilemma of political ambition in its most extreme form. There is some justification for Alcibiades' claim that he desires no more than the kind of mastery over the city that Pericles had. Pericles' rule, however, does not have the same distorting effect on the polity that Alcibiades' does, and part of the reason is a difference in the style of the two men's leadership.

In his eulogy of Pericles, Thucydides says that Pericles was able to encourage the Athenians in distress and restrain them in insolence, that he led them rather than being led by them (2.65.8–9). We see these qualities in Alcibiades' leadership as well; they distinguish Alcibiades and Pericles from the petty demagogues that flourish in their absence. In explaining Pericles' great influence in the city, however, Thucydides says that he restrained the multitude "freely" or "liberally" (*eleutheros* 2.65.8). This cannot be so easily said of Alcibiades, for what Thucydides indicates in part by these words is that in Pericles' time the opinion prevailed that he was no more than a first among equals; hence his advice was always followed with the free and deliberate consent of the Athenians.[50] The belief prevailed, strongly supported by Pericles' own behavior, that his authority came not from the submission but from the constant concurrence of the city. Pericles never appeared to be more than a sage advisor to the city. Alcibiades' predominance in the city, however, and his whole self-presentation, undermines this impression. There are two fundamental reasons for this. First, Alcibiades is more aware than Pericles was of the critical role that leadership plays in the Athenian polity, and partly as a result, he is more frank in pressing his claims. Alcibiades is a purer lover of honor than Pericles: he insists frankly on being honored for what he is. If he wants no more than Pericles' position, he wants everyone to know or admit that he is in Pericles' position, in a way that they did not during Pericles' tenure. Hence, approving Alcibiades' voice, on Alcibiades' terms, is much more palpably an act of submission on the part of the city. Alcibiades insists on being granted the full measure of honor that his position entitles him to; he refuses to concede anything to the sensibilities of the democracy.

Further, Alcibiades shows much greater willingness than Pericles to

---

[50]What Thucydides means precisely by this epithet applied to Pericles' leadership might be a long story. Cf. Finley, *Thucydides*, pp. 163–64; Edmunds, *Chance and Intelligence*, pp. 55–56.

substitute his judgment for that of the assembly. Pericles' judgment just as surely led the city in his time, but Pericles operated more by persuasion; conferring his judgment on the multitude, as it were, rather than simply substituting it for theirs. Alcibiades operates this way too when circumstances are favorable, as they were before the Sicilian expedition; and Pericles sometimes substituted his own judgment, as when he refused to let the assembly convene during the first Spartan invasion of Attica (2.22.1). Yet the difference in their political approaches is a palpable one. Pericles dealt with the *demos* in a much more "liberal" spirit.

Alcibiades, however, is forced to take the approach he does for other reasons that help explain the differences between him and Pericles. Alcibiades' rhetoric is more irritating to the Athenians, because of the frankness that comes from his peculiar love of honor. The Athenians do not trust him as much as they did Pericles, making it more difficult for him to proceed completely by persuasion. The problem of trust is obviously an important factor here, extending beyond the matter of Alcibiades' rhetoric. Thucydides says of the liberal Periclean manner that Pericles had the authority he did in the city on account of his great repute, his judgment, and his obvious superiority to money (2.65.8). The last consideration, which Pericles identifies in his third speech as one of his qualifications to rule (2.60.5), is crucial. Since peculation and the acceptance of bribes are perhaps the most common form that private interest and betrayal of the public trust takes in political men, superiority to those temptations is a powerful sign to the many of public-spiritedness. Being "obviously" above money is a doubly cogent, if vulgar, emblem of disinterest in public affairs. Alcibiades, however, looks very suspicious from precisely this point of view. He proclaims by word and deed his concern with wealth; he even declares his own display of luxury to be one of his public ambitions. This is part of Alcibiades' larger transformation of the role of private interest in political ambition and statesmanship. Thucydides indicates that he forces us to rethink and ultimately reject the presumptive connection between private concern for money and fitness to serve the public interest; he also makes clear how necessarily remote from the city's understanding this thought is. The phenomenon of Alcibiades' public-spiritedness, or perhaps we should say his public usefulness, can never be fully grasped by the city.

When Alcibiades stands before the city and openly claims for himself a position of supremacy, on the basis of arguments that his pursuit of private interest is necessarily in the public interest, in spite of his utter disregard for the conventional ties between the two, his position cannot seem immediately plausible to the Athenians. To the extent that Alcibiades does not appear simply selfish and untrustworthy to them, he is morally an unknown quantity, and putting the city in his hands is a leap of faith on their part. Pericles was by comparison an open book to the Athenians; they freely consented to his supremacy in full knowledge of what they were getting: a public servant, unquestionably tied to the city, and unquestionably devoted to the democracy. Agreeing to the rule of Alcibiades, by contrast, risks falling short of the standard of informed consent, due to sheer uncertainty of what he is. The fact that Alcibiades is such an unknown quantity, combined with the fact that he presses such an uncompromising claim to the public life of the city, make the effective suspension of the democracy under him, as opposed to its effective suspension under Pericles, much more explicit and hence traumatic for the Athenians.

Alcibiades' argument concerning his usefulness to the city is nevertheless valid, for all its implausibility from the point of view of ordinary civic consciousness. This is a discovery of the greatest importance to Thucydides and to all who would understand politics and statesmanship. Alcibiades appears at a time when the selfish logic of Athenian imperialism has run its course, having reached its peak in Alcibiades and in his time. Alcibiades embodies all the lessons learned by the Athenians in the course of the war; his political project is the only one that gives full scope to private interest without destroying the public interest and the city with it. This is not true of all the projects spawned by the Athenian experiment in politics. Alcibiades is similarly the final product of the Athenian liberation of individual talent and ambition, and the Athenians might be considered fortunate to have found in him an individual whose liberated talents and ambitions are capable of encompassing the interests of the city as a whole. By the time of Alcibiades' recall they have ample reason to know that that is not where the dialectic of individualism always leads. The problem for the city is that the triumph of this peak individual paradoxically requires the abridgment or suppression of the political powers of his fellow citizens. The end of the history of individual liberation is the most perfect rule of one.[51]

Alcibiades' return is thus an irony not only for Alcibiades but for the city of Athens as well. The aspirations of both, which are the aspirations of liberated humanity on the level of statesman and city respectively, overreach themselves and in the act of approaching their goals see them vanish. In the city, the greatest immoderation and the greatest individual freedom lead, by necessities of both foreign and domestic politics, to the need for strictest moderation and deference to the rule of one. And the city's claim to uninhibited rule over other cities leads to the individual's claim to rule over the city itself. The city finally produces an individual who not only makes that claim but justifies it, better than the city ever did its title to rule the empire, by reference to the benefit his rule brings to those over whom the rule is exercised, and by a more steadfast dedication to honor than the city itself proves capable of.

For Alcibiades the final irony is not only that his dominance in the city becomes so complete as to vitiate the public life and public speech he so obviously delights in, but that the very vitality of the city as an instrument of power degenerates for the same reasons. It is practically axiomatic that the moderation the city acquires in Book Eight, which makes Alcibiades' recall possible, involves relinquishing the old Athenian daring and eroticism, at least for a time. Those qualities, and the dynamism of imperial Athens in general, were connected to the role that the raucous, unruly, and jealous *demos* was allowed to play in the city. Alcibiades' return is made possible only by the disappearance of those qualities that made the city most Alcibidean. It seems that no city is big enough to contain both a demanding statesman like Alcibiades and a chaotically dynamic *demos* like that of imperial Athens at its height.[52]

---

[51]We should specify that this is the *best* end conceivable for those concerned. The other possible end, which was in fact seen at Athens both before and after Alcibiades, is simply the disintegration of the city. Grene states, in a similar vein, that the real end of the political process at Athens was tyranny (*Man in His Pride*, pp. 33–34); I would say that the end of that process was either a brilliant but overwhelming individual like Alcibiades or tyranny.

[52]Machiavelli's vision of the imperial republic of Rome may provide an instructive comparison here. Machiavelli argues that precisely the chronic feuding between the plebs and patricians, and the resentment of the plebs against the patricians, is what produced the energy that made imperialism possible for that city (*Discourses on Livy*, I, 4). In

Book Eight, and thus Thucydides' History, ends on perhaps the most optimistic note possible with regard to the fortunes of Athens. This may have been intentional; the work's conclusion as it presently stands leaves us with at least a favorable parting impression of the resiliency of the city and the ability of human beings to live together politically.[53] We

---

Machiavelli's presentation this volatile state of affairs was shrewdly managed by the patricians in such a way that they were able to control the city without arousing the worst resentments of the plebs or reducing them to slavishness. They did this by manipulating oracles, dividing the tribunes, resorting to subterfuge in consular elections, and so on. In Athens perhaps a hypothetically cynical and self-conscious Pericles would come closest to this Machiavellian formula. Alcibiades, however, is not a Machiavellian; if he were, he could have been more successful, because more deceitful. Alcibiades does not maintain a demure and disingenuous exterior in order to impose upon the *demos*, and he rejects in particular Machiavelli's overthrow of honor as a genuine or ingenuous link between leaders and people. For Machiavelli the leader is inherently a deceiver because of the gulf that exists between what leaders must do and the moral categories in accordance with which they receive glory. Alcibiades insists on believing that he can receive honor for what he really is. Machiavelli would call this naive, but it is the key to Alcibiades' genuine usefulness to the city.

[53]No one of course can claim to know that Thucydides intended to end the work as he did, and no useful purpose would be served by speculating so (see n. 2, above). It is interesting nevertheless to consider the grounds for suggesting that Thucydides might have considered the work essentially finished as it stands. One is explained in the text—namely, the parting image it provides is of an optimism that could not easily have been produced by ending the narrative at any other point. Even the final detail, the barbarian Tissaphernes sacrificing to a Greek goddess, seems a promising counterpoint to the tragic barbarization of the Greeks during the war. At the same time, Thucydides seems to have shown us everything we need to know to understand the course of the whole war and to understand the characters of the combatants, Athens and Sparta. The supposition that the History ends intentionally where it does might also help explain a manuscript reading that has always baffled editors, namely, the remark recorded in the eulogy of Pericles that Athens held out only "three years" after her defeat in Sicily (2.65.12). All the manuscripts read thus, though the passage has almost always been emended to read "ten years" to bring it to the date of Athens' final defeat. Three years brings us about to the point where the History does end, or perhaps to the episode of the oligarchy, which could be considered a rehearsal so to speak of the final destruction of Athens as it is described in the eulogy, a destruction by faction. A similar suggestion could be made about Thucydides' puzzling remark at 6.15.4 that when the Athenians repudiated Alcibiades they brought the city to ruin "not long after." If the first exile of Alcibiades is meant, the ruin referred to would seem to involve the events of 411 at the latest (cf. Connor, *Thucydides*, p. 164n17). This difficulty is discussed briefly at chap. 2, n. 8, above.

The passage in Thucydides' work that seems to militate most strongly against this suggestion is 5.26, where Thucydides says he wrote down the events of this war, by summers and winters, until Athens fell to the Spartan power. A forced, though perhaps not impossible, reading of this passage would be that it merely means Thucydides was actively writing through the whole war and that the History is cognizant of its whole

have been amply exposed to the grounds for doubt on that score, and Thucydides does not want those doubts simply to have last word. He has already informed us of the fate of Athens and shown us in detail the operation of those causes that will be its undoing. But Thucydides' judgment on the city and politics is not a simply pessimistic or cynical one. Thucydides gives full weight to those considerations which led many of the sophists, his contemporaries, to take a purely cynical or conventionalist view of the city. The final lessons of Book Eight, however, and of the History as a whole, are more complex than that.

One of the themes of Book Eight is the character and conditions of political moderation. The prolonged Athenian experiment in unleashing human nature, which turns out to be an experiment in the possibilities of thoroughgoing political immoderation, succeeds in proving only the city's need for moderation to survive. This moderation seems possible in the cities, but only as a product of artificial, external constraint: thus the moderation of the Spartans and the Chians, the belated moderation of the Athenian allies, and the newfound moderation of Athens itself in Book Eight. The finest product of this Athenian moderation, the regime of the Five Thousand, is brought into being by the greatest terror the city experiences in the war, that produced by the revolt of Euboea (8.96–97). According to Diodotus, moderation comes naturally neither to individuals nor to cities, because human nature is fundamentally lawless and unrestrained. The Athenian experiment seems to corroborate this. If Sparta is the model of moderation incorporated as a principle into the regime itself, albeit under constant duress, moderation compromises human nature in the name of the community and the strength of the community.

Ordinary politics, exemplified by Sparta, is based on a whole series of compromises with human nature and human aspirations, even with some of the most powerful impulses of the city itself. In one respect, it appears that the city, paradoxically, can thrive only under conditions of duress sufficient to force it to moderation and to teach its citizens public-

---

course, not necessarily that Thucydides was going to write down all the events of the war. It is also possible more modestly to suggest that even if Thucydides was forced, or decided belatedly, to cut off his narrative short of the end of the war, he still might have chosen to end it where he does and not elsewhere. He still might have deliberately selected the final image to present and still might have considered the work thematically, if not chronologically, complete. Cf. Strauss, *The City and Man*, p. 227n.

spiritedness. But one of the most important lessons of Book Eight, and of the History as a whole, is that the city also requires a margin of safety for its integrity, a margin that prevents the inevitable questions concerning the relation between public and private, between honor and survival, between necessity or self-interest and justice or piety from being too closely examined or too forcefully raised by circumstances. The conditions of war, and especially of the greatest war, raise precisely these questions, in the most forceful manner possible. The city requires a margin of safety for its stability, but it exists in a world that does anything but guarantee it that safety. The Peloponnesian War is for the cities an experience similar to the plague in Athens, that other great brush with extremity. The rough schoolmaster war, in Thucydides' phrase, teaches human beings to disregard the divine law and the precepts of decency and dissolves cities throughout Greece into barbarous civil war (3.82).

Yet if Thucydides believes the Peloponnesian War to be the most noteworthy war in part because it strains the city in ways the city cannot withstand, still that situation, like the plague in Athens itself, can be said to both reveal and not reveal the character of cities and human nature. War is most admirably suited to revealing the limits, the weaknesses, and the hypocrisies of politics. But it is also a situation in which the greatest human talents can be developed and exploited, in which the considerable resilience of a city like Athens can be displayed, and in which human nobility and valor can be fully manifested. Few readers put down Thucydides with the impression that virtue, or decency, or civilization itself are simple shams. They leave instead with the conviction that they have somehow seen the full range of humanity in a book about a war that does full justice to that range.

The unprecedented example of Athens in this war makes conventional politics seem unsatisfactory. The ever-seductive example especially of Periclean Athens makes it difficult to believe that the rigid moderation required for ordinary politics is in the interests of human perfection. Sparta, when viewed in Athens' light, is seen to rest not only on the suppression of base impulses of nature for the sake of the higher but also on the suppression of some innocuous or even admirable impulses. Athens, for all its difficulty as a political model, still represents a genuine peak of human accomplishment. Its difficulties from this point of view might be described as the difficulties politics has in doing justice to humanity. The natural perfection of men such as Themistocles, Alcibiades, and finally even Antiphon does not fit entirely into the constitution of any city, and in the end that fact must represent as much an indictment of the city as of the men themselves.

Yet in the final analysis, however much difficulty the city has in coping with the most exotic products of its human soil when flourishing, the fact remains that only in the context of the city can human beings flourish at all. However much individual human greatness may be at odds with the community, it is only out of the city, as opposed even to "barbaric" political regimes, that they grow. The prepolitical condition of poverty and instability prevented any such human cultivation; only the long and slow rise of the cities has made it possible in Thucydides' era. Only the rise of the cities has made Thucydides himself and his intellectual project possible. The frightful vulnerability of the city to the pressures of war and the play of human nature, meanwhile, is not necessarily as decisive as it may seem. The development of the political form in Greece culminated in the discovery of humanity, or of the beauty of unadorned humanity, which opened the way for the cultivation of humanity as one of the specific undertakings of Greek civilization. As Thucydides adumbrates it, the Greek ideal, as a human and political ideal, combines with this undertaking a genuine devotion to some notion of modesty or restraint.[54] The decline of the Athenians, and even of the Greeks, in the course of the war results in part from the tension between the cultivation of humanity and the devotion to moderation. This is then a problem within Greek culture as such. Insofar as Greek culture is the model for all high or true culture, the problems of Greek cities reflect the problems of human civilization as such. The fact that the peak they reach is an impermanent one, due to the tensions contained within it, does not spoil the height of the peak or deny its existence. In a world characterized fundamentally by rise and fall, by the alternation of motion and rest rather than by any unitary and unchanging principle; in a world where even the highest phenomena contain contradiction and therefore the seeds of their own destruction, impermanence and even logical incoherence cannot be entirely decisive objections to politics.

This may be the way politics necessarily presents itself to the wise or scientific man who is alive to the genuine human accomplishments of

---

[54]On this point see chap. 1, the section entitled "Thucydides' View of Athenian Imperialism."

the city, to the claims of nobility and of the divine law, before the appearance of political philosophy proper. Thucydides is not a conventionalist, as many of the sophists were, nor does he reinterpret politics or its contradictions in the light of a theoretical principle beyond it or a theoretical life outside it. Whatever we may think of the intriguing example provided by the life of Thucydides himself—not primarily a life of political activity but one of writing and contemplation—that life is devoted to writing a work in which no higher life is proposed or depicted than that of politics and the city. Thucydides is notoriously self-effacing in his book, and if to one way of thinking he is the real hero of it, he seems to do everything to prevent himself from becoming its subject. If Thucydides' project is to educate or to make wise, it seems directed more toward perfecting future statesmen than toward creating future historians or writers on politics, more toward understanding the high and the low in practical politics than toward advancing the cause of a theoretical life for its own sake.

4

Thucydides' Alcibiades

ALCIBIADES is the most ambiguous of political figures. He stands in an ambiguous relation not only to the individual cities in Thucydides' History, but to the city and to politics as such. His are peak political ambitions, but they prove almost incompatible with the integrity of any political community. Thucydides' presentation of Alcibiades makes this comprehensive ambiguity its central theme, and develops it with all deliberateness.[1] Thucydides never gives us a synopsis of Alcibiades' career and character in the History as it stands, and the few general remarks he makes on the subject are notoriously ambivalent. His presentation of Alcibiades does not even make use of many of the categories that

[1]The ambiguity of Thucydides' presentation of Alcibiades is often noted but frequently attributed to confusion on Thucydides' part or changes of attitude as he wrote his History (e.g., Peter R. Pouncey, *The Necessities of War: A Study of Thucydides' Pessimism* [New York: Columbia University Press, 1980], chap. 7). As I have argued already, it seems to me to be a mistake to presume that ambiguity represents a defect of political understanding or composition in Thucydides. Thucydides does not simplify; rather he illuminates the nuances and complexities of political events (cf. W. Robert Connor, *Thucydides* [Princeton: Princeton University Press, 1984], p. 236). Grasping the ambiguity found in Alcibiades and in the events that surround him is, as it were, the last and most difficult lesson in Thucydides, yet one most crucial to the understanding of the History as a whole. Future Thucydidean statesmen will not aspire to be like Alcibiades; but they must understand the fundamental political dilemmas presented by his case above all others.

176

have been developed in the History to characterize and make intelligible the behavior and motivation of other statesmen and cities. Alcibiades is never referred to as daring, or prudent, or intelligent, or virtuous, or erotic, though these are the significant words Thucydides uses to describe other political actors and actions. It is as though Thucydides, having prepared us throughout his History to evaluate the nuances of this most difficult of political cases, forces us now to make use of this education on our own. Alcibiades himself half-humorously indicates that he is outside the realm of Athenian political discourse when he prides himself on his youthful "folly" in his speech at Athens, folly being the Alcibidean equivalent of traditional Athenian daring. If Alcibiades does not fit into the world of Athenian political discourse it is because he is more extreme than the Athenians; yet Athenian discourse and Athenian categories are already very radical versions of political discourse and categories.

It is Alcibiades' extremism that allows him to embrace or encompass the public good of the city within his own, to act for the sake of glory or honor when the exigencies of politics and the war have caused virtually all other public men, Nicias not excepted, to retreat into narrow self-interest. Alcibiades continues to act in the public interest until the final moment of Thucydides' narrative, but his way of doing so remains problematic from the point of view of the city. Thucydides, in his one brief, comprehensive comment on the relationship between Alcibiades and Athens, emphasizes his grandeur of conception and action (6.15); these are the qualities that allow him to embrace the public good within his own. But in the same passage Thucydides connects these qualities to the city's suspicions that Alcibiades' intentions are not compatible with the public good but tyrannical. Thucydides' tone in this introduction, as we noted before, is one of studied ambiguity. The passage is placed between Nicias' speech against the Sicilian expedition and Alcibiades' speech in favor of it; it begins essentially by corroborating Nicias' personal attack on Alcibiades. It ends, however, by indicating that Alcibiades' personal motivations do not prevent him from being the best leader, indeed the best hope, the city has for the war. The Athenians' exile of Alcibiades, on the grounds outlined by Nicias, bring about its ruin. The passage studiously avoids placing blame for this squarely on either Alcibiades or the city.

We have found it useful on a number of occasions to compare Thucydides' treatment of Alcibiades with his treatment of Pericles.

The ambiguous evaluation of Alcibiades cited above can usefully be compared to Thucydides' eulogy of Pericles; the one seems to be something of a counterpoint to the other. The eulogy includes a brief but sweeping analysis of events after Pericles' death, but this account does not seem to correspond entirely with later events as they unfold in the History.[2] The general thrust of it is that the Athenians after Pericles' death did everything contrary to his advice; the decline and eventual demise of the city was due to the fact that his successors were motivated by private ambition and gain; none of them was able to attain the position that Pericles held in the city. Rather, they vied for supremacy by pandering to the whims of the *demos*, and they were led by the *demos* rather than leading it. In effect, they put the control of affairs directly into the people's hands (2.65.10). The result was that the city made a multitude of blunders, in particular the disastrous Sicilian campaign (65.11).

After seeming in this way to prepare for a blanket condemnation of the Sicilian expedition, the greatest single instance of the Athenians' acting contrary to Pericles' advice, Thucydides abruptly changes his tack. The expedition itself was not so much a blunder, he informs us, as was the failure adequately to support it once it was sent out (65.11). This equivocation brings to mind the fact that Thucydides does not here mention Alcibiades, the greatest proponent of the expedition at Athens. Indeed, it is difficult to see where Alcibiades is supposed to fit into this post-Periclean landscape altogether. He is characterized most emphatically by the motives of private ambition and private gain; and his advocacy of the Sicilian undertaking, conditioned in part by these private motives, might well be called a case of pandering to the most extreme desires of the Athenian *demos*. Yet Thucydides refuses to condemn the expedition itself, and in his later introduction to Alcibiades' speech he in fact makes it clear that his leadership was vital not only to the success of the expedition but to the survival of the city. Alcibiades is not on a level with other privately motivated aspirants to leadership in the city.

[2]On this point, see A. W. Gomme, A. Andrewes, and K. J. Dover, *A Historical Commentary on Thucydides*, 5 vols. (Oxford: Clarendon, 1945–81), 2:195–96; Willy Peremens, "Thucydide, Alcibiade, et l'expedition de Sicile en 415 av. J.-C.," *L'antiquité classique* 25 (1956):331–44; H. D. Westlake, "Thucydides 2.65.11," *Classical Quarterly* n.s. 8 (1958):102–10; Wesley E. Thompson, "Thucydides 2.65.11," *Historia* 20 (1971):141–51.

He is not one of the *isoi*, the more or less equal demagogues foreseen in the eulogy of Pericles; and whatever else we may say about him, Alcibiades leads the *demos* rather than being led by it. Alcibiades advocates the expedition for his own reasons, not because it is popular with the people, and he shows amply in his later career that he can motivate or restrain the populace according to his own political vision; he does not follow their whims.

The tone of approval toward Pericles in Thucydides' eulogy, which along with his rendition of the Funeral Oration has led many commentators to conclude that Thucydides was an unqualified supporter of Pericles, gives way only upon reflection to insight into the defects in Pericles' policy.[3] Thucydides' equivocation on the Sicilian expedition is one indication that he does not blindly admire Pericles, but even here the failure of the expedition and the decay of Athens after Pericles' death are seen only in terms of the dichotomy of public and private interest and ambition, where Pericles represents the model of selfless public-spiritedness. The Sicilian expedition failed, according to the eulogy, because of the private intrigues of factious demagogues, which led to the failure adequately to support the expedition once it is sent out (2.65.11). One would never guess on the basis of this statement that the primary subject of the factious intrigue that broke out after the expedition sailed would be Alcibiades' recall from Sicily. Nor would one guess that the only hope for the safety of the expedition, and of the city itself, would be this same Alcibiades, a man who is hardly a model of Periclean selflessness.

[3]Regarding the policy of keeping the city quiet during the war, Thucydides has provided ample grounds for misgivings in Book One, with his portrayal of the Athenian character. See also Gomme, Andrewes, and Dover, *Historical Commentary*, 2:195–96. It is probable that if a careful study of Thucydides' evolving moral teaching in the History were done, Pericles would turn out to represent not the first stage but the second, with a more traditional, Spartan or Nician perspective being the first. Leo Strauss makes this argument, convincingly I believe, about the shifting perspective of Book One itself (*The City and Man* [1964; rpt. Chicago: University of Chicago Press, 1977], pp. 145–63, 179). From the simply traditional moral perspective, Pericles is already halfway down the path that leads eventually to Alcibiades, in virtually every respect. The point has been made at any rate that for someone with Thucydides' aristocratic background, that is, someone of the type intended as the object of Thucydides' moral and political instruction, appreciation of what Pericles represents is already a break with his native outlook. See John H. Finley, *Thucydides* (1942; rpt. Ann Arbor: University of Michigan Press, 1963), p. 30.

But this is only part of the problem with this passage. Its allegation of a failure to support the expedition seems an egregious misstatement since the Athenians in fact unflaggingly sent men and money to their fleet in Sicily. In the light of subsequent events, therefore, this remark can mean only that the Athenians failed to support the expedition in some other, less direct sense. And this must be connected somehow to their failure to retain Alcibiades. What Thucydides says specifically in this part of the eulogy is that the Athenians failed to recognize or resolve upon the measures that were necessary for the support of the Sicilian expedition; becoming involved in factious struggles at home, they conducted affairs in Sicily in a more lethargic fashion. This last corresponds, in retrospect, to the command of Nicias in Sicily after Alcibiades' departure. In the drama of the Sicilian expedition as it unfolds in Books Six and Seven, the scheming and self-interested demagogues bring about Alcibiades' recall, but the fatal lethargy that seizes the expedition in his absence is due to the ascendency of Nicias and Euphemus and what they represent in the public mind at Athens, a kind of recoil from the hubris of the Sicilian project and even of Athenian imperialism as a whole. The immediate and primary cause of the expedition's demise, as portrayed in the later account, is the conservatism, diffidence, and piety of the new command. This return to traditional moralism is the only "lack of support" visible there, but indeed it is the thing that dooms it to failure.[4] The expedition could only have been saved by the brash, self-centered, and amoral Alcibiades. These facts are simply invisible in the eulogy of Pericles, which is written from the quasi-moralistic point of view of a Pericles. Alcibiades represents the possibility, not foreseen in the eulogy, of a self-interested leader whose activity is nonetheless

---

[4]A few remarks are required on the Greek of this passage, since if read in the light of later developments, it does seem deliberately calculated to mislead. The word I have been rendering as "support" to the troops in Sicily (*prosphora*) is of such a concrete derivation that it seems impossible to interpret it as anything but supplies and reinforcements, aid of the most material kind. This is precisely the kind of aid the Athenians did supply. It might be noted for interpretive purposes though that Thucydides has put the word in its more abstract neuter plural form, a form at least more likely to permit the kind of nonmaterial interpretation I am suggesting. Still, other, broader words could be found. For an interpretation of the passage similar to mine, see Dover, in Gomme, Andrewes, Dover, *Historical Commentary*, 5:423–24. The verb Thucydides uses here (*epigignōskein*) can mean either "recognizing" or "resolving upon" the measures necessary for support. On the interpretation of this passage see also Peremans, "Alcibiade et l'expedition de Sicile"; Westlake, "Thucydides 2.65.11"; Thompson, "Thucydides 2.65.11."

salutary to the city, and the necessity, even less foreseen, of accommodating him.

We must pause momentarily to consider one objection to this analysis. The discrepancies between the eulogy of Pericles and the introduction to Alcibiades' Sicilian speech have been considered by some commentators as evidence that Thucydides changed his mind as he wrote the History, and that these changes exist as unreconciled inconsistencies in the text. This line of interpretation has been applied to the whole History, leading to serious and influential attempts to date its various passages. The apparent oversights of the eulogy of Pericles pose a special problem for this approach, however, since this type of interpretation places the eulogy and the portrait of Alcibiades at equally late dates.[5] If Thucydides is not an incoherent thinker or a careless writer, we must assume that the inconsistencies between these two passages are intentional. This hypothesis, the only defensible one I believe, gives us a richer, if a more difficult Thucydides. The inconsistencies between the two passages under consideration are thus doubly instructive: they shed light on Thucydides' presentation of Alcibiades, and they simultaneously help to illuminate Thucydides' method and the character of his writing. The eulogy is written, on the surface of it, from a Periclean point of view; it is indeed a eulogy. Its inadequacies are the inadequacies of the Periclean point of view, which come to light in its assessment of the moral and political ambiguities that appeared especially after Pericles' death. The intro-

---

[5]On the "dating" question, see also the introduction. So far as I know, it is agreed by virtually all those who dissect the History in this way that the eulogy of Pericles and the presentation of Alcibiades are equally late (cf. Dover, in Gomme, Andrewes, Dover, *Historical Commentary*, 5:427). In fact, it was the peculiar character of the eulogy of Pericles that gave rise to much of this speculation in the first place: it appears to digress from the surrounding narrative to look forward to events up to the end of the war. The synopsis of Alcibiades, meanwhile, refers like the eulogy to the end of the war and shows some sympathy for the statesmanship of Alcibiades himself. Dover (5:423–24) discusses the relation between these two passages and tries to reconcile them by supposing some rhetorically motivated omissions from the eulogy of Pericles, though of quite a different sort from those I have suggested. He also interprets 6.15 as more negative toward Alcibiades than I believe is justified.

On the issue of dating, it seems to me that the long obsession with the composition question has been largely based on insufficient sensitivity to Thucydides' subtlety and his method. The line of argument I pursue is typical of the way I believe apparent inconsistencies in Thucydides' History should be explained and understood.

duction to Alcibiades' speech, meanwhile, strikes a note of ambiguity much closer to Thucydides' own perspective. Thucydides thus moves us only gradually away from the ordinary moral perspective into the difficult and disconcerting perspective of unconventional moral nuance, the only perspective from which Alcibiades can be fully understood and properly evaluated. Thucydides' gradual approach is the only appropriate one to a course of moral instruction of this kind.

The comparison of these two passages yields another suggestion concerning the differences between the two statesmen. In the eulogy, Thucydides says that Pericles guided the city in a measured fashion and kept it safe in time of peace (2.65.5). In the introduction to Alcibiades' speech he says that Alcibiades was best at directing the city in the war (6.15.4). Pericles' application of his measured peacetime proclivities to the war was precisely what doomed his strategy to failure. Alcibiades, who arises only under the tutelage of the rough schoolmaster war, is much better suited to coping with its necessities on the strategic level, but he is also the only one who does not succumb to the narrow self-interest and factionalism it bred in Athens and virtually every other city in Greece. This degeneration, caused by the destruction of the notion of honor and of every civic virtue under the pressures of war, is apparent in the civil wars (3.82, 83.1) and in the example of Phrynichus among the Athenians. Concerning the period covered by Book Eight especially, we may presume that a man like Thucydides would ask whether the city could survive this effect of the war at all. That it did, at least for the duration of the period covered by Book Eight, seems to be a fact of real political significance. One cause of its survival is the newfound moderation of Athens, the other is the activity of Alcibiades. Alcibiades' exemption from the decay that makes other prominent men dangerous to the city is connected to his continuing attachment to some form of honor. His form of honor is emphatically not predicated upon any rehabilitation of the traditional virtues, though honor was formerly thought to depend absolutely on the integrity of those virtues. The question of what foundation Alcibiades gives to honor, and whether his reconstruction of it is legitimate or viable, parallels the question whether Alcibiades' vision of the city is a practicable one. The question of Alcibiades' notion of the life of honor is one of the last and most difficult issues encountered in the study of him.

182

Alcibiades and the Rule of Honor

What prevents Alcibiades from becoming corrupt in the manner of many of his contemporaries is, paradoxically, his extremism. In his speech at Athens, he outlines a view of the life of honor whose most obvious difference from the traditional view is its extremism. The statesman gets honor while the city reaps benefit or advantage, as is traditionally the case, but in Alcibiades' view this division of spoils becomes so complete that it virtually eliminates the possibility of a conflict of interest between statesman and city, so long at least as the city agrees to grant the statesman his prestige. We have already seen the political problems created by such an uncompromising desire to dominate the public life of the city: Alcibiades' vision threatens to relegate the others in the city to the status virtually of noncitizens and to reduce the city for most of its members to a society whose goal is mere material advantage. We must look more closely now at some of the ramifications of this view for Alcibiades himself.

Corresponding to the extremism of Alcibiades' view of the place of the man of honor in society is the extreme domination of the love of honor over other impulses in the economy of his own soul. Alcibiades can assert that all of his apparently private extravagance, in horse-racing and the outfitting of choruses for example, is only a part of his quest for honor, because in his case it is. He is truly driven by only one thing: his thirst for acclaim. Alcibiades is an utterly political creature. It is important to recognize that, despite his conspicuous and apparently suspicious devotion to personal wealth, the pursuit of gain or of extravagant display purely as exercises in self-indulgence, are viewed by Alcibiades as corruptions of political ambition as surely as they are viewed so by traditional civic consciousness. This point is vital to Alcibiades' claim that his pursuit of his own interest is not only innocuous to the city but a great boon to it. Alcibiades defines his self-interest wholly in political terms, wholly in terms of honor. This distinguishes him even from traditional men of honor, men like Nicias.[6] Alcibiades'

[6]See Nicias' position outlined at 6.9.2 and the discussion of the admixture of public and private interest in the traditional man of honor and the traditional civic consciousness, above, in chap. 3.

self-defined project does not require any sacrifice of self-interest or ambition on his part because Alcibiades views all his activity in such a
thoroughly political light. Ordinary statesmen, those who divide their
lives more scrupulously or more modestly into public and private
spheres, need the restraints of ordinary virtue to keep their private interests from infringing on their public duty. Pericles' scrupulousness in
this regard was so great that for the duration of his long political career
he virtually had no private life.[7]

Alcibiades' mode of assimilating his public and private interests is
contrary not only to that of Pericles but to that of the other leaders
who succeeded Pericles and who are spoken of in the eulogy of Pericles. The degeneration of Athenian leadership over the course of the
History parallels the degeneration of the Athenian thesis on power
and rule, and to some extent the two are connected. Alcibiades' uninhibited assertion of his own right to rule also looks similar to the
Athenian thesis, but it is precisely here that Alcibiades' superiority
not only to his competitors but to the city of Athens itself becomes
evident. The city's imperialism degenerates when its claim to honor
collapses under the weight of the empire and its rule becomes merely
tyrannical. The Athenians' reaction to the affair of the Hermae and
their partial recoil from the Sicilian project reflect a nascent awareness
of this. Alcibiades never recoils from any of his projects and never
experiences the pious doubts that keep other men in their place.
This, however, is precisely what leads the Athenians to believe that
Alcibiades' ambitions are tyrannical.

The city's judgment against Alcibiades rests in part on the presumptive connection between tyranny and impiety. The traditional
linking of these to immorality makes this connection natural enough
from the city's point of view, yet Thucydides' teaching on virtue and
political expertise calls it into doubt. Concerning piety in particular,
Alcibiades does not fit the paradigm of tyranny in Thucydides' work.
Tyrants are in fact among the most pious people in Thucydides.[8]

---

[7]Plutarch remarks, for example, that from the beginning of his career Pericles scrupulously avoided familiarity with individuals so as to avoid any appearance of favoritism:
he virtually renounced friendship in the name of political integrity (*Pericles* 7). Thucydides
makes Pericles' private life simply invisible. Alcibiades' integration or conflation of public
and private is of a very different character.

[8]See, e.g., 1.13; 1.126; 3.104; 6.54; and Michael Palmer's discussion of this theme

Their piety can be compared to that of Sparta, the most pious city in Thucydides. Spartan piety is part of Spartan moderation, connected by Thucydides to Spartan rule of the Helots, that is, to their quasi-tyrannical domination of a subject population.[9] Theirs is a piety of pessimism and diffidence and implicitly of bad conscience. Tyrants, whose rule over their subjects is similarly coercive and illegitimate, find themselves in a situation in many ways like that of the Spartans: having yielded to the human temptation to do as the gods do and not as they say, to rule absolutely, they become aware of the precariousness of their position and rediscover, as it were, the virtues of moderation and obedience to law. Their retreat into piety and pious hypocrisy only serves, of course, to put the seal on tyranny, since it is used to legitimize or disguise it. With this in mind, we may note that the Athenian *demos* also resorts to professions of piety on the occasion of Alcibiades' exile from the city. When the Hermae are mutilated in the city, the Athenians fear a plot against the democracy, as if piety were the same as dedication to the democracy and to the status quo.[10]

It is a nice irony of this episode that it suggests more the tyranny of the *demos* than the tyrannical intentions of Alcibiades. It is not that Alcibiades does not share the hubris of the tyrant, for it would be difficult to imagine an ambition more complete or overweening than his—but his hubris, if that is what it is, has the paradoxically redeeming feature of being more complete than that of the ordinary tyrant. If Alcibiades and the tyrant have hubris in common, there is at least an implicit dispute between them as to what hubris or rivalry toward the gods truly is. Ordinary tyrants suppose implicitly that the gods rule tyrannically, by force, but perhaps the gods rule not by force, but by honor and acclaim instead. There are indications in Thucydides that the gods support human tyranny;[11] perhaps it could be said that the very idea or ideal of

---

("Alcibiades and the Question of Tyranny in Thucydides," *Canadian Journal of Political Science* 15 [1982]:118).

[9]Cf. 8.24, 40, and my discussion of this point in chap. 3, above.

[10]This presumption of course is inevitably made by all regimes. It is manifestly hypocritical in the case of tyrannies because tyrannies are established by definition in defiance of justice. The Athenian rediscovery of piety as a safeguard of the democracy appears especially naive in this instance, since it seems that many of the Hermes statues in Athens were erected by the Peisistratid tyrants in the first place. See Plato *Hipparchus* 228–29.

[11]The association between piety and tyranny in Thucydides was discussed in the pre-

the gods elicits this desire and this ambition from erotically driven human beings. But that is not to say that the human beings whose attempts are supported or inspired by the gods do not typically botch the job. Typically, honor gives way to the rule of force because human beings simply do not have the status of gods, because honor and persuasion fail, or because the ordinary human ambition to rule, as in the city of Athens, is simply lower and more earthbound, more connected to the desire for profit than it is to honor. Alcibiades' ambition is in a sense to rule as perfectly as tyrants rule, but he is intelligent enough to know that a position of complete supremacy not attained by means of honor or acclaim, is fatally flawed. Alcibiades never moves to impose himself by force on the city, even when the city scorns him. Even after exile has shown him how great the city's resistance to him is, he hopes and plans to return there only "by persuasion" (8.47.1). The extreme character of Alcibiades' hubris consists in his unshakable conviction that he is worthy of the position he aspires to, and that the force of his superiority, made plain by his deeds and his rhetoric, will be enough to obtain and maintain that position for him.

What distinguishes Alcibiades from ordinary tyrants, then, and from the degeneration of ordinary tyranny (including its remorse and pious hypocrisy), is not dedication to honor as such, but single-minded, exclusive—and, we must add, well thought out—dedication to honor. Ordinary tyrants may begin their careers aspiring to honor, but their dedication to it is less pure and less intelligent. This unflagging dedication to honor distinguishes Alcibiades even more strongly from the city of Athens in her own bid for supremacy. Pericles' Funeral Oration, of all the official Athenian pronouncements connected with imperialism, comes closest to interpreting the Athenian pursuit of profit in "Alcibidean" fashion, as only a part of the city's pursuit of honor. Pericles says that the splendor and the brilliance of the city that result from its imperial wealth are part of its greatness and worthiness, its bid for present and future glory (e.g., 2.41). He even comes close to saying that the Athenians rule by acclaim over voluntary subjects (2.41.3, 40.4). Pericles gives this up in his last speech, however, when he admits that the empire is essentially a tyranny (2.63.2), though he still holds that it is glorious

---

vious section from the point of view of the tyrant. For the point made here see especially the story of Cylon the Athenian, 1.126, and Palmer, "Tyranny in Thucydides."

and noble to maintain it (64.3, 6). The last argument proves untenable, and by the time of the Melian Dialogue the Athenians are claiming that they in their imperialism do no more or less than the gods do, making of the gods tyrants like themselves (5.105.2).

Alcibiades' desire to rule does not degenerate like the Athenian desire to rule because it does not have the same independent component of material advantage, the component that comes to predominate in Athenian imperialism. Alcibiades seeks to rule not only for the sake of honor, but by means of honor. Alcibiades believes that he can attain the position that he desires by means of honor or acclaim, by persuasion and without force. He believes in other words that honor effectively rules in the city, overcoming all obstacles (including envy and the wiles of demagogy) and making recourse to other means unnecessary. This is a thoroughly optimistic notion, and his adherence to it is remarkable especially given the course of his career. The importance of this optimism to Alcibiades' politics becomes clear when we consider that it is the only view that allows him simultaneously to maintain his dedication to honor and his political ambition. Without this optimism he would have to abandon his dedication to honor, in the manner of ordinary tyrants, or forsake his ambition. It is important to recognize that Alcibiades has a very high view of politics, perhaps the highest. Only such a view can support such extreme ambitions while shielding them from the temptation to proceed tyrannically. To repeat, the tenacity of this view is remarkable given Alcibiades experience. A Machiavellian might find this naive, but it is this naiveté that prevents Alcibiades from becoming Machiavellian.

An additional feature of Alcibiades' ambition is its embrace of the widest field possible. Alcibiades views the entire political world as a single, universal field, above or beyond any particular city. He implicitly extends his high view of politics to this wider context. If honor rules completely in the city, it rules thus in all cities and over human beings as such. Alcibiades believes that politics among cities can be managed in something like the way that he believes the city can be managed. A distinctive universalism of political method results from this view that is one of the derivatives of Alcibiades' understanding of honor and of the way that honor is capable of directing political events. This universalism is a breakthrough in the practice of international politics, but, as with other Alcibidean innovations, it is more problematic from the point of view of the city as such. This creates a dilemma that Alcibiades ultimately cannot solve.

The Universalism of Alcibiades

It is characteristic of Alcibiades' mode of proceeding in international politics that he prefers what we may roughly call diplomatic means to the simple application of force in accomplishing his designs.[12] He seems even to delight in the manipulation of events by the pure application of his own ingenuity, in living by his wits so to speak. In his speech at Athens before the Sicilian expedition Alcibiades argues that such means avail him in his dealings with foreign powers as well as in domestic politics. One proof of his talent as a leader, and of his title to rule in Athens (according to him) is that he was able singlehandedly to organize and direct a league of Peloponnesian cities that eventually challenged Sparta at Mantineia. The language in which Alcibiades describes these exploits is quite remarkable. He says that his youth and "folly" engaged the Spartan power with fitting words and created persuasion by means of a passion or ardor that inspired trust (6.17.1). What comes through most clearly in this tangled locution is the notion that Alcibiades, both by speech or persuasion and by the simple vehemence or force of his personality, turned events to his will. It is striking that he identifies such a nebulous and clearly idiosyncratic quality as vehemence or ardor as a basis of his power to influence events.[13] Alcibiades' claim is that through a combination of such personal qualities he induced the Argives and others to attack the Spartan power. The way Alcibiades casts the episode, pitting his talent alone against the Spartans, is not entirely misleading, especially when one considers how little initiative of their own the Argives and their allies displayed in the affair.[14]

The image Alcibiades presents in this passage, that of an individual

---

[12]H. D. Westlake characterizes Alcibiades' typical mode of proceeding as "diplomatic": *Individuals in Thucydides* (Cambridge: Cambridge University Press, 1968), p. 223.

[13]The word whose meaning I am attempting to capture here is *orgē*, a word for which I find no truly satisfactory translation in the sense that Alcibiades uses it here. We may take some consolation from the fact that the Greek audience would no doubt be mystified in the same measure and that Alcibiades perhaps intends to mystify.

[14]Cf. 5.43, 46, 52; Plutarch *Alcibiades* 15; Isocrates *De Bigis*.

affecting, if not effecting, events of international scope purely by the force of his own person and talents, may be the most exhilarating or seductive that could be devised for any man of ambition. It is also to be sure the most convenient for Alcibiades' purposes in the speech. But reflection on Alcibiades' other remarks and on his deeds shows that this image reflects quite accurately the kind of achievement he aims for in his political career. This achievement we might describe as the production of the greatest motion, the accomplishment of the greatest political results, solely by persuasion—or, to match the breadth of Alcibiades' formulation, by purely spiritual human forces. Something like this must indeed be possible for Alcibiades to become a real force in international politics on his own account. For in terms of direct, conventional force, it goes without saying that no man can be of any significance next to the power of a city. Hence Alcibiades' preferred mode of operating internationally must be diplomacy, or perhaps intrigue, rather than the simple application of force.

This observation is paradoxical in light of the fact that Alcibiades, as we remarked once before, seems to be always and everywhere an advocate of war. He might even appear quintessentially a man of war—we recall that Thucydides' praise of Alcibiades centers on his usefulness in war. Alcibiades' brilliance as an actual commander in battle is indeed indisputable.[15] But war, as the greatest form of motion, simply provides the greatest opportunity for the kind of maneuvering that Alcibiades describes in his speech at Athens, the greatest outlet for ambition, and the greatest opportunity for distinction. War is Alcibiades' element for these reasons primarily. Even commanding in battle is primarily a strategic exercise, although the means it uses are force. In Thucydides' History as we have it, Alcibiades participates in very few battles himself, in spite of his bellicose image. He spends much more time advising those who are at war and negotiating—with the Argives, the Athenians, the Spartans, Tissaphernes, and the soldiers on Samos—to accomplish his ends. It is also important to recognize that, in his capacity as military advisor, Alcibiades typically recommends the least violent and most

---

[15]This does not mean of course that one could not find a scholar who disputed it: see Edmund Bloedow, *Alcibiades Reexamined* (Weisbaden, Ger.: Franz Steiner, 1973). On Alcibiades as a man of war see Jean Hatzfeld, *Alcibiade* (Paris: Presses Universitaires de France, 1951), p. 73, and Pouncey, *Necessities of War*, p. 110.

diplomatic courses of action possible within the realm of military strategy. His speech at Athens emphasizes the fact that his strategy with the Argive league was entirely safe and required minimal exertion, at least as far as Athens was concerned. He advises Tissaphernes in Book Eight to prevent a conclusive fight in Ionia, using a minimum of exertion (8.46).

The single most illuminating and typical illustration of the gentle warlikeness of Alcibiades is found in his strategic advice to the Athenians on the Sicilian expedition. The expedition is hardly a gentle or peaceable undertaking, and Alcibiades is its most fervent advocate; but the strategy that he recommends is remarkably pacific, given the scope and the aims of the undertaking. It is almost nonmilitary. Alcibiades would use manipulative rhetoric to convince the Sicilian cities as far as possible to capitulate by themselves. He thinks that this strategy by itself is capable of great success, given the disunited and moblike character of the Sicilian cities. Appropriate rhetoric, he argues, could induce factions to deliver those cities to the Athenians (6.17.4). As far as pure military force is concerned, Alcibiades claims that the Sicilians do not have the number of hoplites that they boast of, and those they have, like the men of these cities generally, are defective in patriotism. The plan of action that Alcibiades recommends is reminiscent even of Diodotus' advice to the Athenians to rule by appealing to the factions within cities, advice that is calculated to allow the Athenians to be as gentle or nonviolent as possible within the context of their imperialism (3.47–48). Alcibiades' strategy of course is outlined before Nicias proposes the massive armament that is eventually sent by the Athenians. Alcibiades' strategy does not require such an overwhelming application of force.

After the expedition is under way, when the three commanders, Nicias, Alcibiades, and Lamachus, confer about what strategy they should pursue in Sicily, Alcibiades' proposal is essentially true to his original conception of the campaign. He suggests communicating with the cities of Sicily in order to divide the forces of the island and attach some to their side. Only subsequently would he attack the Syracusans and Selinuntians, with the help of the allies thus acquired (6.48). Thus Alcibiades prefers the use of persuasion, perhaps even to a fault: Thucydides later appears to endorse Lamachus' strategy of immediate frontal assault on Syracuse (6.49, 7.42). The massive armament the Athenians have sent may preclude Alcibiades' subtle and ingenious strategy. If so, his preference for ingenuity may lead him here into a rare strategic blunder.[16]

When Alcibiades is exiled and undertakes to advise the Spartans on their Sicilian strategy, his advice partakes of the same general quality. He insists that the Spartans send a small force of their own to Sicily, and, more important, that they send a Spartan as commander to rally the anti-Athenian forces on the island. These counsels reflect Alcibiades' general preference to achieve political ends by the manipulation of appearances or impressions: the mere presence of a Spartan commander, and the mere spectacle of Spartan resolve, will do much to turn the tide of events in the war. These kinds of devices are in their way substitutes for the raw application of force. Alcibiades' use of what we might today call psychological weapons is a part of his overall project to influence political events not simply by force but by the use of his own talents and faculties. His boast in his speech at Athens that his own splendid victories at the Olympic games, and his splendid manner of living generally, create the impression of power and wealth in the city at large falls into the same category.

These instances suffice to show how much stock Alcibiades places in the careful orchestration of political appearances. It is in Book Eight, however, that Alcibiades' use of this as a political device truly comes into its own. His maneuvers during this period are perhaps the most

---

[16]There has been some debate over the wisdom of Alcibiades' Sicilian strategy, since it is the strategy officially adopted at the first conference of the commanders, and since the expedition subsequently came to such grief. The proper approach to the question, I think, is to tie it to Alcibiades' general strategic approach. It is true that Alcibiades' first attempt at persuasion in the pursuit of this policy, at the city of Messene, is a failure, though it is one that he seems to correct (6.50.1; cf. 6.51.1–2, 74.1). Overall, though, the failure of the campaign cannot be attributed in any significant portion to Alcibiades' strategy, because Alcibiades was not in Sicily long enough to carry it out. The strategy depended on consummate skill in negotiating to replace brute force; in Alcibiades' absence, the strategy simply provides Nicias with another excuse for inactivity.

Many commentators question the wisdom of Alcibiades' plan for Sicily: see John H. Finley, *Thucydides* (1942, rpt. Ann Arbor: University of Michigan Press, 1963), p. 219; Jacqueline de Romilly, *Thucydides and Athenian Imperialism*, trans. P. Thody (New York: Barnes & Noble, 1963), pp. 206–07; G. B. Grundy, *Thucydides and the History of His Age*, 2 vols. (Oxford: Blackwell, 1948), 2:184; Westlake, *Individuals*, p. 221. The bulk of these criticisms blame Alcibiades for underestimating from the start the difficulty of the expedition and the strength and cohesion of the Sicilian cities. Thucydides, however, emphasizes the relative ease with which the campaign could have been made successful.

famous, or infamous, of his career, because they demonstrate his ability to change sides in the war repeatedly, to operate outside any city, and to influence events decisively without a real base of power other than the aura he creates around himself. We need only look at a few of the most outstanding cases of Alcibiades' use of the politics of symbolism or appearance, those connected with his attempts to be recalled to Athens. Here, Alcibiades is acting as a man literally without a country. Thucydides draws our attention several times to the fact that Alcibiades is acting deliberately to create certain impressions or appearances to further his ends. When Alcibiades first begins advising Tissaphernes on the conduct of the war, Thucydides explains that Alcibiades acts as he does in part because he thinks that if he can create the appearance of great influence with Tissaphernes, it will help him to secure his recall to Athens (8.47.1). Thucydides also remarks that the ploy is ultimately successful (47.2). Alcibiades pursues this strategy for some time, even though he has great difficulties maintaining the appearance of influence over Tissaphernes when he is forced to negotiate with Peisander and the oligarchs (8.56). The ruse ultimately fails to work with the oligarchs, but when Alcibiades is recalled by the democratic army on Samos, their opinion of his influence over Tissaphernes is decisive.[17] Once he is reinstated as commander of the Athenian forces at Samos, Alcibiades' orchestration of appearances on all sides reaches its masterful peak. He uses his putative influence with Tissaphernes to awe the soldiers and his position with the soldiers to undermine the oligarchy in Athens. He also uses his standing with the soldiers and Tissaphernes to drive a wedge between the Spartans and Tissaphernes by making it appear that Tissaphernes is now supporting him and the Athenians. The crowning gesture in this Alcibidean campaign of appearances is his sailing to Aspendus, where Tissaphernes had gone with the apparently feigned intention of bringing Phoenician ships to aid the Spartans; Thucydides supposes that Alcibiades does this to make it appear to the Spartans that he and Tissaphernes are cooperating

[17]Cf. 8.76.7; 81.1. Malcolm McGregor suggests that Alcibiades anticipates this entire chain of events: he foments an oligarchic coup, then prevents himself from being made a member of the oligarchy, in anticipation of a democratic backlash that will allow him to return to Athens as the hero of a restored democracy ("The Genius of Alcibiades," *Phoenix* 19 [1965]:42). The scenario is enticing but would be impossible to establish with any certainty, especially since Alcibiades is rather indifferent to the question of regimes throughout. See chap. 3.

to damage the Spartan cause, and in that way to put more pressure on Tissaphernes to join the Athenian cause (88).

This summary indicates not only how systematically Alcibiades exploits psychology and appearances in Book Eight but also how serviceable this means of operating is to him: it more than anything else makes him a power in the war during this period. It is scarcely too much to say that Alcibiades generates power out of nothing but appearances by the use of such devices. If one of the properties of Athenian daring was its ability to create power beyond the conventionally possible, Alcibiades' politics is an unambiguous improvement on its Athenian model. The systematic and ingenious manipulation of appearances, of symbols, and of rhetoric is in fact the primary form in which Alcibiades' political talent or expertise manifests itself in Thucydides.

Politics built around these devices is well calculated to allow the statesman a maximum of influence on the course of events. It is less dependent on the overt use of force and more on the use of wit and ingenuity. These things would seem indubitable advantages, not only for the statesman but for the city. But a problem presents itself if we look once again at the problematic aspects of Alcibiades' leadership of the Athenian soldiers stationed on Samos. Alcibiades' first speech to the soldiers is one of the most striking, and most successful, instances of his manipulation of rhetoric and appearances to attain his political ends. Alcibiades speaks extravagantly of his own ability to bring Tissaphernes over to the Athenian side and of the Athenian soldiers' prospects for the future. Thucydides says that his intention in speaking so was not only to bolster the confidence of his audience at Samos but at the same time to make the oligarchs then ruling in Athens fear him, to facilitate the destruction of the political clubs there, and to sow deep suspicion of Tissaphernes in the Spartans and their allies and undermine their hopes (81.2). He also intends to impress Tissaphernes himself. Alcibiades seeks merely by this rhetorical pose (and by his subsequent message to the Athenian oligarchs: 86) to affect not only the situation in Athens but the political and even the military balance in the war itself. In speaking to the soldiers at Samos, Alcibiades is in effect addressing the whole world.

We are familiar with the problematic character of this episode as an example of public deliberation, and as an epitome of Alcibiades' rule. Alcibiades' tendency to replace persuasion with harangue or even manipulation and to overwhelm any possibility for real deliberation or

193

participation is paradigmatic here. The episode is also typical of Alcibiades' tendency to conceive of the political field in the broadest possible way, indeed as fundamentally unified. His arsenal of devices for exerting personal leadership he applies almost indifferently to the domestic and the broader audience. Alcibiades' vision of the city, where the statesman prevails by means of persuasion and honor or grandeur is only part of his more universal view of politics.

Alcibiades' can be characterized as a high view inasmuch as it is resolutely optimistic about the ability of superior talent to prevail in politics and to direct events over the broadest field with a minimum of violence. Alcibiades' success in this regard represents great progress in the conduct of international politics, as force is replaced as much as possible with wit and guile. These ingenious manipulations are much more questionable, however, as means of securing consent and directing events within the city. Alcibiades' universalism tends to blur the distinction between domestic and foreign politics, if not to dissolve the city completely into the larger political field that he has continually in view. This tendency is visible from Alcibiades' assertion of his stature as an Olympic victor to his elaborate machinations on Samos. It is problematic because it ignores the important differences between politics within and without the city, differences which make a brilliant advance in the field of international politics become a travesty of politics when applied within the city. This is the consequence of Alcibiades' universalism and also its limit, as Alcibiades never fully carries out the program that seems implicit in his universal view. He never actually dissolves the cities into his broader field or even makes any serious moves in that direction. Alcibiades is no Alexander. He is attached to the city as a political platform, as the true home of politics, even while his ambitions and his conceptions lead him to transcend it in almost every way. Alcibiades' universalism remains incomplete, even inconsistent.

Imperialism could be called the form of universalism characteristic of cities. It is one kind of universalism that Alcibiades unhesitatingly and unequivocally advocates. Yet, as we have discovered, Alcibiades' universalism differs from that of the city because of its superior dedication to honor rather than profit, and its use of nonviolent devices. Given Alcibiades' views and his methods, it is not an accident that he does not anywhere call the Athenian empire that he champions a tyranny, though doing so has almost become commonplace among Athenian statesmen in the History. Alcibiades does not regard the empire as a tyranny, and his conscience is as clear about recommending exploits like the Sicilian expedition as it is about claiming preeminence for himself at Athens or in the Greek world as a whole. He seems to regard his leadership of Athens, and through Athens of the Athenian empire, as two essentially similar things. His own unique universalism makes this view possible, but the difference between the universalism of Alcibiades and the imperialism of the city is obviously a problem of some importance in assessing Alcibiades' statesmanship as a whole.

The Universalism of Alcibiades and the Imperialism of the City

Typical of Alcibiades' imperial policy at Athens during his first tenure there is his advocacy of the greatest imperial expansion, to be carried out in the gentlest or most pacific way possible. His activities with the Argive league, as summarized in his speech at Athens, as well as his strategy for the Sicilian expedition, rely on a minimum of force. This gentleness reminds us of the advice of Diodotus to the Athenians, except that Diodotus does not advocate expansion of the empire. This of course is not an insignificant difference. Alcibiades, in the same speech in which he outlines his plan for the "gentle" conquest of Sicily, even anticipates the argument of Machiavelli that powerful nations must expand without limit. And Alcibiades cannot escape the fact, whatever his own views on the character of empire, that it is the empire of Athens that he is furthering here. In the final analysis, when Alcibiades advocates imperial ventures in the name of Athens or any particular city, he necessarily advocates something harsh, not gentle. Inasmuch as Alcibiades is the most ardent supporter of imperial ventures in Athens, that makes him, almost in spite of himself, an advocate of violence and indeed of tyranny.

This is reflected in many ways in Thucydides' narrative. In spite of Alcibiades' own disinclination to anger, for example, he does on the occasion of his first appearance in the History incite the city to rage (at the Spartans) in order to obtain the vote he wants (5.45.4). Anger is not a significant part of Alcibiades' psychology, but it is necessarily involved in the actions of a city. Thucydides says of Pericles that he was able to move the city to fear or boldness when occasion demanded (2.65.9); he did not characteristically move the city to anger. Cleon

195

moves the city to anger (3.36–40). Alcibiades cannot on the whole be compared to Cleon, but when he acts in partnership with the city, he is implicated necessarily in the city's ways.[18] This might be seen even in Thucydides' presentation of the most egregious of all Athenian misdeeds, the action on Melos: he mentions briefly an unrelated act of Alcibiades, then launches immediately into his account of the Melian campaign (5.84). The effect is to exempt Alcibiades rather pointedly from any connection with the Melian episode itself, while mentioning him in the same breath, as it were.[19]

This is as good a way as any of depicting the problem of Alcibiades' relation to Athenian imperialism. Alcibiades does not regard the Athenian empire as a tyranny because there is no room for such a notion in his view of his own activity. When Alcibiades speaks of the empire, he thinks of his own rule and not that of the city, or perhaps he blurs the distinction between the two. The only evident way to overcome this problem in the imperialism of Alcibiades would be to transcend the city in such a way as to create in effect a new imperial community over which Alcibiades would stand in his accustomed position as leader. The closest Alcibiades comes to articulating such a vision in Thucydides is in the peculiar conclusion to his second speech, where he offers the Spartans the prospect of "hegemony" over all the Greeks, "voluntarily and without force, by good will" (6.92.5). This is precisely the way Alcibiades would envisage his own rule over an empire; but this promise, delivered to the Spartans, can only be reconciled with his desire to return to Athens, which he professes in the same speech, if we imagine Alcibiades ruling simultaneously over Athens and Sparta. This would require the transcendence, and the dissolution, of both cities, if only because both have

[18]Nevertheless, Alcibiades' moving the city to anger is a very rare event in Thucydides; the case mentioned is the only instance. The signal service that Thucydides lauds Alcibiades for at Samos, meanwhile, is the calming of the anger of the soldiers who wanted to sail immediately against the oligarchs at Athens (8.86; cf. 82). Cleon, on the other hand, characteristically operates by means of violence and anger (3.36.6; 5.16.1).

[19]Thucydides' treatment of this detail draws our attention partly because Plutarch connects Alcibiades directly to the eventual decision to slaughter the Melians (*Alcibiades* 16). Thucydides refrains completely from implicating Alcibiades in the deplorable Melian incident (cf. Romilly, *Athenian Imperialism*, p. 195). The deed of Alcibiades that Thucydides mentions "in the same breath" as the beginning of his narration of the Melian episode is the taking of some Argive hostages to guarantee against an oligarchic coup in that city. These hostages are later killed—in the anti-oligarchic hysteria connected with the incident of the Hermae, the same hysteria that exiles Alcibiades (6.61).

proven their incompetence, as cities, to fulfill any ideal of voluntary rule. Alcibiades' attachment to the polis prevents him from seriously contemplating this, but his whole cast of mind lends itself to grave rhetorical and practical dilemmas of just this kind. Only a statesman can rule in the way Alcibiades has in mind, but it is by no means clear that such rule can be extended as far as Alcibiades wants to extend it.

What seems to rest behind Alcibiades' species of universalism is the supposition of a possible community among cities, a real common good. The implicit premise is that from a point of view sufficiently high—which is of course Alcibiades' own point of view—all interests can converge or at least be reconciled. For Alcibiades this is not only true within the hypothetical context of his own greatest hopes; it also functions as a guiding principle for his practical political activity. The typically Alcibidean thought, when confronted with apparent conflict of interest in the pursuit of his ambition, is that no real conflict exists. This is certainly true of his activity in Athens. When we first see Alcibiades, he is recommending an Argive alliance to the Athenians, because, says Thucydides, he believes that the alliance will suit his interests and will be best for the city as a whole (5.43.2). The whole premise of Alcibiades' activity as a statesman in Athens, as he openly proclaims, is that his own interests and the interests of the city cannot diverge. That premise is strained, to say the least, when Alcibiades is exiled from the city and becomes advisor to the city's worst enemy. Yet he continues to insist on it nonetheless, causing in the peculiar difficulty just discussed in his speech at Sparta, a difficulty that can be reconciled in logic only if the interests of Alcibiades, of Athens, and of Sparta all three are compatible.

This kind of thinking runs as a thread through Alcibiades' entire career, even to Book Eight, where, predictably, it is stretched thin indeed as Alcibiades serves successively every side in the war. Thucydides draws attention to Alcibiades' thinking when he moves from the Spartan camp to become advisor to the Persian Tissaphernes. The advice he gives Tissaphernes to start with is not to support either Athens or Sparta too much but to wear one down against the other. Thucydides remarks, in an echo of earlier passages, that Alcibiades gave this advice both because he thought it best for Tissaphernes and because he was beginning to prepare his way back to Athens (8.46–47). Alcibiades believes that no fundamental divergence of interest will prevent this policy being best for Tissaphernes, for Athens, and for himself; nor does he doubt that

197

by his machinations he can make it so in the long run. Alcibiades believes at this point that he can genuinely serve these two masters (or rather, clients) as well as himself. At least he has given up temporarily the idea that he can serve the Spartans as well. That this supposition plays a role in Alcibiades' advice is made conspicuous later when it proves a great stumbling-block to Alcibiades' plans as Athenian commander. Tissaphernes learns too well from Alcibiades' original good advice and proves absolutely intractable to Alcibiades' attempts to bring him forthrightly into the Athenian camp.[20]

Alcibiades' overly optimistic belief in the compatibility of all political interests, drawn from his own view of politics and empire, allows him to move from one camp to another without feeling guilty of outright betrayal. It also facilitates his belief in the effectiveness of rhetoric and other manipulations as substitutes for brute force, insofar as the divergences of interest they are designed to overcome are not adamant and perhaps not entirely real. Divergences of interest, however, are both real and adamant, as the phenomenon of war demonstrates. Contemplation of these Alcibidean thoughts and actions necessarily leads us to the conclusion that Alcibidean politics, taken to its full extent—the attempt to rule perfectly, by honor and acclaim, and to extend one's rule over the broadest possible field—must ultimately fail, if brilliantly and even generously. In the end, Alcibiades' view of the possibilities of international politics is too high. Alcibiades' successes as an international statesman, guided by this view, are impressive but limited. Implicit in his speech and political activity, as a kind of keystone to the entire edifice, is the notion that he can somehow transform imperialism into a nonoppressive and nontyrannical thing, that he can somehow bring all interests together and stand over the whole merely by appealing to good will, without the use of compulsion. This would seem to be the purest,

[20]8.56, 87–88. I suggested earlier that Alcibiades' initial advice might be understood as the most pro-Athenian advice he could give in this context (see chap. 3, n. 16, and text). That, however, does not alter the fact that Alcibiades gives this advice according to Thucydides because he sincerely believes it best and most compatible with his prospective service to Athens. The argument of McGregor, that Alcibiades is not so much convinced that he can serve all these interests as he is hatching an exquisitely clever plot for his return to Athens, is discussed briefly in n. 17, above. No one is more impressed with Alcibiades' cleverness than I, but I believe that he also has some characteristic blind spots linked precisely to the more generous aspects of his political outlook. His unjustifiably sanguine belief in the compatibility of political interests is one of these.

as well as the highest and the most extreme, form that political ambition takes. There was an element of this in Athens' own aspiration to empire.

Alcibiades, in other words, is a political idealist, though of a peculiar kind. His remarkably durable idealism preserves him from the corruption that affects so many actors in the History, but it has certain untoward consequences of its own. To hear Alcibiades called an idealist would perhaps shock those in the History who regard him as a simple cynic, but after all it is a tendency of excessive idealism to turn in practice into a simulacrum of its opposite. It takes an intellectual grasp like that of Thucydides to perceive the idealism that lies behind Alcibiades' actions, to see that it springs from statesmanlike ambitions pushed to their extremes and that it proceeds on the supposition that such ambitions can indeed be consummated. But they cannot, and that fact caps Alcibiades' many brilliant successes in foreign politics with ultimate failure, giving his whole project even a kind of incoherence. It dooms Alcibiades' aspirations in domestic politics to even greater frustration, since their triumph would mean effectively an end to the political life of the city as such.

The Honor and the Hubris of Alcibiades

At the core of Alcibiades' idealism lies his abiding commitment to the life of honor as he sees it. Alcibiades remains attached to this notion even after the events of the war seem to have all but driven honor from the world; hence he appears at the end of the History as the one man able to reconstruct the public good in the city of Athens, after the depradations of the oligarchs in particular. This "reconstruction," however, has problems of its own. Some of the difficulties created by Alcibiades' pursuit of honor we can identify as archetypal problems in the relations between great statesmen or seekers of honor and their communities. As Alcibiades says, such men are always vexatious to their contemporaries while they are alive (6.16), and they always have certain distorting effects on the communities in which they operate. This jealousy and distortion haunted even the career of Pericles. The problems with Alcibiades' presence go considerably beyond this, however, for reasons that have to do with the peculiarity of his notion of honor and the question of exactly what it is that he desires. For although he holds fast to an ideal of honor, Alcibiades redefines it substantially, and perhaps unconsciously, after his own fashion. Hubris is the error of those who step beyond the limits of what is appropriate to human beings, even if they do so in the name of a mistaken or excessive love of honor. And Alcibiades' new ideal of the life of honor looks more than a little like hubris.

What we must bear in mind is that the traditional life of honor had traditional, public-spirited virtue, as well as traditional piety, as its core and its substance. The eclipse of these at Athens led to the demise of honor and consequently of statesmanship there. What makes Alcibiades uniquely serviceable to the city in this context is his continued devotion to some notion of honor, but if we examine his speeches and actions with a view to discovering just how he conceives of this honor, we find anything but the traditional notion. Alcibiades' concept seems much closer to simple splendor or grandeur, or perhaps to a kind of height. The means Alcibiades uses to attain the position he desires certainly include some that are difficult to distinguish from simple material splendor or grandeur. He conceives of the place of honor, moreover, as a place so high that from its perspective the world appears a single field, and his own interest becomes so global as to embrace all those beneath him. But honor is not the same as height, grandeur, or splendor: it also includes virtues that define and limit its "height." Alcibiades does not bring these to his reconstruction of honor.

Alcibiades' immoderation, his spirit of excess, is curiously a key both to the success of his restitution of honor and to its apostasy. We have remarked more than once that Alcibiades' extremism is instrumental in preserving him from the corruption that destroys others. The Athenians certainly recognize Alcibaibes' dedication to the life of grandeur, but they fear that, far from being a sign of his love of honor, this grandeur augurs tyrannical ambitions in him (6.15.4). Alcibiades' bid for grandeur is founded largely in his material extravagance, which appears self-indulgent to the Athenians, and contrary to, if not incompatible with, the traditional pursuit of honor. The question of extravagance is doubly serious since Thucydides regards moderation as a key element of Greek culture, a quality important in particular to the achievement and perfection of political community. Alcibiades, not only in his dress,[21] but

[21]Thucydides says nothing about Alcibiades' dress specifically, but Plutarch claims that it was one of the most conspicuous forms his extravagance took—and also one of the most irksome to the Athenians (*Alcibiades* 16).

in his entire manner of life, appears to flout that reserve. The Thucydidean character that Alcibiades resembles most in his lavish mode of life is not Pericles or Themistocles but Pausanias. The extravagant manners and dress that Pausanias adopted reflected indeed a repudiation of Greek moderation and a desire to rule as an oriental despot.

Within the broad context of the History, Alcibiades' extravagance blends suspiciously well with the incipient decay of Greek ideals and of Athenian political life in his own time. It even looks like a characteristic misapprehension of the nature of honor that grew out of the decay of Athenian imperialism. The Athenians began the war with the notion that their empire was honorable, but shadowing this notion of honor as it were, especially in the mouth of Pericles, was the more general notion of splendor or brilliance. As honor faded, this more morally neutral or even immoral notion took its place. The transition seems complete by the time Thucydides describes the stunning éclat of the expedition sent to Sicily, that is, its material splendor. Honor plays no part in this; but brilliance does. Alcibiades' self-proclaimed pursuit of honor seems to resemble most the splendor of this "Alcibidean moment" at Athens.

Alcibiades' project is as hostile to restraint as is the Athenians', and as much a stranger to traditional virtue. But Alcibiades' arguments in defense of his behavior are to the point here. His use of extravagance to dominate the public life of the city, according to Alcibiades, is an expedient to secure a voluntary rule in the city, that is, it is precisely the contrary of tyrannical force. Extravagance for Alcibiades is part of a self-conscious project of political and not tyrannical rule. It is not, as it was for Pausanias, the trappings of a tyrant, nor is it an exercise in self-indulgence for its own sake. Alcibiades' profligacy must at least be distinguished from ordinary profligacy. In his case, paradoxically, it reflects continued devotion to some form of the Greek political ideals identified by Thucydides. In fact, Alcibiades' project might be understood to have its source in the very core of the Greek ideal, especially in its Athenian pole.

At the center of the Athenian experiment in politics is the uncovering and liberation of as many human faculties as possible, coupled with the kindred attempt to push human power to its limits. Alcibiades' ambition has the same characteristics, with the initial difference that Alcibiades' project much more boldly relies on and projects the power of one individual. The Athenian project, uncovering and relying on humanity, seems a natural and legitimate outgrowth of the Greek discovery of humanity as a worthy object or ideal in its own right.[22] The humanistic Greek ideal was connected simultaneously with a spirit of modesty and reserve, as against barbaric or pre-Greek lavishness, but this modesty has proven perishable, as Athens and Alcibiades show. The unguarded ambition and energy that the Athenian project unleashes proves excessive in every way and ends in tyranny, the tyranny of Athens over its subjects and the tyranny of the Four Hundred within the city. It is rather more difficult to think of Alcibiades' excess as simply illegitimate, although it is strictly parallel to that of Athens. All of Alcibiades' excess is dedicated to his project of political rule, and the rule of one man over others, as Alcibiades conceives it, is much more legitimate than the rule of one city over others. The only way Alcibiades as one man can hope to bring his project to fulfillment is by becoming in every way bigger than life. This he does in part through an opulence that for any ordinary, "private" individual would be the height of unjustified, even boastful, self-indulgence.

The Athenians, according to Thucydides, feared and suspected Alcibiades' extravagance because of its lawlessness, its affront to accepted standards of civic behavior (*paranomia* 6.15.4). In Alcibiades' defense of his activities before the Athenians he makes one literal rebuttal of that charge, etymologically speaking, when he claims that all his extravagances—in Olympic horse-racing, the subsidizing of choruses, and so on—are in fact things that bring honor "by law" or according to accepted convention (*nomō* 6.16.2). The statement is intended to reassure the Athenians that his extravagances are engaged in only for the sake of honor and that as such they are not only lawful but downright conventional. In that sense, we would have to add, they are even moderate, since they are governed by a rule or law of honor and rigorously integrated into Alcibiades' larger political project. This is a legitimate form of moderation, although the Athenians can doubtless be excused for not recognizing it. It appears excessive because of the unparalleled grandeur of Alcibiades' ambitions and of his political project. Questions about Alcibiades' personal conduct, therefore, must be referred to that

[22]See the discussion of this point in chap. 1, "Thucydides View of Athenian Imperialism."

political project as a whole. The question of the excessiveness of his personal conduct, and thus the defensibility of the notion of Alcibidean moderation, is tied to a judgment about the defensibility of Alcibiades' ambitions and his political views altogether. Alcibiades' self-justification on the count of lawless excess makes sense only if the project to which it is tied is a legitimate one.

Thucydides does not provide any single, simple answer to this question. Alcibiades' project, in comparison to the corresponding Athenian project, is both more viable and more defensible. Yet we have been forced to admit its simple impossibility. In international politics, one man, no matter how grand his stature, cannot induce all men and events to follow his prompting. Individual human faculties cannot reach so far, even with the extravagant prostheses. One of the reasons for Alcibiades' overstated, exaggerated character is precisely that he is possessed of an ambition that throws him against the limits of impossibility. Alcibiades' may in one sense represent the highest or purest form of political ambition, but if politics is truly the art of the possible, his ambition could in another sense be regarded in effect as nonpolitical. There is a certain manic or driven quality to Alcibiades' activity and especially his extravagance that stems from the ultimate impossibility of his project. This is perhaps harmless enough—it does after all signify Alcibiades' fundamentally nontyrannical bent inasmuch as extravagance substitutes for the brute use of force in his political manipulations. But Alcibiades' political project remains fundamentally hubristic. Alcibiades does quite well given the audacity of his project, but the project itself remains an exercise in mere audacity. Its scope and its daring—its "folly," to use Alcibiades' terminology—doom it to failure. The project of ruling the world, whether tyrannically or not, is appropriate only to a god.[23] The fact that Alcibiades seeks nontyrannical rule only makes his rivalry with the gods more complete, if more innocuous to his fellow human beings.

Alcibiades' personal extravagance participates in this hubris at least indirectly, as part of his project. The Athenians perceive the hubris in Alcibiades' extravagance, but they mistake its cause. Alcibiades' extravagance of manner and of conception reflect not a tyrannical ambition but an ambition to do more and to rise higher than is possible and appropriate for a human being. We have remarked that Alcibiades' extremism,

[23] Cf. Aristotle *Politics* 1326a30–35.

paradoxically, saves him from corruption and tyrannical temptations. His extravagant view of what it is possible to accomplish by statesmanlike means, and of the rewards forthcoming to those who live the life of honor, preserve and nurture his peculiar brand of idealism. But this view places him hypothetically in a position that only a god can occupy, a position so high that its occupant could be given all honors indifferently without dishonoring his constituents and could enjoy a perspective from which all political interests, indeed all human interests, converge.

Alcibiades' views are so extreme and uncompromising that in effect they make better theology than political science. Yet his ambitions somehow reflect the fondest dreams or aspirations of all statesmen. Alcibiades simply crosses a line that ordinary men of honor do not cross—they shrink from openly daring as much as Alcibiades does. A man like Nicias simply believes that there are limits to what human beings may aspire to, because man is not the highest being in the cosmos. Pericles thinks that boasting is a danger for the city. Alcibiades is led to abandon all the old forms of restraint and to undertake every form of overstatement because he attempts to fill a role that no man can fill. His bid for supreme honor finally takes on an appearance radically different from those models of statesmanship that Alcibiades claims to emulate.

There is more at stake here than appearances, though, for in the process of conceiving and executing his project Alcibiades ends up substituting a new standard of honor for the old one, which is virtually destroyed by the events of the war. The old notion of honor, which depends on the traditional virtues and piety, is vulnerable to precisely the kinds of attacks that the war and Athenian sophistication leveled at it, and is limited in what it will undertake, at least compared to Athenian and Alcibidean daring. When Alcibiades tells the Athenians, and himself, that he is pledged to a life of honor, it is honor of a significantly new and different kind. It is in this that the true depth of his hubris consists. It might be the work of a human being to rediscover the possibility of a life of honor, that possibility having been forgotten; but to construct or reinvent it in the way that Alcibiades does might be more, even, than the work of a god.

The question reappears, then, of the precise content of Alcibiades' notion of honor, and of its foundation, absent the traditional standards of virtue and piety. Let us return to Alcibiades' personal extravagance, apparently lawless but proclaimed by Alcibiades to be a lawful part of his pursuit of honor. We have to this point given full credit to Alcibiades' claims that his personal extravagance is merely part of his political project, that it is subject to the rule or law of honor, and hence implicitly that it is even informed by a kind of moderation. This claim needs to be evaluated more critically. Alcibiades is not attached to this extravagance, which after all costs him so dearly, purely for the sake of political utility. The impetus for it comes more from within. The source of Alcibiades' principles or standards, in the absence of traditional honor, is actually his own tastes and inclinations, his idiosyncratic nature.

Here as elsewhere, Alcibiades' revolutionary innovation begins as nothing more than an idiosyncratic reflection or diffraction of traditional political models. On the one hand, great statesmen and men of honor are always a rule unto themselves, in Aristotle's phrase[24]; for such men, following their inclinations is doing the correct thing. On the other hand, the rule these gentlemen carry within themselves has its origin, and is understood by them to have its origin, outside of themselves, in the gods or in some objective and transcendent standard to which they are subservient. This is what Alcibiades has failed to reproduce in his version of the life of honor. According to Aristotle, the life of the gentleman is predicated on painstaking habituation or the cultivation of the proper inclinations and tastes. Alcibiades proceeds on the basis of inclinations that are untutored, to say the least; his nature is a veritable cauldron of diverse passions, leading in all different directions, each demanding full and ostentatious gratification.

In the economy of Alcibiades' soul only one passion reigns supreme, that for political achievement and immortal glory, his political ambition. All his other inclinations are strictly subordinated to this—thus can Alcibiades claim that all his extravagant indulgences are subservient to his general project of garnering fame and honor. His argument becomes nearly circular, however, once it is understood that the standard Alcibiades implicitly uses for determining what is honorable is to a large extent simply his own undisciplined nature. Rather than saying that Alcibiades' appetites are strictly subordinated to his political project, it is closer to the truth to say that they are all taken up into his political project, becoming part of his notion of what greatness and hence honor is. Alcibiades follows such conventional avenues to honor as horse-

[24]*Politics* 1284a14.

205

racing, but even here he is as much governed by his own impulsiveness as by any convention. Other parts of his outrageous way of life, which he defends as instrumental to his political project, are still further from the conventional.

Alcibiades' instincts or appetites are so strong that they exclude self-doubt from his nature, impelling him to an unshakable belief that he is a model of natural perfection and needs not restrain or discipline himself in any way. Whatever his overwhelming passions impel him to do must be admirable and honorable. Yet it is hubristic in the purest sense to replace the old law of honor with an essentially self-generated standard. In this sense most fully, therefore, hubris and the life of honor are identical for Alcibiades. Alcibiades makes himself a law unto himself not in genuine conformity to the standards of nobility, as he claims, but in all his idiosyncrasy. Hence it is not merely that Alcibiades aspires to raise himself to the position of a god by his activity; his activity seems rather to presume that he is a god to begin with, inasmuch as his reconstitution of the life of honor amounts simply to giving his nature the most ostentatious free reign. He may presume himself even more than a god. Alcibiades makes his nature the standard for honor itself, but it is an open question whether the gods are a rule unto themselves in this way.

This is not to say that Alcibiades is aware of these implications of his views and his activities. The case of Alcibiades does not prove that it is possible to live self-consciously by a self-generated, or even a merely human, standard. Alcibiades genuinely thinks of himself as a simple heir to the tradition of great statesmanship, with perhaps some minor adjustments. But he occasionally makes remarks that come close to making the character of his hubris explicit. In his speech at Athens, Alcibiades explains that good fortune itself justifies his looking down on those less successful than himself. Good fortune is something that simply belongs to Alcibiades as a natural gift (6.16.4). Alcibiades here casts himself in the traditional role of the beloved or favorite of the gods, the well-fated man (*eudaimōn*), even though he does not believe in the existence of the gods. A pious man would see presuming on the favor of the gods so far as to boast about it as the blindest kind of hubris. For Alcibiades to assign himself this role, without divine authority, is the perfect example of Alcibidean hubris beyond hubris. In other ways as well, Alcibiades conceives and speaks of his success, talents, or gifts as essentially individual or idiosyncratic traits. He names his "youthful folly" and his "passionate intensity" or "ardor" as the qualities that explain his success. He intends these words to describe his talents more or less comprehensively, but in fact his statement is a nonaccount of those talents. Alcibiades seems to treat them as ineffable, unaccountable in the strictest sense. Yet it is on the basis of these qualities, thus expounded, that he lays claim to the Athenians' confidence and devotion and proclaims that he deserves to rule in the city.

The fact that Alcibiades, in addition to thinking this way, should present himself this way to the city is indicative in itself of the problem with his notion of honor. We remarked before that some of the problems with Alcibiades' leadership in the city spring from the fact that, from the Athenians' point of view, Alcibiades is largely an unknown quantity; acquiescing in his claims is a leap of faith for them. Gentlemanly honor of the traditional sort at least provides a set of clues to the character of the statesman who has it. Whatever may be said about the defectiveness of the city's judgment when it comes to recognizing and endorsing the true talents of statesmanship, the traditional understanding of honor does provide a bridge of sorts, a channel of communication as it were, between statesman and city. It is conventional, it does not truly correspond to political talent, and it is in many respects crude—one of the major themes of Thucydides' History is the character and extent of its inadequacies—but its faults are the inadequacies of the civic consciousness, which is unable to transcend the simple identification of political merit with conventional virtue and patriotism. Such a standard indeed sacrifices the peaks of political brilliance in the name of safety or regularity of leadership, but it is fair to say that only one of the functions of traditional honor is to serve as a test and standard for statesmen. The other is to help provide a basis for community in the city.

When Alcibiades displays his political talents and the rest of his brilliant nature before the city, insisting on being honored and given power on that basis, he makes a claim that is in one sense politically justified but in another sense it leaves the political community out of account. Alcibiades' new pattern or rule of honor is cogent for those, like Thucydides, who can see Alcibiades' natural brilliance and take the point of view of nature. But Alcibiades, indeed a plausible model for natural perfection or "virtue" of a certain kind, allows for no possible community. Although he sufficiently demonstrates his awareness of the need

207

for conventional virtues like moderation and discipline for the health and success of the community, this view leads only to a pervasive double standard in his political outlook, one standard for great and successful men, the other for ordinary citizens. According to Thucydides, viable political community, one of the crowning achievements of the Greeks as they rose out of barbarism, was made possible only by a generous forbearance in the conduct of the wealthy and successful few (1.6.4, 18.1). Alcibiades, who is otherwise very attached to the political form and the political opportunities of the polis, is quite ignorant of this lesson.

Alcibiades represents one of the most illuminating, if most difficult, presentations of the question concerning the harmony or disharmony between political community and human nature, that most important of Thucydidean themes. The spectacle of Alcibiades' career suggests answers that encompass both sides of the issue. Alcibiades' natural impulses are hardly governed by conventionality, yet he is strongly impelled toward the political life and is captivated by a vision of nontyrannical political achievement. This fact in itself suggests that political life is not simply based on convention. Within the context of the later parts of the History especially, after the oligarchy of the Four Hundred has run its course, Alcibiades appears to redeem the notion of political community. The politics that he longs for is one of the common good, of persuasion, and of community. To the extent that this is shown to be a chimera by the History, the stock of tyranny as a serious political alternative would rise. Thucydides' sympathetic treatment of the Peisistratid tyranny points in that direction.

Problems arise in Alcibiades' politics only from his excessive love of political rule in the nontyrannical sense, yet this is paradoxically the aspect of Alcibiades' career that places the political community in the most questionable light. One of the most significant lessons to be drawn from his career is that political aspirations, when given the freest rein, when allowed to appear in their greatest and most uncompromising form, prove self-defeating or destroy the object of their longing in the very act of attaining it. The history of Athenian imperialism tells a similar story. At the level of individuals, tyranny is perhaps the most common form of this self-defeating excess, as the tyrant effectively dissolves the political community in the act of possessing it. Alcibiades is wise enough to avoid the self-defeat of tyranny, but he faces the same dilemma in a

208

different form: even voluntary supremacy in a community, if that supremacy is complete and unqualified, makes community apolitical and makes rule of it unsatisfying for any truly political ambition. It looks as though only by placing external, conventional restraints on political ambition can it be prevented from thus overreaching itself.

Another difficulty in Alcibiades' politics has less to do with the internal tensions of politics, more with the relation of the city to human nature. Alcibiades' nature contains driving political ambition but also a wild variety of other passions and desires. He synthesizes all these into what he takes to be a comprehensive political project, but in fact this project goes beyond politics in significant ways. Yet Alcibiades, in spite of this excess, cannot be understood as simply corrupt. On the contrary, with all his vehement robustness, Alcibiades seems in Thucydides' presentation to embody vibrant health: that is to say, he exhibits a natural, not a conventional or a moral, perfection. Without it, he would not be the interesting figure that he is for Thucydides and for us. Alcibiades is the final product of the Athenian liberation of human nature, a project that produced a number of questionable results but some real natural brilliance as well. When Thucydides uses the word *virtue* to describe the Peisistratid tyrants and Antiphon the oligarch, among others, he indicates sufficiently the problematic character of reducing human virtue to ordinary moral qualities. He also indicates the difficulty of confining that virtue within the four corners of political community.

From the point of view of nature, Alcibiades' virtue or excellence may be unmatched. If there is not room for him in the city, it is because politics does not do full justice to human nature. Thucydides cannot say, with Aristotle, that man is by nature a political animal. Aristotle's dictum suggests that to domesticate human nature in political society is to perfect it; Alcibiades on this view would necessarily appear defective or corrupt.[25] Thucydides' presentation of Alcibiades, and of politics in

---

[25]I do not mean by this to slight or underestimate the subtleties of Aristotle's analysis of these issues, but only to make use of the simplest or most obvious part of his teaching for illustrative purposes. Aristotle does not simply take the point of view of the city. Political life is not the highest form of life for him, and one must reconsider the extent to which man is a "political animal" in the light of that. The point in the text is nevertheless valid enough for present purposes.

Aristotle seems to avoid the subject of Alcibiades, if I may put it so, in his political works. Alcibiades is not a convenient example, perhaps, for what Aristotle is interested in teaching in these books. The few references to Alcibiades that are scattered through

general, does not point in that direction. But it does not point in the opposite direction either. There is nothing so clear in Thucydides' History. it seems to me, as his fundamental admiration for the human achievement that the politics of the city represents, with its shared community, its deliberative public speech, and the virtues it does cultivate. The city is unambiguously superior to the barbarism that preceded it and that still surrounds it. One of the emblems of its superiority, paradoxically, is that it can cultivate even those human peaks that escape its limits and destroy it. Thucydides offers no solution to the problem thus indicated, no "best regime" of the philosophic type that puts all political aspirations in order, if only in speech. His view of history would have to be called cyclical, if by that we mean that cities and nations rise to the peak of culture only to be destroyed by their own progeny. Such a view seems to border on the tragic. But Thucydides' History does not have the aura of tragedy either; his perspective is more philosophic, so to speak. Alcibiades, whose career embodies all the most futile aspects of politics, is far from a tragic figure. The inevitable disappointment of his hopes do not even enrage him. Indeed, one of the most striking paradoxes of Alcibiades' character is his ironical view of the whole political scene, even in the midst of the most strenuous exertions to realize his political designs. One never fully loses the sense that for Alcibiades politics is a game, albeit one he is intensely interested in winning. The quasi-divine height from which he surveys the political scene, which takes him beyond the world of any particular city, almost puts him above considering political life a serious matter. In Thucydides' presentation we can see the Alcibiades who more or less retired from politics after his second break with Athens (although that took place after the History ends), as well as the Alcibiades who stops at nothing to keep control of the entire war in his own hands. There is only a fine line in his soul between intense devotion to political action and the most sovereign irony toward it. The fact that Alcibiades is above simple attachment to any particular city puts him nearly beyond attachment to the life of the city as such. In that respect he reminds us of Thucydides himself, the man beyond politics who still takes political life with the utmost seriousness.

---

his works, however, show ample appreciation of his virtues. See, for example, *Rhetoric* 1390b29, *Posterior Analytics* 97b17–20. The latter passage makes Alcibiades and Socrates examples of magnanimity, though it seems of different, if not opposite, types.

Selected Bibliography

Adcock, F. E. *Thucydides and His History*. Cambridge: Cambridge University Press, 1963.

Adkins, W. H. *Merit and Responsibility*. Oxford: Clarendon, 1960.

Andrewes, A. "Spartan Imperialism?" In *Imperialism in the Ancient World,* ed. P. D. A. Garnsey and C. R. Whittaker. Cambridge: Cambridge University Press, 1978.

Betant, E. A. *Lexicon Thucydideum*. Hildesheim, Ger.: Franz Steiner, 1973.

Bloedow, Edmund. *Alcibiades Reexamined*. Weisbaden, Ger.: Franz Steiner, 1973.

Bluhm, William T. "Causal Theory in Thucydides' Peloponnesian War." *Political Studies* 10 (1962): 15–35.

Bowra, C. M. "Euripides' Epinician for Alcibiades." *Historia* 9 (1960): 68–79.

Bradeen, Donald W. "The Popularity of the Athenian Empire." *Historia* 9 (1960): 257–69.

Bruell, Christopher. "Thucydides' View of Athenian Imperialism." *American Political Science Review* 68 (1974): 11–17.

Bury, J. B. *The Ancient Greek Historians*. London: Macmillan, 1909.

Cairns, Francis. "Cleon and Pericles: A Suggestion." *Journal of Hellenic Studies* 102 (1982): 203–4.

Chroust, Anton-Hermann. "Treason and Patriotism in Ancient Greece." *Journal of the History of Ideas* 15 (1954): 280–88.

Cochrane, Charles Norris. *Thucydides and the Science of History*. 1929. Rpt. New York: Russell & Russell, 1965.

Cogan, Marc. *The Human Thing*. Chicago: University of Chicago Press, 1981.

211

———. "Mytilene, Plataea, and Corcyra: Ideology and Policy in Thucydides, Book Three." *Phoenix* 35 (1981): 1–21.

Connor, W. Robert. *Thucydides*. Princeton: Princeton University Press, 1984.

Cornford, F. M. *Thucydides Mythistoricus*. London: Edward Arnold, 1907.

Delebecque, Edouard. *Thucydide et Alcibiade*. Aix-en-Provence: Centre d'Etudes et de Recherches Helleniques, 1965.

de Ste. Croix, G. E. M. *The Origins of the Peloponnesian War*. London: Duckworth, 1972.

Dodds, E. R. *The Greeks and the Irrational*. Berkeley: University of California Press, 1951.

Edmunds, Lowell. *Chance and Intelligence in Thucydides*. Cambridge: Harvard University Press, 1975.

Ehrenberg, Victor. *From Solon to Socrates*. London: Methuen, 1968.

———. "Polypragmosyne: A Study in Greek Politics." *Journal of Hellenic Studies* 68 (1947): 46–67.

Euben, J. Peter. "The Battle of Salamis and the Origins of Political Theory." *Political Theory* 14 (1986): 359–90.

Finley, John H., Jr. *Three Essays on Thucydides*. Cambridge: Harvard University Press, 1967.

———. *Thucydides*. 1942. Rpt. Ann Arbor: University of Michigan Press, 1963.

Fustel de Coulanges, Numa Denis. *The Ancient City*. 1864. Rpt. Baltimore: Johns Hopkins University Press, 1980.

Galpin, Timothy J. "The Democratic Roots of Athenian Imperialism in the Fifth Century B.C." *Classical Journal* 79 (1983–84): 104–15.

Glotz, Gustave. *La solidarité de la famille dans le droit criminel en Grèce*. Paris: Albert Fontemoing, 1904.

Gomme, A. W. *Essays in Greek History and Literature*. 1937. Rpt. Freeport, N.Y.: Books for Libraries Press, 1967.

———. *More Essays in Greek History and Literature*. Oxford: Blackwell, 1962.

Gomme, A. W., A. Andrewes, and K. J. Dover. *A Historical Commentary on Thucydides*. 5 vols. Oxford: Clarendon, 1945–81.

Grene, David. *Man in His Pride*. Chicago: University of Chicago Press, 1950.

Grundy, G. B. *Thucydides and the History of His Age*. 2 vols. Oxford: Blackwell, 1948.

Hatzfeld, Jean. *Alcibiade*. Paris: Presses Universitaires de France, 1951.

Hegel, G. W. F. *The Philosophy of History*, trans. J. Sibree. New York: Colonial Press, 1900.

Hobbes, Thomas. *Hobbes's Thucydides*, ed. Richard Schlatter. New Brunswick, N.J.: Rutgers University Press, 1975.

Hooker, J. T. "*Charis* and *Arete* in Thucydides." *Hermes* 102 (1974): 164–69.

Huart, Pierre. *Le vocabulaire de l'analyse psychologique dans l'oeuvre de Thucydide*. Paris: Librairie Klincksieck, 1968.

Hunter, Virginia. "The Composition of Thucydides' History: A New Answer to the Problem." *Historia* 26 (1977): 267–94.

———. *Thucydides the Artful Reporter*. Toronto: Hakkert, 1973.

Immerwahr, Henry R. "Pathology of Power and Speeches in Thucydides." In *The*

Speeches in Thucydides, ed. Philip A. Stadter. Chapel Hill: University of North Carolina Press, 1973.

Jaeger, Werner. *Paideia: The Ideals of Greek Culture,* vol. 1, trans. G. Highet. Oxford: Oxford University Press, 1939.

Lang, Mabel. "The Murder of Hipparchus." *Historia* 3 (1955): 395–407.

McGregor, Malcolm F. "The Genius of Alcibiades." *Phoenix* 19 (1965): 27–46.

Momigliano, Arnaldo. *Essays in Ancient and Modern Historiography.* Middletown, Conn.: Wesleyan University Press, 1977.

Orwin, Clifford. "The Just and the Advantageous in Thucydides: The Case of the Mytilenaean Debate." *American Political Science Review* 78 (1984): 485–94.

Palmer, Michael. "Alcibiades and the Question of Tyranny in Thucydides." *Canadian Journal of Political Science* 15 (1982): 103–24.

———. "Love of Glory and the Common Good." *American Political Science Review* 76 (1982): 825–36.

Pearson, Lionel. "Prophasis and Aitia." *Transactions and Proceedings of the American Philological Association* 83 (1952): 205–23.

———. "Three Notes on the Funeral Oration of Pericles." *American Journal of Philology* 64 (1943): 399–407.

Peremens, Willy. "Thucydide, Alcibiade, et l'expedition de Sicile en 415 av. J.-C." *L'Antiquité Classique* 25 (1956): 331–44.

Pouncey, Peter R. *The Necessities of War: A Study of Thucydides' Pessimism.* New York: Columbia University Press, 1980.

Pusey, Nathan Marsh. "Alcibiades and *to phiolopoli.*" *Harvard Studies in Classical Philology* 51 (1940): 215–31.

Quinn, T. J. "Thucydides and the Unpopularity of the Athenian Empire." *Historia* 13 (1964): 257–66.

Raubitschek, A. E. "The Speech of the Athenians at Sparta." In *The Speeches in Thucydides,* ed. Philip A. Stadter. Chapel Hill: University of North Carolina Press, 1973.

Rawlings, Hunter R., III. *The Structure of Thucydides' History.* Princeton: Princeton University Press, 1981.

Romilly, Jacqueline de. *Histoire et raison chez Thucydide.* Paris: Societé d'Editions "Les Belles Lettres," 1956.

———. *Thucydides and Athenian Imperialism,* trans. P. Thody. 1947. Rpt. New York: Barnes & Noble, 1963.

Saxonhouse, A. W. "Nature and Convention in Thucydides' History." *Polity* 10 (1978): 461–87.

Seager, Robin. "Thucydides and the Charge of Aiming at Tyranny." *Historia* 16 (1967): 6–18.

Shorey, Paul. "On the Implicit Ethics and Psychology of Thucydides." *Transactions of the American Philological Association* 24 (1893): 66–88.

Strauss, Leo. *The City and Man.* 1964. Rpt. Chicago: University of Chicago Press, 1977.

Thibaudet, Albert. *La campagne avec Thucydide.* Paris: Editions de la Nouvelle Revue Française, 1922.

Thompson, Wesley E. "Thucydides 2.65.11." *Historia* 20 (1971): 141–51.

Wallace, W. P. "Thucydides." *Phoenix* 18 (1964): 251–61.

Wardman, A. E. "Thucydides 2.40.1." *Classical Quarterly* n.s. 9 (1959): 38–42.

Westlake, H. D. "Athenian Aims in Sicily, 427–424 B.C." *Historia* 9 (1960): 385–402.

———. *Individuals in Thucydides*. Cambridge: Cambridge University Press, 1968.

———. "Phrynichus and Astyochus (Thucydides 8.50–51)." *Journal of Hellenic Studies* 76 (1956): 99–104.

———. "Thucydides 2.65.11." *Classical Quarterly* n.s. 8 (1958): 102–10.

Wettergreen, John A. "On the End of Thucydides' Narrative." *Interpretation* 9 (1979): 93–110.

White, James Boyd. *When Words Lose Their Meanings*. Chicago: University of Chicago Press, 1984.

Woodhead, A. Geoffrey. *Thucydides on the Nature of Power*. Cambridge: Harvard University Press, 1970.

Index

Library of Congress Cataloging-in-Publication Data

Forde, Steven, 1954–
    The ambition to rule.

    Biblography: p.
    Includes index.
    1. Alcibiades. 2. Imperialism. 3. Greece—History—
Peloponnesian War, 431–404 B.C. 4. Statesmen—Greece—
Athens—Biography. 5. Generals—Greece—Athens—
Biography. 6. Thucydides. History of the Peloponnesian
War. I. Title.
DF230.A4F67 1989   938'.05'0924 [B]   88-47919
ISBN 0-8014-2138-1 (alk. paper)